"*If Eve Only Knew* challenges pervasive evangelical teaching about 'biblical' womanhood and manhood, arguing that it is both damaging and unbiblical. Authors Kendra Weddle Irons and Melanie Springer Mock are great teachers and fine writers, and this engaging book shows their depth in understanding the contemporary conversation, biblical teaching, and historical theology. This fun, disturbing, and hopeful read will help both men and women explore the wonder of what it means to be made in God's image."
 – Howard R. Macy, George Fox University

"Kendra Weddle Irons and Melanie Springer Mock lay out the big picture view of evangelical Christianity's long patriarchal hold on the minds, bodies, and voices of girls and women. In an important indictment of the culture of shame and silence, the authors trace the detrimental effects of (often for-profit) enterprises such as complementarian gender binaries and the purity movement on both women and men. Raised fundamentalist evangelical, I found myself relating deeply to each scenario, considering my own history and journey, and cheering the series of insights that call out the religious infantilization, oppression, and abuse of females in the United States. *If Eve Only Knew* is a crucial text for everyone who values and upholds the freedom, equality, and justice of the Gospel of Jesus."
 – Jennifer Crumpton, Author of *Femmevangelical*

"Whether you are new to egalitarian readings of the Bible that set women free, or whether you are a long-time Christian feminist who is unaware of the hugely popular attempts to keep women in their subordinate roles, *If Eve Only Knew* will supply you with hundreds of fresh insights. Like the Gospel's Canaanite woman who convinced Jesus that he needed to expand his mission, Kendra Irons and Melanie Mock present expansive challenges to contemporary Christianity. Don't miss the excitement!"
 – Virginia Mollenkott, William Paterson University; author
   of *Sensuous Spirituality: Out from Fundamentalism*

"In *If Eve Only Knew,* Melanie Springer Mock and Kendra Weddle Irons give us all a great gift by helping us see our faith tradition with new eyes and, along with it, our place within that story. They provide we who claim Christ a better lens by which to penetrate decades, sometime centuries, of unhealthy, unhelpful teaching on gender and to peer into the true richness of our shared humanity as those made in God's image."
        – John Pavlovitz, Pastor, Blogger, Founder of The Table
          online community

"Men and women ill at ease with complementarian models of family and church life should welcome this book. By analyzing popular evangelical messages and offering faithful ways to interpret scripture through an egalitarian lens, the authors provide a way forward–a way of faith, freedom, and fulfillment that refuses to silence half the church. Given the strong emotions that often characterize debates on this issue, I especially appreciated the book's sound scholarship and judicious tone."
        – Gary Tandy, Author of *The Rhetoric of Certitude*

"This new book by Irons and Mock tackles the biblical and contemporary aspects of Evangelicalism and other conservative strands of Christianity that denigrate and subordinate women. Not only do they succeed in showing that the Bible often does not say what conservatives claim, but they also show that their notions of modesty and purity originated much more recently than in biblical times. The toxic effects of these allegedly biblical views, which are used to silence and control others, are exposed. The message of *If Eve Only Knew* needs to be heard far and wide, for the sake of not only women but people of all genders who are being misled by harmful teachings masquerading as biblical truth. The information in this book probably won't bring an end to patriarchy and oppression, but it should at least make more people aware that those who justify their view of male superiority as simply 'what the Bible says' are in fact ignoring and distorting the Bible left, right, and center."
        – James McGrath, Butler University

To Letha Dawson Scanzoni and the "Sisters of Summer,"
inspiring teachers and companions on our journeys as feminists
and Christians.

To Robert Muthish —
Best Wishes to You!

Melanie
Springer Mock

IF EVE

ONLY

KNEW

FREEING YOURSELF FROM
BIBLICAL WOMANHOOD AND BECOMING
ALL GOD MEANS FOR YOU TO BE

KENDRA WEDDLE IRONS
MELANIE SPRINGER MOCK

CHALICE
PRESS

ST. LOUIS, MISSOURI

Cover illustration: Natalie Turri
Cover design: Jesse Turri

www.chalicepress.com

Print: 9780827216709   EPUB: 9780827216716   EPDF: 9780827216723

Library of Congress Cataloging–in–Publication Data

Irons, Kendra Weddle.
If Eve only knew : freeing yourself from biblical womanhood and becoming all God means for you to be / Kendra Weddle Irons, Melanie Springer Mock. – First [edition].
    pages cm
Includes bibliographical references and index.
ISBN 978-0-8272-1670-9 (pbk.)
1. Feminist theology. 2. Feminism--Religious aspects–Christianity. 3. Women–Religious aspects–Christianity. 4. Sex role–Religious aspects–Christianity. I. Title.
BT83.55.I76 2015
248.8'43–dc23   2015015960

Contents

Introduction

Becoming What We're Meant to Be

The airplane was completing its late-night descent into Indianapolis, the hot summer air making the landing a little more textured than I preferred. My seatmate, a woman in her sixties with a swooping hairstyle and a voice laced with Midwest twang, turned to me.

"What brings you to Indy?" she asked.

For much of the flight, she'd been reading *Guidepost* magazine, a monthly publication that offers "true stories of hope, faith, personal growth, and positive thinking." My own grandma had once stored *Guideposts* by her toilet, because—I suppose—everyone can use a dose of positive thinking in the bathroom. Though the magazine promises to be nonsectarian, it is prized by many conservative Christians—its true stories involving loads of prayer, references to Scripture, and miraculous Divine intervention.

I wasn't sure what I should tell this *Guidepost*-reading grandmother about why I was visiting Indianapolis. My itinerary was free of debauchery; there would be no all-night benders on riverboat casinos or anonymous hook-ups at Indianapolis's downtown bars. But I hesitated, carefully mulled my answer, then said:

"I'm speaking at a Christian women's conference."

She nodded and smiled, because we were compatriots. I smiled, too, a little more weakly. If only she knew.

An airport hotel in Indianapolis seems an odd place for a Christian feminism conference. The Midwest isn't always considered a hotbed of progressive thinking. Yet there I was, at a hotel surrounded by a culinary wasteland, with the restaurant trifecta of Bob Evans, Cracker Barrel, and Denny's providing a nice buffer to the highway noise nearby.

For the most part, the participants at this conference looked like the stereotypic Christian woman: older, grayer, wearing slacks and cardigans, hair nicely coiffed into a short bob or perm. A few men followed their wives into the conference room, but this crowd was mostly female. The participants reveled in the companionship found at the conference, and spent time before and after meetings catching up, standing in clumps to visit, gossip, and gather warmth from decades-old friendships.

Most significantly, these women believed ardently in Jesus.

This may be where their similarity to a good many Christian women, including my airplane seatmate, ended. Those at the Christian feminism conference were teachers and pastors, social workers and doctors, mothers and grandmothers, wives and partners, straight and lesbian. They believed in Jesus, certainly, but not the mean, angry, judgmental Jesus some of this country's Christians seem to follow. The feminists' Jesus was a loving social activist, subversive in his time—and in ours.

So, yes, I was speaking at a Christian women's conference. But how do you tell a stranger, reading a conservative Christian magazine on an airplane, that those sharing the dais would include an eighty-two-year-old lesbian, a noted expert on transgendered folks in the church, and several other women exiled from their denominations for asking hard question about the policies that excluded them?

Kendra and I had come to the conference to talk about the effects evangelical popular culture has on the students we teach at our respective colleges. We wanted to help Christian feminists understand what they are up against: a Christian culture that continues to tell women they need to be submissive, silent, docile, and focused not at all on an outside-the-home career, but on raising children and caring for husbands. This was God's exclusive design for women, and those who followed a different path were outside God's will.

As professors, Kendra and I work with women excited about their vocations but faced with the pervasive message they've often been given by their evangelical upbringing, by their families, their churches, and by Christian popular culture. Our students learn early that women—by virtue of their biological relationship to Eve—are more deceptive, more prone to sin and impurity, more emotional, and less capable of making decisions than their male peers. A woman's primary role is as a helpmeet, raising children. Lifelong vocations are for the very few women who do not marry. Any vocation involving church leadership is reserved for men, no matter what a young woman's calling.

Given the persistent thrum of these messages, it is little wonder conservative Christian women struggle to find a voice in their church communities and to feel affirmed in their life choices. It's also no wonder that women graduating from evangelical Christian universities often express less confidence than their male peers, and their sense of vocational call is less clear upon graduation. Women who visit our offices seeking guidance often seem less self-assured about their futures, especially if they haven't found the "Mrs." degree they are told is imperative with a conservative Christian college education. They often exhibit a lower level of self-competence than do their male peers.

The evangelical blogs, magazines, and books these young women read, the music they listen to, and the organizations to which they belong send clear messages about who or what they should be. And all of it is delivered with the conviction that it's godly, because "the Bible says so."

Christian feminists also believe the Bible tells us so: that Scripture is an important guide to how people of faith should live, and how we should relate to each other and to God. While it might be easy to assume Christian feminists disregard the Bible and its role in the faith journey, this is not always true. We may understand Scripture differently than other evangelicals, seeing it within its social, historical, and cultural context. Following the model of early Christian feminists such as Letha Dawson Scanzoni and Nancy Hardesty, whose ground-breaking work in the 1970s invited people to re-examine the Bible without the presupposition that God endorses patriarchy, we see the Bible as a living text, opening up to us again and again and allowing us to see the Divine in new and powerful ways. Rebecca Kiser, writing for *Christian Feminism Today*, describes the Bible as one form of authority, and asserts that Christian feminists also "affirm the continuing work of the Spirit of God in unfolding the truth that is written in the Scriptures."[1] Understood in this manner, the Bible does not demand that women act a certain way, and men another; instead, the Bible offers us freedom to explore the very gifts God has given us, allowing us to be all God has meant us to be.

And still, this liberating vision is stifled by the more pervasive message of God's ordained plan for women–plans that include a prescribed way of living. Such messages are difficult to ignore not only because they are so prevalent but also because of the power inherent in peer pressure. Despite the voices of Christian feminists offering an alternative understanding of Scripture, gender, and God's call on our lives, messages about biblical womanhood continue to dominate Christian culture. Such messages provide easy answers to the messy, complicated question of who God wishes us to be, but they are also quite lucrative. According to the CBA (formerly Christian Booksellers Association) state of the industry report, in 2009[2] Christian products sales were reportedly $4.6 billion. Women assume a significant portion of this market share. Speakers such as Joyce Meyer draw large audiences–and large sums–by ironically preaching in mega-churches and to mega-audiences around the country about the primacy of women's domestic domain. Telling women and girls how they are to act, and what godliness *must* look like in those born female, is big business, especially when packaged as "God's design."

The commodification of the Bible and its presumed message to women becomes even more problematic when we consider that taking the Bible seriously doesn't necessarily mean its function is to add Divine approval to any number of personal preferences. Instead, the Bible invites readers to plumb its depths for meanings and paradoxes, for difficult conundrums and unanswered questions. This depth of analysis, however, is almost always missing from the messages embedded in evangelical popular culture. In its place are cultural assumptions reflecting a contemporary society motivated by a mass consumer-driven market. Using the Bible in this manner becomes a trump card, compelling young people to accept the messages they're fed without critically analyzing those messages or considering the potential that the Bible itself can be misinterpreted, used to support a particular worldview absent from Scripture itself.

We support a counter-message, one that encourages Christians to think about the popular evangelical culture they are ingesting, and about the contradictory, confusing, and sometimes wrong messages offered there. Relying on the biblical hermeneutics offered to us by the Christian feminist movement, this book challenges readers to understand the Bible in a new way. We want to offer a different, richer, and more complex reading of the Bible: one that allows women and men the freedom to be all God intended for them.

Each chapter looks at messages popular evangelical culture sends us about who it believes the Bible demands we be, given its interpretation of Scripture and church tradition. Could there be a different way to understand the biblical texts? We will critique and rebalance evangelical culture with a reading of Scripture that provides a fresh perspective on the Bible, Jesus, faith, vocation, and the self; and help our readers find new strength in pursuing what God meant them to be.

Feminists are often maligned by evangelical culture as the bogey who would make every woman a self-absorbed, man-and-child-hating harpy; however, what we *really* want to offer is a way to know God more deeply, and to live more richly. While *If Eve Only Knew* analyzes some of the most potent messages in evangelical popular culture about a woman's role in marriage, child-bearing, homemaking, and vocation, the book also argues that God—and God's revelation through Scripture, tradition, and experience—creates all of us to celebrate our abilities rather than confine ourselves by some ill-defined gender roles from the biblical manhood/womanhood movement.

Thankfully, many evangelicals ceaselessly work for gender justice and equity in their vocations, strive to maintain egalitarian relationships in their homes, and believe the Bible unequivocally empowers women to be all God means them to be. In our work at our colleges and for evangelical organizations, many share our commitment. I am married to an evangelical who, in thought and deed, seeks to assure that equity reigns at home and in the workplace, believing that is how God intended the world to be. And, in recent years especially, younger evangelicals such as Rachel Held Evans and Sarah Bessey have carried the mantel of Christian feminism that was first raised high by Letha Dawson Scanzoni and Nancy A. Hardesty, challenging the patriarchal systems that continue to demand women remain in roles far different than those enjoyed by men.

When we write about evangelical culture, we are not critiquing these individuals or the good work they do to make a better place for us all. Instead, we critique evangelical *culture*—and, specifically, the views and actions some bigoted women and men espouse: the messages they promote, informed by the books and blogs written by their leaders: their beliefs and consumer slogans promoting their theology to those who will plunk down a few bucks. We cannot underestimate the destructive power of these pervasive messages, even as we trust the individuals who work for gender justice, including those who have made a vast difference in our own lives.

Messages about gender are knit into the very language we use to talk about our religious experience. Using exclusively masculine language in our discussions about God—and even progressive churches can struggle with inclusive language—shapes how we understand God and ourselves. If divinity is always referenced as masculine, we convey God is male and, thus, men as more Godlike than women.[3] Using patriarchal language also denies the many feminine biblical metaphors of God, conveying that those metaphors figuring God as female are less significant than the masculine traits.

For the foremothers of the Christian feminist movement, the women who I met at the Evangelical and Ecumenical Women's Caucus Gathering in Indianapolis in 2012, discovering inclusive language was a significant part of their spiritual journey, helping reshape and transform their relationship to God, to each other, and to the church. These women had an important vision for the evangelical church: that women and men could be understood as equal, because they were created that way. Their vision of gender equity within the church is an important one, but even more significant is their idea that women and men are both created in God's own image. Believing this affirmation—found right there in the book of Genesis—means we cannot fall prey to the counter-idea that God designed specific roles for women and specific roles for men, a sensibility now rampant in evangelical popular culture, and which limits what women can do to reflect God's image within them.

If women and men truly are going to be all God means for them to be, we need to call out those aspects of evangelical popular culture that send women and men negative messages about gender. We need to show that the evangelical understanding of biblical womanhood and manhood is not, in fact, biblical. We need to provide women and men with an alternative message: that they are fearfully and wonderfully made in God's own image, providing them freedom to explore fully who God intends them to be.

Chapter One

Saving Eve

Most evangelical children learn early and often that Eve is the real villain in the Genesis story. Forget the talking serpent, depicted in Sunday school curricula wrapped around a tree, his forked tongue whispering lies into the woman's ears. Forget Adam, standing in the garden, unable to clearly decode God's message. The real culprit of the first sin, the fall, and everything bad that's happened since, is Eve, her beautiful alabaster hand delicately holding the red apple up to Adam, who unwittingly takes a bite.

Biblical literalists who construct such Sunday school curricula stumble into at least one factual dilemma: the Red Delicious could never be indigenous to the region where the garden of Eden presumably existed. Children learning about Adam and Eve are also rarely told there are two Genesis narratives to consider, each figuring the story in a slightly different way. Or that, when Genesis is read with the appropriate acknowledgment of its complexity, its relationship to other creation accounts, and its own puzzling contradictions, the predominating message of Adam and Eve is not necessarily a straightforward tale about a talking snake, a woman's deceitfulness, and humanity's fall into sin.

Never mind all those things. If evangelical popular culture is right, then Eve represents all that's gone wrong from the very beginning, her disobedience a clear indication of the ways women were designed, and her hubris a sign that men, rather than women, need to be in charge.

Forever, if possible.

7

Messages about Eve's culpability are legion in Sunday school curricula, and they are also ubiquitous in evangelical books and blogs for girls, in sermons preached about the Genesis story, in Bible study programs for young women. In other words, messages about Eve—and, by extension, Eve's daughters—are everywhere, letting women know they are the cause of sin in the world; that they are more deceptive and more easily deceived than men; and that Eve's initial disobedience, her wily ability to misguide, shows an unnatural order of the way things should be: a wife leading a husband.

Paradise lost, the result of sin, is the theme upon which evangelicals stake their claim, and gender is inextricably linked to this worldview. Those early Sunday school lessons about a beautiful woman in the garden, tempting Adam, are the foundation for every other message evangelical women receive about who and what they are, about how they walk through the world, and about their place in God's intricate ordering of gender roles. Ultimately, these messages let women know where they stand in relationship to God and to the beings they managed to deceive, from the world's very beginning.

Reading Genesis primarily as a story about sin is advantageous for some evangelicals. It provides an explanation for evil's existence in the world, a formulaic way to contend with life's complexities. If the garden is literal, and Eve the locus of sin, then evil can be readily explained, its presence not random and unpredictable but pinned to a woman who chose listening to a serpent over following God. In this view, evil comes from sin. Sin comes from making bad choices. Eve is the example of making bad choices and thus the model of what not to do.

More significantly, interpreting Genesis in this way exclusively implicates women, making them the conduit through which evil enters the world. Because Eve, the first female, made the wrong decision, all women after her are prone to act likewise. In this particular worldview, women are more likely to be deceptive and to deceive. They are guided by their hubris, and their desire for control. They will tempt and torment men into doing what men, by their very nature, do not want to do. To establish a successful society, men, not women, need to be in charge. When this happens, even some kind of paradise can be restored.

The Chasm Eve Created

Just how much havoc did Eve cause in the garden of Eden? Some Christians can draw a ubiquitous diagram used to visually articulate just how wide and deep the gulf is between an all-powerful and loving God and wayward humanity. A large chasm stretches across a page while an isolated individual (drawn in small scale) stands on one side of the deep ravine and the large Divine figure is found on the opposite side. There is no way for the two to come together without something—a miracle, really—to bridge the gap.

Fortunately for the narrative and for the visual image, a cross with its wide beam seems to fit just right, a bridge the faithful are invited to fearlessly step upon, drawing us close to the Almighty. Fundamentally, evangelicalism argues the death of Jesus on the cross provides the only reasonable bridge bringing humanity and divinity together, restoring and healing the chasm created by Eve's (and subsequently Adam's) disobedience.

Everything about the faith is founded on this idea, and those reared in evangelicalism—even those who claim a progressive theological understanding—seem to accept this premise as God's own truth. For Christians outside the evangelical bubble, it is baffling to hear so much focus on sin and its taint in humans as the gospel's central concern. They may rightly wonder why the gospels are called "the good news" if read through the lens of human depravity, wickedness, and a resulting separation from, presumably, a loving God. What's so good about all of that?

Many evangelicals argue their understanding of Genesis, and in particular of its third chapter, is rooted in biblical truth, and that the text speaks for itself. However, most theologians acknowledge a more complicated understanding of Genesis, recognizing that the Defective-Eve-and-Original-Sin interpretation can be traced to a few male theologians writing at a time when women were believed to be less than fully human.[1]

During the second century, for example, a Christian theologian, Tertullian, put forward the idea that all women were just as guilty as Eve. "Do you not know that you are Eve?" he wrote. "God's sentence hangs still over all your sex and His punishment weighs down upon you. You are the devil's gateway; you are she who first violated the forbidden tree and broke the law of God."[2] John Chrysostom, writing a couple of centuries later, continued this misogynistic claim when he charged, "The woman taught once, and ruined all. On this account... let her not teach. But what is it to other women that she suffered this? It certainly concerns them; for the sex is weak and fickle.... The whole female race transgressed."[3]

Most famously, though, is Augustine of Hippo, the church father whose theological shadow remains firmly in place especially among evangelicals, and whose rendering of Genesis 3 identified sexuality with sin. Interpreting the text through the lens of his experience, including a life with a long-time mistress, Augustine struggled with competing desires of sex without familial constraints and commitment to fatherhood versus recognition within the Christian faith—recognition that in his mind required celibacy. Women's bodies, he claimed, were so evidently sexual that women themselves represented sinfulness in ways far transcending males, whose minds rather than bodies were indicators of their godlikeness.

According to Augustine, women, as primarily sexual beings, could serve only one real purpose. He once asked, "Now, if the woman was not made for the man to be his helper in begetting children, in what way was she to help him?"[4] The answer? No other way. Augustine instituted a perspective about women evangelicals echo today: women are made *from* men; women are made *for* men; women are less like God than men because women are more sexual. And, thus, more sinful. The first book of the Bible, the argument goes, makes this so.

Sin Is All That Matters

As soon as young girls begin dressing themselves, they are told in myriad ways that their bodies reflect a propensity for sin. From purity rings and balls to princess websites, where girls are instructed to measure the lengths of their skirts and shorts and to wear blouses that aren't revealing too much skin or budding breasts, the message is clear: their bodies are a problem. Girls and young women hear they need to be wary of their sexual nature because, unbeknownst to them, Satan will use their bodies to make boys and men fall into the deep chasm of sin. And when this happens, girls are clearly culpable, their very physical selves a temptation to the spiritual well-being of the boys and men around them.

Augustine and other Christian writers may have established this sin-filled theme from Genesis, but contemporary evangelical leaders continue to perpetuate it, presenting this ideology as gospel truth rather than the machinations of early church fathers. For example, John Piper, a leading figure in the complementarian movement (a sub-group of evangelicalism), argues a fundamental shift occurred in the nature of humanity.* Prior to the Genesis narrative, Piper claims, Adam and Eve were morally upright, but, after they ate the forbidden fruit, they became corrupt by nature, enslaved to sin, and morally unable to delight in God and overcome their own proud preference for the fleeting pleasures of self-rule. The reason for this massive shift—one so all-encompassing that it changes the essence of what it means to be human—is disobedience.[5]

Similarly, Nancy Leigh DeMoss and Mary Kassian, promoters of the *True Woman Manifesto* and well-known conference speakers and writers, relate a comparable understanding of humanity. They say sin not only separated God and humans but it makes people unable to reflect the image of God, a characteristic granted to humans in Genesis 1. In their understanding, the reason Jesus is the antidote to this altered reality is that he represents a sinless state and his vicarious death makes possible a new opportunity for the otherwise now fundamentally flawed humanity.[6]

Many popular evangelicals promote the idea that when Adam and Eve sinned in the garden, they so angered God that She or He rightly could have punished them with death. Since disobedience to God's command indicated a desire to go beyond the authority given to them, the first humans deserved to be punished for their lack of humility, for their extensive pride. This way of thinking is a pattern we find troubling, one in which a crucial link exists between a theology built upon sin and subjugating women to men.

Blaming Eve

It isn't just that sin has marred humanity and the world. We must remember who started this chain of sin: Eve. Evangelical popular culture has created Eve as the scapegoat, her one act in the garden a reason evil exists in the world, causing heartbreak, pain, and a need for redemption to everyone ever born. We need to blame someone, and making Eve culpable for *everything bad* means Adam (dupe that he is) does not have to bear the same mark of shame. He's a man, and needs to take charge. The stain of guilt would only drag him down.

---

*Throughout *If Eve Only Knew*, the term "complementarianism" will be used to describe a Christian ideology asserting that God created men and women to exist in separate, but equal, roles, and that these distinct roles are to complement each other. Egalitarian Christians, on the other hand, believe in gender equity, and that women and men are to live fully into their callings, not based on gender but on the gifts God has given them.

Many evangelicals find support in the New Testament for seeing Eve as the conduit through which evil entered the world by looking to 1 Timothy and the negative portrayal of Eve presented there. According to the author of 1 Timothy, women should be silent and submissive, having no authority to teach because Eve was formed after Adam and was deceived; subsequently, the author of 1 Timothy writes, she transgressed God's commandment. Although the Hebrew translation of Eve is "mother of all living," evangelicals have discovered in this progenitor not life but sin, an idea that has been carried through Christian tradition and embraced by much of contemporary evangelical culture.

And since in evangelical lore Eve's most notable attribute is her propensity for sin, Eve is blamed for every social ill, not just a few thousand years ago (although there are no firm dates for origin narratives), but for today. Speaking at a True Woman conference, Kay Arthur recently said women have entangled themselves with the affairs of life because of Eve. True Woman events have taken place for several years in multiple venues—and have birthed an entire franchise of True Woman blogs, books, videos, and study curricula—so thousands of women have heard they are mired in their lives because of Eve.

Arthur claims that Eve made a fateful decision to usurp God's power; and, similarly, when women today decide to have careers outside of the home, they are deliberately choosing the wrong path, likewise transgressing the rules of God's design. Arthur also says that when so many women are making these choices—as is evident in the recent employment data—this is evidence of how much sin exists in the world. Women who make choices deemed problematic by evangelicals are thus, again and again, re-enacting that first unwise decision made by someone born female.[7]

Nancy Leigh DeMoss teamed up in a book with Dannah Gresh targeting teens to take Eve to task for everything gone wrong with our world. *Lies Young Women Believe: And the Truth That Sets Them Free* has on its cover that always-present apple, letting us know immediately who the genesis of those lies is going to be: Eve, of course. In the opening chapter, called "The Deceiver," Gresh and DeMoss provide a somewhat unbelievable scenario about a teenager who develops a romantic relationship with her "church-going father," who offers her crystal meth, saying "God wants us to be happy." When the teen starts reading the Bible, the father gets angry, saying "I am God," hoping to sway his daughter to the evil dark side.

Here is apparently the biblical parallel: In Genesis, Eve also took some "crystal meth," in the form of the "forbidden fruit," from someone who wanted to be God. Eve listened to the serpent and his lies, and was easily deceived. She, in turn, was able to deceive her husband. In other words, Eve, being easily deceived, has made all women into deceivers, and brought down all of humanity by making her husband sin. Young women reading Gresh and DeMoss's book will discover that, first of all, "Satan targets women with his lies." We may not understand exactly why Satan wants to go after women, but, the authors write, "The facts are the facts." They are willing to acknowledge that "it may feel like a bad rap" for women to be targeted, but argue women will just have to live with the facts, because "there was something in the way Eve was created that made her more vulnerable to deception." So there we have it. Women are more inclined to be deceived, and to deceive. According to *Lies Young Women Believe*, young women believe lies because they are more inclined to do so.[8]

Similarly, John and Stasi Eldredge, popular authors and speakers, also build upon the Genesis narrative, blaming Eve for negative traits running through all women. In their book, *Captivating: Unveiling the Mystery of a Woman's Soul*, they say Eve's transgression confirms women want to be captivating, want to gain the attention of others. Eve did this when she talked with the serpent. According to them, the serpent and Eve had a flirting exchange, and out of their desires to mesmerize the other, Eve succumbed to temptation, doing exactly what the serpent wanted. Since Eve is the symbolic representation of all women, any woman born since then is prone to flirt and to be captivating, all of which will lead to no place good, unless women strive for the approving gaze of God.[9]

Blaming Eve and her daughters for introducing evil into the world thus provides evangelicals opportunity to assert the need for male dominance and female submission, while also abrogating the need to consider other potential causes of societal ills: the privileging of those already in power, or greed that drives people to treat others poorly, or even institutional racism and sexism that reinforces hierarchies oppressing the "weakest of these." As long as we blame Eve, everything else–including misogyny within the church–can remain the same.

Eve, The First Feminist

In the eyes of some evangelicals, the contemporary expression of Eve's sinfulness is feminism. According to them, Eve was the first feminist, her willful disobedience of God and man/Adam is clearly reflected in a movement that challenges women to assert themselves, to voice their own desires, and to fight for equity. Some evangelicals draw a direct line from Eve to feminism, believing feminism is the current cause for all that is wrong in the world.

The Council on Biblical Manhood and Womanhood, the flagship complementarian organization, was founded in 1987 as a response to evangelical feminists who argued for gender equity in the church. According to its own site, CBMW was "established primarily to help the church defend against the accommodation of secular feminism." Because secular feminists got their wily hands on some evangelicals, though, the CBMW and its definitive Danvers Statement became a way to argue for "God's design" in gender roles; otherwise, CBMW founders believed, the "heart of the gospel is in jeopardy." Feminists, secular or evangelical, were playing fast and loose with the authority of Scripture and biblical translation, the health of the home and church, and the advance of the gospel. CBMW formed to fight against the scourge of feminism's broad reach.[10]

It's no wonder that the contemporary CBMW site continues to publish articles denouncing the evils of feminism and tying those evils to the Genesis story. In May 2013, Courtney Reissig, claiming to be a recovering feminist, posted an anti-feminist article on the site. "Feminism started in a garden in the Middle East thousands of years ago," she asserted. And, thus, "Feminism is at the very heart of our fallen nature and manifests itself in many different forms." And while Reissig believes the "first feminist, Eve," is the root of this satanic movement, she also argues the continuing source of the problem is within women themselves, who see themselves—not God—as the "authority of all."[11]

Because feminism is so powerful and evil, it needs an entire website dedicated to its opponents. Ladies Against Feminism, founded in 2002, intends to "publish thoughtful, biblical responses to feminism and to encourage other women in their God-given roles." To that end, correspondents for the organization write about how to encourage husbands, keep an impeccable home, raise and teach children, and maintain a "well-ordered family," all presumed goals anathema to feminists. Ladies Against Feminism provides links to other like-minded organizations, as well as promoting online sites through which readers can purchase t-shirts to voice their antipathy toward this "devil's tool." Three options provide a decent sampling of the possibilities: "Birth Control is for Sissies," "Militant Fecundity," and, "I Refuse to be a Victim of Feminism."[12]

This idea is a consistent message in evangelical popular culture. Applying pervasive stereotypes of feminism that have long colored the culture at large, a good many evangelical advice books targeting young and old women rely on a composite "feminist" character: she is often an academic teaching lies to college students and pushing them to seek careers rather than spouses. She is sometimes single and likely childless, because feminists decry marriage and family. On occasion, she is a lesbian, because feminists have these tendencies. She hates the Bible and God, makes decisions independent of anyone but herself, and sees herself as her own "authority of all," just like the first feminist, Eve.

Rather than questioning the ways their stereotypes about women and feminism might send problematic messages to young Christians, both female and male, evangelical apologists often critique mass media for endeavoring to destroy each generation. In Mary Kassian's "You've Come a Long Way, Baby!" True Woman 101 lecture she illumines the downward spiral of American culture caused by the onset of feminism and illustrated through television programming, beginning with *Leave it to Beaver*, which she believes is a portrayal of how things *should* be in the hearth and home; to Mary Richards of the *Mary Tyler Moore Show*, who was, in Kassian's assessment, a little too independent; to Murphy Brown, a self-absorbed, loud-mouthed atheist who was pregnant but chose not to marry; to Ellen Morgan on *Ellen,* with her in-your-face lesbianism, *Friends* with all of their sexual promiscuity, and *Sex and the City*, in which women live neurotically and completely for themselves. Feminism resides at the heart of this destruction, with characters such as Ellen Morgan and Murphy Brown telling young women they can be autonomous beings, successful and strong. Little in Kassian's lecture suggests a consideration of the ways evangelical popular culture has also conveyed problematic messages to young women, nor how an ideal like "True Woman" can be in its own way complicated, because it's easier to blame feminists— and their foremother Eve.[13]

Femininity: The Antidote to Eve

If Eve and feminism represent the defectiveness of women, what options for wholeness and a fulfilling life remain for women? Although many Catholics may have Mary, the mother of Jesus, as a female icon, the evangelical Protestant tradition has long kept Mary at arm's length, believing any attention to her life and witness might turn to idolatry, a criticism often leveled at Catholics. Indeed, while other female characters in the Bible—Ruth, Esther, the nameless Proverbs 31 woman—are lifted up in evangelical popular culture as the godly women to emulate, little focus is given to the godly woman who bore Jesus.

With Mary contained in the background, evangelical women are told to see their own femininity as the corrective to Eve. Kassian and DeMoss tell women to counter the evils feminism has wrought by embracing femininity and working on their inner beauty. They should become receptive to the needs of others and should serve them, especially men; women should also avoid nagging—a trap into which they will fall when placing their own needs first. In this way, women will glorify God, the highest calling for a Christian. Additionally, women should find their fulfillment and life's purpose first and foremost at home. In contrast to Eve's initiative, godly women embrace being helpers, especially in their relationships with their husbands.

Kassian explains this rationale extensively in "The Genesis of Gender."[14] Here Kassian says "Man" was created first, which means he is the primary feature of Genesis, and now responsible for all things work-related. He is to protect his home like a castle. (This medieval framework recurs in a lot of evangelical writing, and is discussed more in chapter 8.) Man is to be in control, having a God-given right to make decisions—presumably because he will make better ones than Eve (and those of her gender). Because of being created from the rib of Adam, women are made as instruments for men. They should exalt in this position, especially given the ways Eve potentially mucked up the helper role. As a man's helper, a woman will want to defer to him in all things, realizing she is weaker than he, softer than he, and certainly only meant to support his dreams and desires. Since the woman was made not in the desert but in the garden, readers should realize women are vulnerable and need a husband's protection in all times and places.

Christian tradition has long supported the idea that women are inferior: their brains are smaller and thus they do not have the mental capacity of men; they are physically not as strong as men; their hips are wider than men's, suggesting their sole duty is to bear children; they are supposed to keep house and so their need for education is limited to the domestic arts. Why study history or natural sciences when the only necessary knowledge is cooking three square meals a day and making bathroom fixtures shine?

Some contemporary evangelicals continue to perpetrate notions of women's inferiority as well, making claims about women's special but limited roles and asserting that God has specifically designed women—their bodies, their minds, their spiritual gifts—for these roles. Some young evangelical women also assert that women's inferiority, again, given their relationship to the first woman, makes them more suited to roles that do not require much intellect, leadership, or strength. For example, Elizabeth and Anna Sofia Bodkin, young authors, speakers, and curators of the Visionary Daughters website, advocate that women remain under the tutelage of their fathers until they are married and can be led by their husbands.[15]

Complementarians argue that women should hew to the roles God designed for them, roles perverted by Eve's actions in the garden, roles against which feminists have been fighting since the world's beginning. This includes embracing a type of femininity, excelling in the domestic sphere, and leaving the "heavy lifting," figuratively and literally, to men. In evangelicalism, those women who chafe at these prescriptions are often marginalized and shamed, their inability to comfortably fit within God's design a sign they identify with Eve and her sin, and also with feminists, whom evangelicals revile.

Not all women are necessarily feminine (by societal standards, at least) and may, in fact, be masculine in a number of ways; gender theorists have long acknowledged that gender occurs on a spectrum, and that a number of traits formerly considered irrefutably biological are actually the result of social conditioning. Virginia Ramey Mollenkott, professor emeritus of English at William Paterson University, in her groundbreaking *Omnigender: A Trans-Religious Approach*, uses Scripture to explain how most people exist outside of a binary gender construct deserving more interrogation than evangelicals are willing to give it.[16] And yet, writers such as Kassian and DeMoss see Scripture verses in Genesis as a textbook of sorts for the world's origins. In this sense, they teach that God determines gender, and that to reject or doubt one's gender is tantamount to dethroning God (notice the medieval imagery again).

To rebuff God's gender gift is, for them, sin. And once again, it all comes back to Eve.

The Devil Made Me Do It

Eve may be the culprit for all the sin in the world, but the devil is at least partly to blame in the evangelical reading of Genesis. Conflating the terms "serpent" and "satan" and then freely interchanging "satan" and "devil," many evangelicals make interpretive leaps with the Genesis narrative that are not necessarily embedded in the text itself (serpent is the term used in the account). And because the reading of Genesis is tied so specifically to gender, the serpent is figured as male, the seducer of Eve, their sublimated sexual tension foreshadowing the fraught relationships always existing between men and women. In places where these claims are made, however, there is no serious interrogation—no questioning at all, really—about the ways evangelicalism itself might be contributing to the negative messages young women receive.

Despite the evangelical preoccupation with a deceiving serpent who tricks the unguarded humans into sin, the entire remainder of the Hebrew Bible fails to refer to Genesis 3 as the fall; fails to build upon the idea of the serpent as a tempter, leading subsequent humans down a path of destruction; fails to explore more fully the concept of "original sin." The fact that the Hebrew Bible does not maintain these themes should suggest these themes were not ones the original author or authors had in mind. Maybe the devil is no devil after all, and the serpent's encounter with Eve and Eve's encounter with us needs to be understood in a different way.

Adam: Men Will Be Men

If women have been the inheritors of the fallout from Eve's first choice, evangelicals have used Adam to justify the placement of men above all—women, children, animals—in the universe. Although a close reading of Genesis shows Adam was present during the entire conversation Eve has with the serpent, Eve gets the blame for her disobedience and Adam's own culpability is often minimized. Instead of belaboring Adam's sin, some evangelicals use Genesis to justify patriarchy, zeroing in on Adam's God-given duty to lead, essentially because of the presumed created order. Because Adam was apparently created first, he is meant to be the one in charge.

In his role as first human, Adam becomes the model for all subsequent men. He is instructed by God to take care of the garden and the animals, a prescription for "being in charge." Mark Driscoll, former pastor of Mars Hill Church in Seattle, Washington, uses an apt analogy to make the point. "Men are like trucks—they drive smoother and straighter with a load.... Real men don't look for other men, organizations, and governments to carry their load. Real men carry their own load."[17] A real man is thus supposed to cultivate gardens, caring for beast and women alike. This means working hard on the land, making sure that it—and wives, too—will be fruitful and multiply. Michelle Wallace elaborates on men's roles via Adam by arguing the duty of all men is to "carry out husbandry." In the beginning, she explains, God put man in the garden to take care of it. The garden represents man's sphere of influence or territory, his labor in the public sphere separated from the woman's role. This sphere continues to exist now for men, as progenitors of Adam.[18] Owen Strachan, the executive director for the Council for Biblical Manhood and Womanhood, echoes Wallace, claiming men having specific roles within marriages. He argues men are called by God to be providers and "if a man can physically work, and if he is able to keep employment, then it is his special, God-given call to devote his strength, his intellect, and his attention to providing for his family. In following this pattern, we're responding directly to Scripture, and also to the worldview taught us in our bodies."[19]

Though some see Adam as an exemplar for real men, others find in him a model of failed manhood, believing his deception by Eve reflects a brokenness other men are called upon to mend. Robert Lewis, in *Raising a Modern-Day Knight*, imagines Adam might have acted manly in the garden, killing the serpent and restoring order in paradise. Instead, Adam represents failed manhood, reflected in his passivity. Lewis acknowledges Adam was standing next to Eve when the serpent deceived her, but sees in his lack of action his fallen nature (an ironic assertion, given that Eve's act was supposed to have been what precipitated the fall). Adam was "naturally aggressive," Lewis writes, but when he was challenged with a moment of "authentic manhood"–the opportunity to protect his wife and his land–he chose passivity instead. Men have been following Adam's example "ever since," choosing to shirk their God-given roles. Lewis believes it is only Jesus who sets manhood right, because he initiated action rather than remaining passive, fighting sin by dying on the cross.[20]

The idea of Adam's failed manhood being made right by Jesus is found throughout evangelical popular culture, especially in the Real Man movements that attempt to provide for men what the True Woman movement provides for women: a model for godliness. In an article on the Lifeway Books website, Robert Lewis examines what makes a real man, arguing fathers need to teach their sons the biblical meta-narrative of fall and redemption through the figures of Adam and Jesus, failed man and man made right. Adam's inability to act as a man when confronted by the serpent–he "ducks behind Eve" instead of fighting back–shows not just moral weakness, but also manly weakness. Jesus here provides the "polar opposite": he who "held firm" despite "facing challenges far greater than Adam."[21]

So the cross represents redemption, but also provides a new model of manhood, which "includes rejecting passivity, accepting responsibility, leading courageously, and expecting God's greater reward." Gender becomes the lens through which we are supposed to see the most important theme in Scripture: our fallenness and our need for Christ's saving act on the cross. If Eve's culpability and her willingness to deceive is based on her femaleness, then Adam's passivity and willingness to be tempted is based on his maleness. In the Genesis narrative, gender becomes all, the center of the story guiding every other aspect of evangelical Christianity.

Taking Another Look

Eve-as-temptress and Adam-as-wimp is foundational to evangelical beliefs about gender. Using Genesis to define all relationships between men and women, evangelicals establish clear gender roles. Because Eve disobeyed, her willingness to allow sin into the world means women must be guided by men. Guided, but also controlled. The pervasiveness of this interpretation of Eve creates in women a clear sense of their unworthiness to be fully human. And why wouldn't it? Hearing for your entire life you've inherited Eve's deceitfulness and propensity to sin is no doubt erosive to one's sense of self. Being told that your foremother is at fault for all that is wrong in the world? No wonder so many Christian women struggle with feeling unworthy.

But, what if?

What if we read Genesis without a preconceived idea of Eve as a bad woman? Is it possible to consider her as someone created in God's image rather than primarily as a temptress? By setting aside our assumptions about Eve–what we have been taught to believe–we may find the story opens up to us with new insights.

The so-called biblical evidence for gender roles, with men as appointed leaders, is based upon interpretations most privileged by evangelicals and tied to Genesis 2, where the man is told God wants to create for him a suitable helper. This narrative of woman-as-helper subsequently results in women bearing the burden of becoming domestic assistants: the cook, the cleaner, the parental figure in charge of children. And, while much has been made in recent years to revise this concept of helper by explaining its Hebrew term, *ezer*, there remains much work to do to re-evaluate this patriarchal rendering of the text.

Ezer is a word suggesting help, but it refers to a specific type of assistance: the kind God offers–seen, for example, in Psalm 121:2: "My help (*ezer*) comes from the LORD, / who made heaven and earth." Or, Psalm 146:3, 5a, which states, "Do not put your trust in princes, / in mortals, in whom there is no help (*ezer*)… / Happy are those whose help (*ezer*) is the God of Jacob." In each case, the help is not from an inferior assistant but rather from the Divine: the kind of help we trust because of its source. To read Eve's help in contrast to God's is to see her through a patriarchal lens not supported by the narrative. She is no mere second-hand assistant; her help is likened to God's.

Not only is her help on par with God's, there is no biblical evidence to suggest Eve is subordinate to Adam because of her ability to help. Sixteen times in Scripture the word *ezer* clearly refers to a superordinate–not subordinate–helper, an insight Letha Dawson Scanzoni and Nancy Hardesty point out in their book published almost forty years ago, called *All We're Meant to Be*.[22] In Genesis 2:24, *ezer kenegdo* reveals the relationship of the primordial pair. Without its modifier, the noun, "helper," can indicate "an assistant" or "an expert." However, with the modifier as it appears in 2:24, it means "an equal helper." The Hebrew words in this well-worn narrative, therefore, do not indicate a hierarchy between Adam and Eve. Rather, mutuality is expressed: this helper is suitable, is "bone of my bones," is able to provide assistance–not as one lower, but as one equal to the other.

Eve's bad rap stems not just from seeing her as an inferior "helpmeet" but also because of her supposed predisposition to be deceived. While such a rendering is commonplace, this understanding masks her decision-making process. In the narrative, Eve carefully considers whether or not to eat the forbidden fruit; she weighs the result of doing so, which is death, with the advantage, which is knowing good and evil. She realizes the tree holds the potential for food, that it was a "delight to the eyes," and that it had the ability to make one wise. In other contexts, people would readily admit all of these are good reasons to partake of the fruit. Eve does the reasoning work of a theologian and determines the best path, deciding through her problem solving that knowledge of good and evil is worth the risks involved. Alternatively, Adam does none of this: he eats unreflectively.[23]

Of course, the final assault on Eve's character comes from the so-called punishment she receives: pain that is multiplied in childbirth and magnified by men who point out that with every birth women are reminded of their subordinate place and propensity to sin. Such admonishments fail to account for the difference between something that is prescriptive (what should be; i.e., punishment) versus something descriptive (what will be, i.e., result).[24] Since the Bible is the result of Divine inspiration and human experience, we realize that its authors were trying to make sense of their lives, lives that in this case involved significant pain during childbirth. As readers we cannot make an uncritical leap from how these writers understood their experience to confirmation that their perceptions were the same thing as God's will. But because numerous people have failed to make such distinctions, they overlook the powerful insight conveyed in this narrative, choosing instead to blame Eve for sin and to point to childbirth as evidence of her disobedience.

Still, there is the potential now for better understanding. Eve's example is that life comes from the courage to fully participate in something new. In order to gain, we must be willing to lose. Eve's "yes" to life foreshadows Jesus' in the gospels. Isn't the resurrection itself one all-encompassing call to overcome death for the potential of new life? Rather than cowering in the face of danger, Eve opted for life, even with its pain.

If there is one other figure who gets blamed almost as much as Eve for all that is wrong in the world, it is "satan," the talking serpent in Genesis. Seen by evangelicals as a devil who tricked Eve and Adam into their life-altering decision, a closer look reveals a different possibility. The serpent in fact does not mislead, nor tell a lie. Rather, reading Genesis through the lens of its relation to other ancient texts suggests the serpent is symbolic rather than literal, its place in the narrative less about evil than something much more significant. The mythologist Joseph Campbell points out that a serpent has the ability to throw off the old and embrace the new, much as a snake sheds its skin. Instead of a temptation to do evil, the serpent, rather, is an image of life. "Life sheds one generation after another, to be born again."[25] In the Genesis story, the serpent shows Eve and Adam the truth. Eating the fruit of the forbidden tree represents moving beyond an idyllic existence into the true reality of life, one that comes with an awareness of good and bad. This shift occurs for all of us. We migrate from a state of innocence into a state of maturity marked by realizations that nothing is truly good or truly evil, but that all of us, indeed all of life, are a commingling of both.

Understood this way we realize the serpent is an agent of transformation, of what it takes to become a new creation. The ability to shed the trappings of an old way of thinking or being for new ways of thinking or being is a process. Such a transition requires the ability to comprehend paradox and inequity, to understand complexity and to discover that life, despite its wonder and beauty, is sometimes simply unfair and cruel.

What Eve and Adam learn from the serpent is that life is more complex than they had imagined, and in order to function in their world, they had to realize paradise was not what they thought it was. Paradise represented innocence, a time of bliss. But can paradise produce transformation? Most likely not. The best place, the environment where we will more fully develop into what we are meant to be, is one in which hard realities exist, where the painful process of shedding one's skin is the only way to stay alive.

Looking at the passage with fresh eyes reveals other significant details, too. Trees and gardens, for example, were common motifs in ancient Near Eastern traditions, and were symbols of feminine fertility and of wisdom. By eating fruit from the tree, Eve might not necessarily be succumbing to the wiles of a crafty serpent. She may, in fact, be choosing to live a different kind of life: one less idyllic, but one imbued with the complexities of wisdom. In such a reframing, Eve is an example of a wise woman.

In Genesis 2, God forms a being out of the dust. The Hebrew term for this being is *adam*, closely related to another Hebrew term, *adamah*, which means of dust from the ground. We might say God forms a dust creature or, as one translation suggests, "man from the dust of the ground." So, there are three possible ways to translate the Hebrew word: Adam (personal name), man from the dust of the ground, and dust creature. Two of these choices are masculine, while one is androgynous without any clear reference to sex distinction.

This acknowledgment about sex is important because it is not until the end of Genesis 2 that there is a clear distinction of sex made by the narrative. The terms for this differentiation are *ish* (male) and *ishah* (female): "This at last is bone of my bones / and flesh of my flesh; / this one shall be called Woman (*ishah*), / for out of Man (*ish*) this one was taken" (Gen. 2:23). Careful observations allow a counter-narrative to emerge. An androgynous being is created to care for the earth and to establish relationships with the animal world. From that one being another one is born, one that is intimately connected to the first and yet has its own distinctiveness. There is no hierarchy or primacy here. Instead, the picture of cooperation and true sharing poignantly reflects the Divine image these humans are said to possess.

We can also reasonably deduce from Genesis that the presence of sinfulness, without a preoccupation with it as evangelicals promote, is healthy and helpful. Genesis points to an undeniable paradox, one we experience every day. Humans are fundamentally good and yet prone to make mistakes. We reach out to others, expressing love, generosity, and grace, and at the same time we misunderstand each other—we withhold love, we fail to be generous, and we can be intensely selfish. Although Augustine all those years ago decided sinfulness and sexuality were inseparably linked, we do not have to embrace and perpetuate this notion by focusing on "the fall," and on seeing every human act through that lens. More to the point, we do not need to have girls growing up believing that they—and their bodies—are responsible for the entrance of sin in this world, nor that they need to somehow redeem Eve's mistake by protecting the thing most valuable to them: their virginity—i.e., their "purity."

Like Eve, we can be the protagonists in our lives, an idea suggested by Susan Niditch.[26] Feminist theologians have challenged the male-centered notions of sin as primarily expressed in pride, egoism, and self-love. Since men are often socialized to be independent, the excessive problem of that independence readily explains this view of sin. At the same time, however, women are normally socialized not for independence but for serving others, often men. The excess of giving to others is not pride, egoism, and self-love, but rather self-abrogation, self-denial, even self-loathing. Taking women's experiences seriously enables a revision to the Eve-as-sinner motif and instead suggests Eve's autonomy and agency are skills women should embrace. They are traits that lead to life, even with all of its complexities and challenges.

While many evangelical leaders use Eve to prop up patriarchal versions of the Christian faith, convincing scores of young women and girls to be servants to men and boys, to promote a good society by staying home and rearing large families, this relies on reading the Bible in a particular way. If women want to be all they were meant to be, they can start by throwing off the blinders their leaders and teachers have been encouraging them to wear and begin embracing the liberty offered to them evident in the Bible, modeled by a woman who chose life over living in a box, even an idyllic one.

Chapter Two

Waiting for Boaz and Other Myths of Love

Almost any Christian college graduate knows the dating rituals that inform campus life. Having been told the best place to find a mate is at college, and with only a few years standing between matriculation and graduation, evangelical college students learn it's best to start the spousal search immediately, with first-year orientation, when many college women begin their quest to find Mr. Right: someone with good-Christian-boy looks and an at-ease mien; someone who prays ardently; someone who plays guitar soulfully, strumming Christian choruses just loud enough for everyone in the campus quad to hear.

Someone, in other words, like Boaz.

Yes, that Boaz: the older man in the biblical book of Ruth who has become, for many evangelicals, the model of a Christian man whom all godly women should strive to find and marry, and before college graduation, if possible. He knows how to treat women, and is wealthy, hard-working, and successful, all traits good Christian women want in their men. When women seek their Boaz, they are hoping for Mr. Right, perfect in every way.

"Waiting on your Boaz" has become the evangelical catchphrase for patiently praying for the man of one's dreams. Presumably, "someday, my prince will come" seems far too secular a principle for an evangelical woman who wants a godly man, not Prince Charming. And who better to represent that Christian ideal than Boaz, an actor in what some might claim is the best love story the Bible ever told. Not one, but two, Facebook pages invite women to wait for their Boaz, with one page garnering 23,000 members by offering encouraging slogans for those who linger in their singleness. Although the sites promise to help people "pursue God relentlessly before and after the waiting process," and although they suggest both men and women are each seeking their Boaz, the site's intended purpose is clear. Someday, your Boaz will come. And, until then, members of the Facebook pages are to "dance with God," knowing that "he will let the perfect man cut in."

If Boaz is the perfect Christian man, then naturally his counterpart, Ruth, is the godly woman to whom all Christian women should aspire. Ruth was apparently a woman of integrity and sacrificial love, someone who waited patiently for "The One" without the help of two Facebook pages to sustain her; women are encouraged to be just like Ruth, assured that when they develop Ruth's character, they make themselves more attractive to the Boaz-men they seek.

In recreating the book of Ruth as a guide for dating and marriage, evangelicals overlook the many complex cultural components in the text, starting with this most basic of facts: that both Boaz and Ruth existed before Jesus' ministry and therefore cannot be considered models of "Christian" perfection. Instead, the "waiting for Boaz" interpretation of Scripture (and its companion, "Ruth as godly woman") is read through the lens of contemporary culture, of twenty-first–century and Western romantic ideals. As a result, women and men are asked to fit into some imagined biblical model that does not exist, and which the biblical characters Ruth and Boaz would probably not recognize.

Ruth as Godly Woman

What specifically about Ruth makes her a godly woman? Of all the female characters in the Bible, why has Ruth been chosen as a key model for biblical womanhood, especially in regards to love and romance? And why have so many evangelicals focused their attention in the story on Boaz, when Ruth is the protagonist and actor in her own narrative?

Those cultural artifacts highlighting the Ruth story often turn initially to her virtue and her steadfast commitment to her mother-in-law, Naomi. Ruth is seen as embodying the character traits of perfect womanhood—traits that Christian women are called to emulate. Websites devoted to explaining the book of Ruth focus their study on Ruth's doggedness, loyalty, and industry, suggesting a godly woman is not relentless in her activity outside the public sphere but in her pursuit of family and relationship. Thus Ruth's efforts to save herself and Naomi are seen as righteous, her work outside the home necessary only in its ability to secure a husband, saving Naomi and Ruth from a lifetime of labor.

Ruth's connection to the Proverbs 31 woman is so strong that at least on one site, Ruth is called the ultimate Proverbs 31 woman: talk about mixed biblical metaphors! In a blog post on the site, figuring Ruth as a Proverbs 31 woman, a writer at the Unlocking Femininity website suggests we need to understand Ruth primarily in terms of her lineage to Jesus Christ—a common reason writers suggest Ruth deserves our attention. Also, because in the Hebrew Bible the book of Proverbs and the book of Ruth are in close proximity, readers are to understand that Ruth becomes a "real life" model of the Proverbs 31 woman.[1] This, despite the fact that the location of Ruth after Proverbs was made for different reasons entirely: Jewish authorities made their placement decision as a way of reinforcing community rituals, thus grouping it with other festival scrolls—including Esther, Song of Solomon, Ecclesiastes, and Lamentations.[2]

How did Ruth exemplify the ultimate Proverbs 31 woman? While Ruth was a strong woman who toiled in the fields from day to night, this work was always selfless, meant to feed her family, which initially included only Naomi. The unstated assumption is that contemporary women who work outside the home may be strong, but consider only themselves, not their families. As the site explains, "A Proverbs 31 woman works to provide food for her home and she works hard, never leaving an idle moment. She is resourceful, intentional, and productive. She knows the value of time when taking care of a family and she doesn't waste it, making sure her family doesn't suffer because of her laziness."[3]

In addition to being a hard worker, Ruth is also a woman of faith and compassion, someone who trusted God to provide her with all her needs—including her Boaz. She is also said to have waited for God's blessing. Women seeking to live a godly life thus have to be everything to all people—a hard worker, a provider for the family, a faithful member of a community, someone who never rests—and, in doing so, they will be given their Boaz: the perfect man. These descriptions of the perfect godly woman make Ruth sound more like a Disney Princess, ready for her Boaz-like Prince Charming. Evangelical popular culture often figures the book of Ruth as one of "the greatest love stories ever told," the courtship and marriage of Ruth and Boaz revealing them to be "a couple after God's own heart." One pastor in his sermon about

Ruth and Boaz described their courtship as a "love story written by God," a prominent theme as well in a number of books about biblical stories and the godly models for marriage they can provide.

In the marriage-motif readings of Ruth, her humility is praised as the one characteristic all women should seek to cultivate while waiting for their Boaz. Brad Anderson, writing for faithcycleministry.org, suggests Boaz was so impressed by Ruth's humility that he failed to realize her outer beauty. In this case, Ruth's bow when she initially meets Boaz after gleaning in his field indicates she has treated this eligible bachelor with the appropriate deference all good Christian women should have.[4]

But these romantic notions of Ruth misrepresent the biblical narrative. Ruth is loyal, fiercely so, but not in the way most highlight. Ruth's determination to accompany her mother-in-law from Moab to Naomi's hometown of Bethlehem is especially interesting, given that the loyalty she is acclaimed to have is not initially given to Boaz, but to Naomi, a woman. The popular phrase—often used in marriage ceremonies—where Ruth tells Naomi, "Where you go, I will go; / where you lodge, I will lodge;… / your God [will be] my God" (1:16), is reminiscent of the "leave and cleave" language in Genesis—save that here, the words are not what readers generally expect to find between women, especially because most readers are encouraged to see a traditional love story in Ruth and Boaz that simply is not there. And so readers seldom pause when the narrative takes a bizarre twist: Naomi responds with silence to Ruth's determination to join Naomi on a treacherous journey, one that easily could have been their demise (1:18). Mythologies about Ruth's love story also show little consideration to Naomi's statement given to her hometown friends upon their safe return to Bethlehem. There she laments she has returned home empty. This, despite the fact Ruth is standing beside her, having left her country and family to do so.

So, it is Naomi, in fact, who represents the epitome of so-called biblical womanhood: she, rather than Ruth, defines herself in terms of being a wife and having children. Ruth epitomizes an independent spirit: she goes against the cultural norms by choosing to embrace her mother-in-law rather than remaining within her own culture. The only way readers might use the book of Ruth to support a traditional love story is to eschew the book's central plot, and to ignore the ways Naomi fits the traditional model of biblical womanhood that are often ascribed to Ruth instead.

Ruth isn't the only person in the biblical narrative to embark on a long journey. Abraham, the great patriarch of Christian tradition, responds to the Divine command to leave his home country and travel to an alien place. His decision to do this results in a reward of land, children, and a prominent place in history. As a contrast to his story, Ruth embraces her journey not because of a Divine order but because of her loyalty. There is no promised reward for her; it is her own initiative she follows, a selfless decision made on her own. Ruth is not lauded for who she is but instead for whom readers want her to be. She leaves her home, choosing to cleave to another woman. Rather than explore the complexity of female friendship and companionship, evangelicals shift the focus to the relationship between Ruth and Boaz, perhaps fearing close friendships between women might reflect lesbianism.

But consider this: Ruth chooses autonomy over submitting to the decisions of someone else, seeking her own fortune once she arrives in Naomi's hometown. By ignoring the initiative and determination of Ruth, readers gravitate to the romantic potential between a woman in need of help and a man in the position to give it. Rather than noting that, at every turn in the narrative, Ruth creates the opportunities she needs, another tale gets spun: that Ruth's future is secured because she knew how to patiently wait for Boaz to make the godly move.

The narrative's denouement suggests something far different than a great romance to emulate. Only when Ruth gains security for Naomi and herself through Boaz can she finally exemplify the so-called biblical model of a godly wife by becoming silent. Throughout the entire plot she has been the driving force: making decisions, finding food, providing a means for two single women to live. And yet, once she is presumably married to Boaz and gives birth to a son, Ruth doesn't just fade into the background, she disappears. Naomi nurses the baby; the locals rejoice, "A son has been born to Naomi" (4:17); and they name him. In becoming a wife and a mother, Ruth ceases to be the protagonist in her own drama.

Alas, Ruth can be praised as the quintessential biblical woman only when viewed through a lens that presumes being mother is all that matters, as well as being married to someone like Boaz.

Bozo Versus Boaz

One popular concept traveling through the evangelical internet relies on a cleverly worded comparison, challenging women to find the Boaz in their lives, not the Bozo. The Bozo is the clownish reject no woman would ever seek to marry. How exactly does a woman recognize that her man is a Boaz rather than Bozo? A Boaz will be obviously single and unattached, with no past baggage weighing him down; a Bozo has loads of history, and maybe even a woman he's willing to leave when something better comes along. A Bozo doesn't recognize the worth of women, and is out only to please himself. He has no self-control, while Boaz is patient and guarded, unwilling to jump into the sack with just anyone. Boaz's qualities certainly make any person attractive, male or female; in many ways, they are character traits we should all strive to achieve: fidelity, compassion, thoughtfulness, the knowledge that sexual intimacy demands emotional maturity.

Beyond these appealing qualities, though, Boaz is also a man's man, at least according to Steve Farrar in *Real Valor: A Charge to Nurture and Protect Your Family*. The biblical character is a model for valor men today can turn to, giving men the clear answers they need about what it means to be a man of God. Boaz is a little rough around the edges and a little unrefined, but at his heart he is all a woman will need: a savior and protector, providing Ruth with financial help at a critical time. He steps into Ruth's story and changes the course of her life. Farrar believes Boaz is so much a man of valor that the biblical book is misnamed and should be the book of Boaz.[5] Who wouldn't want a man as the central actor in a crucial biblical story rather than giving the leading lady central billing?

Christian marketers intend to help women deal with impatience while they wait for manly perfection, emblematic in the descriptor "Boaz." If you investigate these products, you will note that character traits of Boaz seem strikingly similar to those men of Hollywood construction we also find perfect. While Christian writers generally avoid describing Boaz's appearance, they are quick to note his other defining characteristics: that he is selfless and sacrificial, kind and thoughtful, a caretaker and a protector. Boaz is also morally pure, his sexual relationship with his first wife notwithstanding.

Who wouldn't want a man like the Boaz described by evangelicals? Judging from descriptions of the contemporary Boaz, there is no way in which such a man will be found wanting. In the same way that the Proverbs 31 wife has become the model of godliness for evangelical women, Boaz is becoming for evangelical men the standard to which they must aspire: perfect in every way, right down to his willingness to protect the woman who shows up at his feet—or, who somehow has been waiting at his feet all along. Boaz has become so pervasive a model of godly perfection, in fact, that some women are starting Pinterest boards that describe the clothes, shoes, even smoking jackets that will be worn by their Boazes, and include as well images of the wedding attire a metaphoric Boaz and Ruth might wear, and the beds upon which they will have passionate sex with their Boazes. On the "For Boaz, Not Bozo" Pinterest board, one woman has pinned a number of very snazzy Italian suits and leather shoes for her Boaz, presumably not worried about the dust on her threshing floor.

Studying the mass of Boaz cultural artifacts in their totality, we might want to ask why there is such an intensive focus on Boaz? Why has attention turned to Boaz in elevating the book of Ruth to the "best love story ever told"? And what does this say about evangelicals' understanding of love stories, period?

The Evangelical Idea of Waiting

Embedded within the Boaz meme is a deeply held ideal about women's roles and about who and what women should be. Ideologies about biblical womanhood take perceptions about gender roles, then apply those lenses to the biblical text—in this case, the book of Ruth. Instead of seeing Ruth as an actor in her own story, as someone who pursues Boaz out of her own need, she has become a woman who waits. Boaz becomes the man worth waiting for.

The mythology that compels this understanding goes something like this. Because women are to be passive and submissive, without agency or autonomy, it is important for this God-designed role to also operate in dating and marriage relationships. Women are not to show interest in men, ask them out on dates, or pursue them in any way. To do so would abrogate the clearly delineated roles presumably in the Bible: that men are to be the dominant actors, and women the passive ladies-in-waiting, hoping and praying that their Boazes will come.

While many evangelicals love to claim this as a biblical ideal, the sense of a passively waiting woman really is a nineteenth–century phenomena, a Victorian principle that has been revived for new generations. Initially named after a poem by Coventry Patmore, "The Angel in the House" ideal reflects in many ways the characteristics evangelicals see in the Ruth and Boaz story, and indeed informs many definitions of godly womanhood now prominent in evangelical popular culture. For those in the Victorian era—and for many evangelicals now—this model of godliness figures a woman as docile and submissive, graceful and charming, devoted, and sexually pure. She also cannot act on her own, meaning she is to avoid pursuing a romantic relationship with men, because this is not her godly role. This submission is all-encompassing: a woman interested in dating a man is not to call him first, but must wait for him to call; she cannot ask him on a date, but must wait for his first move; she cannot pursue him after a date, but must wait for him to call again. She certainly cannot suggest marriage, for it his duty to ask her father first, then ask her.

The ideal, perhaps even idol, of a woman waiting patiently for her Boaz to come has become an important part of evangelical dating advice, which gives complete agency to men, who are responsible for asking, organizing, and paying for a date, and must always pursue women. Deeply embedded in the dating advice is the sense that women are to wait for men to pursue them, a theme explored *ad nauseam* in evangelical popular culture, from John Eldridge to Mark Driscoll to *Boundless* podcast regular Candice Watters, who encourages women to "pray boldly" for some future spouse. In her book, *Get Married: What Women Can Do to Make It Happen*, Watters urges women to make themselves marriage material, then essentially sit back and wait. If they've taken the right steps toward improving their eligibility to marry, then waiting for the right man to come along will be part of God's plan.[6] This requires making themselves perfect godly women, the Proverbs 31women/Ruths whose every attribute will be made attractive to the men God intends for them to marry.

According to a number of sites intending to help women prepare for marriage, this means praying ardently for one's future spouse. Even before meeting this man, a single Christian woman should be asking God to protect, nurture, and prepare him, too; even single women can practice the power of the praying wife before they've married. Waiting also requires that women inventory their weaknesses as potential wives and work on improving those weaknesses so that future spouses will not find them wanting. Women who struggle with domesticity should seek ways to strengthen their housekeeping muscles, making meals for friends, cleaning their family homes, perusing websites for ideas about how to enhance home and hearth.

Practice may also take the form of learning submission—something a Christian woman will definitely need to do once she is married. Because many evangelicals believe contemporary women have been destroyed by feminism, practice in submission is especially vital. Women should find men to whom they can submit: generally, one's father can provide a good testing ground. Beyond this, Christian singles are told that God (or, in some cases, Jesus) is the husband on whom to try submission—until an earthly husband can be found. One Christian singles website says, "God is your husband for now. Seek His guidance and ask His permission before doing or committing to various activities."[7] Only this kind of submission will prepare a woman for when it will be necessary to ask her spouse to make every kind of decision, from when they will have children to what kind of food she will cook.

Because, of course, she will have children, and she will cook.

These days, an Angel in the House has all kinds of evangelical cultural artifacts at her disposal, including those ubiquitous social networking sites that promise encouragement for women while waiting, lifting followers up with white-washed photos of women in solitary places, thinking deep thoughts about trusting God's timing; stories of those who were rewarded for their long waiting; and reminders that, while people wait, it's important for them to stay invested in their own lives.

What evangelicals don't have, however, is biblical evidence to support this notion of waiting. And, without this, they are compelled to shift their focus from Ruth, the protagonist of her narrative, to Boaz. By placing their attention on the male in this narrative, they can more successfully promote their idea of biblical womanhood.

Boaz and Purity

In evangelical mythology, waiting means not only passivity for women as they wait for their Boazes but it also means purity, as in no sexual intercourse until Boaz has tied the knot. Indeed, the ideal of "waiting" is so prominent a part of evangelical popular culture that an entire industry has been built up to convince young women to remain virgins until marriage.

Boaz and Ruth are seen as the ideal couple who presumably avoid sexual contact until after their nuptials. John Piper, a prominent evangelical leader, interprets the book of Ruth on his Desiring God site by exploring "strategic righteousness." Boaz, "a God-saturated man," and Ruth, "a God-dependent young woman," are placed in a situation in which they could do evil. After all, an older man and a younger woman, alone on a threshing floor? Why would Naomi put a young woman into such a potentially sexually compromising position? To show her purity and strength in the face of temptation! Piper writes, "The situation is one that could lead us into a passionate and illicit scene of sexual intercourse or into a stunning scene of purity, integrity, and self-control." Using "strategic righteousness," both Boaz and Ruth are able to create a romantic situation that is subtle, righteous, strategic, beautiful. Piper concludes we need to be like Boaz and Ruth, "profoundly in love" and "powerful in self control."[8]

This perspective of sexual purity fails to find support in Scripture, because Ruth seeks an encounter with Boaz that many evangelical readers ignore: an interpretation generally supported by most biblical scholars who read the story within its historical and cultural context.

At one point in the narrative, when the harvest is almost over, Naomi tells Ruth she should wash, put on perfume and her best dress, and go to the threshing floor, a place associated with extramarital sexual activity.[9] Once there, Ruth should wait until Boaz has finished eating and drinking and only then present herself to him. Finally, Naomi says, "When he lies down, observe the place where he lies; then, go and uncover his feet and lie down; and he will tell you what to do" (Ruth 3:4).

Ruth, however, only partially follows Naomi's instructions when she dresses up and goes to meet Boaz. Once she arrives, rather than waiting for Boaz–as Naomi had wished–Ruth uncovers Boaz's feet, then tells him what to do, that he should "spread your cloak over your servant" (Ruth 3:9).

Two details in this narrative shatter the evangelical myth of sexual purity: the threshing floor as the place for sexual encounters, and the use of the term "feet," a literary euphemism for male genitalia. Look to most any study Bible, and you will see an explanation of this euphemism, widely accepted by biblical scholars. An examination of the same scene in the *Zondervan NIV Study Bible*, the flagship text for many evangelicals, however, will reveal a startling silence about Boaz's feet. Instead, there are strong intimations that Ruth and Boaz were sexually pure that night, desiring not each other but their impending marriage.

Even without knowing about the euphemism employed, the narrative itself reveals the potential vagaries of this episode. Why does Ruth prepare to meet Boaz at dark by dressing up, if not to be physically enticing? Further, why does Naomi tell Ruth to present herself to Boaz only after he is content with a full belly and plenty to drink? Finally, does it really make sense to imagine a woman going to the trouble of wearing her best clothes, of using rare perfume, to meet a man by uncovering his feet? Of course not, *unless you are ignoring all of the reading clues.*

While the story doesn't spell out whether or not there is actual intercourse, it is difficult to imagine the scene any other way. And yet, in a quest for "purity," the predominant evangelical narrative about Ruth ignores these aspects of the story, happy to have a dressed-up Ruth meet Boaz in the middle of the night to uncover his feet (not his genitalia) and be her redeemer. Knowing these important narrative clues, it isn't difficult to understand why evangelicals shift their gaze away from Ruth in order to make this a "safe" biblical story. There is too much here that contradicts popular assumptions about women and sex. "Waiting for Boaz" is obviously more beneficial: there is no independent woman, just one who is fiercely loyal; there is no serious threat to livelihood, just a poignant love story between a patient woman and her God-fearing, soon-to-be husband.

Taking Another Look: A Great Love Story

The book of Ruth may be "the greatest love story ever told," but not for the reasons many suppose. If readers allow the narrative to unfold in light of its cultural context, the concrete manifestations of love emerge. The book of Ruth poignantly displays how one woman— an outsider because of her ethnicity (a Moabite traveling into an Israelite setting), her family (a widow who is her mother-in-law), her gender (a woman in a staunchly patriarchal society), and her religion— becomes an insider. Despite her multiple ostracizing factors, Ruth travels not only to a new locale but also into new levels of acceptance.

Her decision to be loyal to Naomi at all costs debunks any notion that only Jews knew how to treat others, how to love someone else more than oneself. Ruth is not just loyal to her mother-in-law, she is dedicated to someone very different from herself. Ruth's journey to Bethlehem is a powerful image of crossing barriers, of learning that culture and ethnicity do not need to separate us. Upon her arrival in Bethlehem, Ruth is able to find food, gleaning in the fields of Boaz. She is allowed to do this because of specific laws put in place to provide sustenance for the destitute that also required that people work to gather the food they needed. Even though Ruth is not an Israelite, this provision of care extends to her, a tangible example of what it means to love a stranger. This cultivation of love and compassion is a dominant theme throughout Scripture and in Jesus' ministry. When readers twist the story into one about a romantic quest and pining for Boaz, the real message of love and loyalty is lost.

In the Ruth story, once another person has been identified as the "next-of-kin" and Boaz must negotiate the law in order to solidify his relationship with Ruth, we see evidence of a second law stipulating that those most vulnerable in the society, usually women and children, would have a social safety net. Even though the book of Ruth reveals an ancient society, what it also conveys is a society that has already established strong family values: the values of sustenance, of social responsibility, of caring for one's family.

When evangelicals look for romance and purity in the lives of Ruth and Boaz, not only do they establish warped visions of biblical characters, they also create harmful ideas of perfection and purity. These ideas, while intended to be helpful, can be extraordinarily damaging to women and men, compelling Christians to aspire to problematic notions about what it means to be godly women or men. Boaz-and-Ruth mythologies also send messages to young people about love, marriage, waiting, purity, and autonomy that are not accurate reflections of the biblical narratives. Instead, the moral underpinnings of biblical narratives are disregarded in favor of Western, individualistic, religiously conservative notions of what it means to be a good person, ideas that would have seemed foreign in the biblical contexts from which they have mutated.

Consider instead how women and men might understand themselves—and their relationship to God—differently, were they to read the book of Ruth in an alternative way. Women might not need to assume a position of passively waiting for Boaz, nor would they feel the shame of their shortcomings—of their inability to live up to some supposed model of female godliness embodied in Ruth. Men might no longer feel the pressure to be as Boaz, the exemplar of manliness, steadfast and strong in his well-pressed suit. Rejecting the evangelical mythology of a happily-ever-after Ruth and Boaz love story might allow both men and women to be all God intends them to be, and to enact what Christ himself says are the greatest commandments: loving God with a loyalty similar to that which Ruth loved, and loving your neighbor (Moabite or otherwise) as yourself.

Perhaps the book of Ruth is a poignant love story, after all.

Chapter Three

What's Wrong with Proverbs 31?

In December 2011, a student at Baylor University discovered there were only two kinds of women: either they were virtuous, or they were sluts. Even though women have been categorized by these unfortunate polarities for centuries, the Baylor student felt his idea unique, and like others of his generation, he immediately produced a YouTube video, sharing his astounding epiphany: he would "rather have a Proverbs 31 woman than a Victoria's Secret model."[1]

And thus the Live 31 movement was launched. Targeted primarily to young people, the Live 31 movement hoped to encourage others to see women's inner virtue rather than their physical beauty. The YouTube video quickly garnered over 200,000 views, and its Facebook page reached over 13,000 "likes" within a month's time.[2] The video and the Live 31 site outline exactly who this enviable Proverbs 31 woman should be. So that college students can begin looking for the "wife of noble character," they are told they should use Proverbs 31 as their guide.

The video encourages young women to be Proverbs 31 women, telling the young men in the audience seeking to date that they should look for a Proverbs 31 woman, and that they "shouldn't settle for anything less." The divorce rates in this country will go down, we are promised, because men will be marrying something other than just the Victoria's Secret aesthetic.

There is nothing wrong with critiquing the Victoria's Secret mindset, and the video is no doubt right in noting that young women express constant insecurities about their appearances because of events such as the Victoria's Secret fashion shows. But the response to the ideal image of physical beauty presented by Victoria's Secret is to argue that women need to set their sights on the woman of virtue found in Proverbs 31, and use her as the model for rightful living. What the Live 31 movement doesn't seem to realize is that there's a different kind of pressure, mostly unacknowledged, in taking that approach.

It's a method evangelical popular culture has found quite useful to pressure women into conforming to an unattainable model of perfection. The myth of the Proverbs 31 woman is a useful tool for making women feel the need to be all things to all people: beautiful and strong; virtuous and docile; an extraordinary housekeeper who does everything for all people; a savvy business person who works from home in order to also tend to children and husband; a woman attuned to health and fitness, who wears the right fashion with modesty and grace. Websites and books on the Proverb urge women to live by its principles. Entire industries have sprung up to help women live the Proverbs 31 perfection by selling purses and whatnot from home, all the while raising babies who hang off both modestly covered breasts.

Evangelical popular culture has provided models for men to follow as well, but the Proverbs 31 mythology has become so pervasive that even those with only a glancing knowledge of evangelicalism know pretty much who and what women are supposed to become: the Proverbs 31 wife, able to accomplish more before the sun rises than any other female imaginable. Proverbs 31 products fail to interpret the Scripture within its cultural context, and also shackle women to an impossible standard by setting up such a model of "Christian" perfection they must attain, else they will surely sink to the status of a Victoria's Secret model.

A Biblical Martha Stewart

For the last few decades, Martha Stewart has been synonymous with impeccable home décor, effortless crafting, and making gourmet meals for dozens every night of the week. Her vast business empire reaches into publishing, broadcasting, and marketing, and—at least for a while—into shilling housewares for Kmart, so that those with low coin could aspire to her decorating beauty and grace. Even a guilty verdict for securities fraud with five months of incarceration was only a small blemish on Stewart's career.

In many ways, the Proverbs 31 woman is evangelicalism's Martha Stewart, minus the jail term. The Proverbs 31 woman decorates her home well, dresses in fine clothes (marked by the K-mart brand if necessary), and makes fabulous meals for her family. Compare many of the Proverbs 31 websites with Martha Stewart's *Real Simple* magazine, and you see little difference: images of beautiful (white) women standing in well-appointed homes (or, inexplicably, in fields of grain); links to recipes, decorating ideas, and child-raising tips; and day-by-day resources to help make a woman's life manageable and perfect.

Proverbs 31 Ministries might well be the mother ship as far as Proverbs 31 information is concerned, and its likeness to the Martha Stewart empire is indisputable. Started in 1992, Proverbs 31 Ministries has developed a significant outreach to women worldwide. In addition to providing resources, blogs, books, and devotions on its website, Proverbs 31 Ministries sponsors "She Speaks" conferences intended to help women "answer God's call on your life" which, according to conference materials, means helping women get trained in speaking, writing, and leadership; guiding them in developing platforms; and encouraging women who are looking for agents and editors who will publish their material.[3]

In this sense, Proverbs 31 Ministries is an equipping organization, helping to empower women who are pursuing professional goals. Beyond the She Speaks conferences, Proverbs 31 Ministries includes training materials that promise to equip women to "write, speak, and lead with excellence," and provides professional coaching as part of its services. Seeing in the Scripture clear avocation for professional work of a sort, Proverbs 31 Ministries hopes to create a godly woman who, like the "real" Proverbs 31 woman, works hard to bring income into the home. The Bible tells us that the Proverbs 31 woman works diligently with her hands, that she buys fields using her business acumen, and even that she makes and sells fine linens—kind of like Martha Stewart, selling household goods to the bargain-shopping masses. For many adherents of the Proverbs 31 model for feminine godliness, having some kind of professional life—especially a platform intended to save souls for Christ—is an acceptable reading of Scripture.[4]

Yet organizations such as Proverbs 31 Ministries offer another message about what it means to be a woman of virtue, and this message is stronger and more pervasive than messages about the Proverbs 31 woman's vocational choices. The passage also suggests that the Proverbs 31 woman is a consummate wife, so perfect in her spousal duties that her husband will stand at the city gate, praising her name. She is an industrious woman in her own home, and her children call her blessed because she is an amazing mother whose daughters share her virtue. Proverbs 31 Ministries has a coalition of bloggers, almost all beautiful (white) women who provide advice on everything from child rearing to decorating tips, often times with exquisite photography that appears to be right out of Stewart's *Real Simple* magazine.[5]

Although Proverbs 31 Ministries seems to accept the belief that a godly woman can be both consummate mother and successful professional, this idea is not shared by many other advocates of the Proverbs 31 model for women. The more prominent evangelical reading of Proverbs 31 downplays a woman's professional work while highlighting other parts of the passage that assert the woman's in-home acumen, reflecting the persistent narrative that God has designed women to live within the domestic sphere, provided for by men who are designed for the professional world.

A Proverbs 31 Business Plan

The "contemporary career woman" is a reviled character in the evangelical narrative of God's design for women, because she has been wooed by feminism to leave her biblical realm and venture out into a man's world, ignoring her children and husband in the process. Because of the idea that women who work outside the home are also outside of God's plan, a different way of reading Proverbs 31 was needed, one that understood her work as a business woman differently. The Proverbs 31 woman was *not* like today's career woman, one article asserts, as she did her work from home, spinning flax so she could be close to her children, thereby allowing her husband to work in a public role. Her work, the extra pin money she made by weaving linen at home, gave her husband more freedom to fulfill the vocation to which he had been called. She is his helpmeet, and everything she does is in relation to him, for "he is the center of all she does." Like other "contemporary career women," who leave their families to pursue their own selfish monetary and professional gain, the Proverbs 31 wife is really, truly staying within the godly sphere outlined by

Scripture.[6] For this reason, as evangelical considerations of the Proverbs 31 wife have become more ubiquitous, so too have at-home businesses catering to women who need a vocation, but who want to stay true to God's presumed design for women by doing their work within the home.

The woman who works inside the home at a Proverbs 31–inspired business can make extra money for her family if they are in financial difficulties. The idea that a woman can "help out" her husband by running a business within her home has been carried as well in the platforms of pseudo-secular-religious figures like Dr. Laura and Dave Ramsey, both who seem to preach a similar stay-at-home business model for women, arguing mothers (at least) should find some kind of work inside the home if the family needs a financial boost. While the impulse to work within the home is necessary for some families, given their circumstances, some savvy entrepreneurs have used this ideology to their fiscal advantage, creating at-home businesses catering to those who want to remain true to a particular reading of Scripture. And so now women can sell Proverbs 31 gifts, Proverbs 31 handbags and purses, P31 key fobs and purses, and skin care products and clothing, all from the comfort of their own homes, the P31 label itself branding the at-home business as godly, above reproach.

The more significant message is in the ideology underlying Proverbs 31 at-home businesses: that the biblical woman will stay at home and, if necessary, work from home, even if that means taking on sales jobs that do not in any way fit her gifting. Imagine a woman who would be miserable trying to sell anything, and who is being told the godly model for womanhood demands that she become a marketing consultant, trying to sell purses that are somehow sanctified by the Proverbs 31 label.

Many other evangelical women have used Proverbs 31 to justify their own home-based businesses, even if the Proverbs 31 stamp of approval is not part of the business name. One business woman offers an extended justification for a Proverbs 31–inspired home business, arguing that by staying home and making extra money through her skin care product line, she both follows closely the Proverbs 31 wifely model and has more freedom, a freedom "feminists don't want to acknowledge." She is certain that the money she makes from her skin care products is part of "God's design" for women, allowing them to live into their calling and to help their husbands with financial needs.[7] Another woman shared her story about how Proverbs 31 compelled her to become a Beachbody Fitness coach, writing that the Scripture passage describes a "warm, wise woman who works with willing hands, has a healthy body for her tasks, brings nutritious food for her household from afar, wakes up when it's still dark out to prepare for the day, her husband loves her and her children call her blessed! She also serves others and her community with her abundant blessings."[8] She now manages 150 other Beachbody coaches, using the Proverbs 31 philosophy—being a stay-at-home mom, running a business, and making money—to give other folks the beach-hot body they deserve.[9]

The idea that a toned body might be part of the Proverbs 31 wife's goals may at first appear inconsonant: the scriptural passage doesn't say anything about reaching fitness goals, nor does having fitness goals seem wholly compatible to the evangelical mythology that glorifies mothers as self-sacrificial, willing to put everyone's needs before their own. Yet another significant component of Proverbs 31 marketing is self-help products, intended to encourage women to become their perfect, most godly selves: through better diets, better fitness plans, better make-up and fashion choices, and better—that is, more organized—closets.

Apparently, although the biblical passage says little about the Proverb 31 wife's closet, it's presumed she would have had her shoes in order. And so, by extension, the godly woman will, too.

Scriptural Self-Help

The Proverbs 31 wife has become an excellent way to resolve any complicated feelings evangelicals have about self-improvement, providing a nifty biblical framework through which self-help gurus can peddle advice. Laying out a self-improvement plan following Proverbs 31 isn't about self-centeredness, but about being biblical. Women seeking to enhance their figures, wear nicer clothes, and become friendlier people are simply doing so because of biblical instruction, *not* because they want to be an improved version of themselves.

Embracing this mindset means that books such as the *90-Day Guide to Living the Proverbs 31 Life* (Donna Partow) can thrive in a Christian marketplace somewhat suspicious of self-help plans. The author promises that a woman who follows her advice will learn to live "with purpose and passion," and can "become the woman God wants you to be" in only 90 days! The book's introductory chapter suggests the author herself had her doubts about the Proverbs 31 woman. She writes, "Somehow I thought the Proverbs 31 woman was a mythological creature or worse—I thought she was a weapon spiritual leaders use to make all of us ordinary Christian women feel bad about ourselves." Subsequent chapters outline what and how a woman should eat, including directions for how she is to follow a "cleansing diet," purifying her body of all toxins before she begins her pursuit of wholesome eating, and that a simple daily fitness plan is an important part of being a godly woman. Day by day, advice is shared for what a woman needs to do to reach Proverbs 31 perfection: developing godly habits by decluttering messy spots in the home, collecting the right home-cleaning gear, making menu plans and grocery lists, and surveying clothing and make-up choices to assure that the appropriate color palettes are being followed.[10] Concurrently, a woman wanting to become a Proverbs 31 wife (in 90 days!) needs to also attend to husband and children, consider finances and plan for retirement, and potentially start a home-based business.

The Christian book marketplace is crowded with similar selections offering self-help instruction packaged in "easy-to-accomplish," biblical goals. Women can learn how to be a *Proverbs 31 Wife* (Lara Velez) using a handbook that allows them to interrogate their own daily activities and transform themselves by changing their bodies and their hearts, all to please the men in their lives. (And God, too, it goes without saying.) A Bible study called *Pursuit of Proverbs 31* (Amy Bayliss) helps women learn the "truth" about the proverb, and the perfect woman praised within. Women discover how to "live up to your God-given potential" by looking "into the heart of God and the reality of the words in the Bible."[11]

Other books echo this promise, suggesting that (1) the Proverbs 31 woman is a perfection about which others can only dream, but (2) to be a Christian, we must aspire to become a Proverbs 31 woman, because (3) doing so is biblical, and draws us closer to Jesus. And although married women with children are the primary audience for these self-help books, so much so that the Proverbs 31 woman has become known as the Proverbs 31 *wife* (as if those terms are interchangeable), publishers have found other lucrative markets to whom they can peddle their presumably biblical advice. Now, even women who have not been "blessed" by a husband can find strength, succor, and practical tips in the Proverbs 31 model through books such as Alice Giraud's *The Single Proverbs 31 Woman* and *A Guide to Waiting for the Single Proverbs 31 Man*. And, yes, there is apparently something called a "Proverbs 31 Man," giving rise to books such as *In Search of the Proverbs 31 Man* (Michelle McKinney Hammond) and *The Proverbs 31 Man: The Man at the Gate* (Stella Immanuel). Such books offer advice for both men *and* women, letting men know who they should be, and what they need to do to get there; and telling women exactly who they should be looking for in a spouse.[12] The Proverbs 31 man has been under assault by feminists, we are warned, and these books provide an important antidote, letting men know exactly who they need to be, especially if they want a godly Proverbs 31 wife.

The fundamental message in these self-help books is somewhat confusing, as the books provide advice to help women achieve that which evangelicals also argue she is designed to do: be a perfect wife and mother, her godliness centered in these roles. Even the books for other audiences–ostensibly for men, and for single women–work toward a similar goal, which is to create women who, like the Proverbs 31 figure, are all things to all people, or at least to their husbands and children. Understanding this, we recognize that the evangelical interpretation of the Proverbs 31 woman is really an interpretation of the Proverbs 31 *wife*, and that any messaging about this particular passage will ultimately focus on what evangelicals believe are the best, most biblical, most godly roles a woman should assume: those of wife and mother.

The Model of Wifely Perfection

Some Christians tend to use "wife" and "woman" interchangeably to describe the female figure in Proverbs 31. Thus any prescriptions about what it means to be a biblical woman, following the Proverbs 31 model, assume marriage–or, at least, the promise of nuptials at some point in the future. And prescriptions about the Proverbs 31 wife are everywhere: in evangelical women's Bible studies, in the conferences they attend–even on the Pinterest sites they visit, where they can pin easy-to-access checklists about what makes a godly woman, and step-by-step guides to creating a godly home. If those checklists aren't clear enough, women can make line-by-line comparisons between the character traits of a "virtuous woman" and that of a "voluptuous woman," a list that makes us wonder whether its compiler has considered that some women are voluptuous by godly (and/or genetic) design.

Everywhere in Proverbs 31 messaging for evangelical women, similar binaries are established: one is either voluptuous or virtuous;

a home breaker or a homemaker; self-centered or self-sacrificing; contemporary career woman or a biblical, godly wife. Prescriptions about the Proverbs 31 woman often center on these binaries, as if women can choose either the awful "ways of the world" or *the only* model for female godliness found in the Bible, in the figure of the Proverbs 31 wife. Over and over again, Bible studies on the Scripture passage focus on what the Proverbs 31 wife is, but also what she is not, highlighting her character traits through negation. She is a business woman, but does not work outside the home. She is a strong wife, but remains submissive to her husband. She is well clothed and physically fit, but her beauty definitely comes from within. She is humble and demure, but proud of her life as a Proverbs 31 wife.

So proud, in fact, that a number of Proverbs 31 products have been created to announce her primary status as Proverbs 31 wife. There are the plaques and paintings and needlepoint keepsakes that announce one's wifely virtue, but in the most humble way possible. What would be more godly than some nicely apportioned throw pillows announcing one's identity as a Proverbs 31 wife? What more would need to be stated to prove one's godliness? Christian marketers have also developed clothing lines allowing women to announce their own godliness through allusions to the proverb. Women can wear shirts labeling themselves as a "Proverbs 31 Wife" and tops proclaiming the wearer is "Clothed in Strength and Dignity." Those wives who want to appear somewhat culturally relevant while also standing above the secular fray can wear a "I'm a Real Housewife of Proverbs 31" shirt, or even one emblazoned with a Superman insignia, with "Proverbs 31 wife" superimposed on the giant pink "S."

Above all, the Proverbs 31 wife is superhuman, an ideal to which women can only aspire. Proponents of a presumably Proverbs 31 lifestyle will be forthright in this assertion: that the wife in Proverbs is perfect in every way, the standard for the "Good Christian Woman." And what exactly does this mean? According to at least one writer, the "Good Christian Woman" never complains about her husband, and she runs an impeccable home, in which she takes great pride. She represents her husband and family in what she wears, and in how she appears. And, most significantly, she "takes instruction from God, and always considers her husband."[13] Other Proverbs 31 propaganda echoes these sentiments: that a godly—that is, Christian—wife will have these self-sacrificial traits, focusing most on what she can do for her husband, his instruction being almost on par with God's.

Becoming a Proverbs 31 wife can be a heavy burden for women to carry, but plenty of Christians seem content hoisting the weight of Proverbs 31 onto their backs and walking through life, always aware that they are falling short of what they've been told is God's plan for them.

Filtering Down to Youth—Live 31 Movement

Like most Internet sensations, the Live 31 movement started red-hot and burned out a year later, so that, now, the URL for the movement (live31.org) directs users to a Japanese used car auction house. In its heyday, though, Live 31 got plenty of media attention, including a shout-out from a Victoria's Secret model, who decided to quit her modeling career, convicted that she needed to focus on her faith, and on becoming the Proverbs 31 woman God was calling her to be. Subsequently, she wrote a memoir about her experience. *I'm No Angel: From Victoria's Secret Model to Role Model* presumably details Kylie Bisutti's conviction that she needed to quit being a Victoria's Secret model and become, instead, a Proverbs 31 wife.[14]

After the release of the Live 31 video and website in December 2011, larger Christian publications began featuring the movement, and—in a PR-worthy twist—Bisutti took up the cause, telling her story of giving up Victoria's Secret for the Proverbs 31 lifestyle. She was interviewed by *Good Morning America* and Glenn Beck, Fox News, and *CBS This Morning* because, she said, the Live 31 "message is so biblical and Christ-centered, and it is exactly what I'm striving to be." Such a statement, one echoed by the campaign itself, revisited too much damaging ground: that there are only two kinds of women in this world, and you're either a slutty model or a Proverbs 31 saint; that women need to rehabilitate themselves primarily for the spouses who will marry them; that the standard to which women must aspire is one that focuses on submission, caring wholly for others, and sustaining the virtue of their homes and families. It's important to recognize, too, that these were college-aged men who drove the Live 31 movement, and that they presumed authority over their same-aged peers, letting women know how they are expected to act and be.

Teenage girls in evangelical settings hear about these expectations not only from their male peers, but from many other channels, telling them to be preparing for the Proverbs 31 life early, because the most godly trajectory for their future is one as the scripturally perfect wife and mother. Bible studies geared to teens focus on this message. Even on Pinterest and Instagram, the new online hangout for teens, girls can discover inspiration cheering them on to self-actualization as Proverbs 31 girls, including ideas for Proverbs 31 tattoos that girls can ink to their skin, permanent reminders that becoming "God's girls" means conforming to a scriptural pattern already clearly defined for them.

For those who are worried that Proverbs 31 is a little anachronistic—or perhaps intended only for the older set—a spoken word video convinces young women that Proverbs 31 can be relevant to them. Called 31 Status, the poem and its accompanying website remind teen girls that they should not conform to the beauty standards offered by today's world, and that, "like Eve," they have been deceived to follow the wrong advice, straying from Scripture. Rather than compromise, and be part of the world, girls are supposed to accept status as Proverbs 31 women. The artist Janette...ikz relies on maternal metaphors to let girls know they are "barefoot in the kitchen of grace, pregnant with purpose, baking up praise." Presumably, being a barefoot and pregnant teen in the kitchen of grace is morally acceptable, especially if praise is in the oven.[15]

When a teenage girl struggles to achieve the standards set by Proverbs 31, she can always turn again to the Proverbs 31 Pinterest sites for teens, where she can find all manner of inspirational pins, letting her know she is clothed in strength and dignity, and that her value is far above rubies and pearls. Important messages for sure, ones that teen girls especially need to hear every moment of every day. But when coupled with information on how to paint the kitchen, patterns for Christmas needlepoint pillows, and prescriptions for how to become the most godly Proverbs 31 woman possible, these messages become a little more muddled.

Muddled, but also persistent, thanks to Christian products that tell girls at an even earlier age what their highest aspiration should be. Girls can play with Proverbs 31 dolls and read Proverbs 31 children's books to know exactly who they are to emulate. Although the line has apparently been discontinued by the Blessed Toy Company (who has switched to a "God's Girls" doll product), the P31 dolls were advertised as having "similar features to the popular American Girl dolls but with a more pronounced biblical message," and were intended to "encourage young girls to pursue biblical womanhood." And what exactly was the message? Apparently, that if a girl wants to pursue biblical womanhood, she needs to get into the kitchen, pronto, because each doll came with its own "accessory kit, containing a Bible lesson (based on Proverbs 31:20), two cookie-cutters, a cookie recipe, and a list of exciting activities." Playing with the P31 doll inspired a girl to "look for good deeds she can do to help everyone around her," because at the heart of the Proverbs 31 wife is a desire to always help others; of course, being helpful isn't a bad characteristic, but is one *all children* should be taught, not only young girls, who learn the concurrent message that their God-given role is as servants to the men who instruct them.

Another line of Proverbs 31 dolls hopes girls will "act out godly themes in their play," which include "basic sewing, cooking, and crafting skills." Girls can also learn about their godly role by practicing "simple homemaking skills" through Ruby's miniature market basket, her garden tools, a doll-sized sewing kit, and linen sashes Ruby can pretend to sell (no doubt through her home-based business). Accompanying the doll is a workbook allowing a girl to learn what it means to be a Proverbs 31 woman of virtue, and to apply Proverbs 31 skills "in her own young life," as well as a Proverbs 31 Bible study that teaches principles such as "the law of kindness," "the bread of idleness," and what it means to reach "forth our hands to the needy."[16]

Christian marketers have also produced children's books to remind girls what their role is, or will be, and to teach them character traits they will need if they ever hope to become Proverbs 31 Women of Virtue. A book such as *God's Wisdom for Little Girls: Virtues and Fun from Proverbs 31* (Elizabeth George) instructs girls (in a fun way!) about the "qualities their moms strive for," which include helpfulness and thoughtfulness. The corresponding book for boys, called *God's Wisdom for Little Boys,* (Jim George and Elizabeth George) relies on the rest of Proverbs to provide "Character-Building Fun." We might be tempted to ask why boys need instruction from all parts of Scripture, but girls apparently need only attend to Proverbs 31, as if it alone provides the exclusive mold into which little girls should pour themselves.

By the time a daughter in an evangelical family reaches maturity, she has heard countless times that there is one woman especially in the Bible upon whom she should focus her attention. Forget those women who served as prophets and disciples, leaders, ministers of the gospel; their stories are admirable, but they are not as the Proverbs 31 woman/wife, upon whom some evangelicals seem to place all their expectations about women. So many idealistic expectations, we could *almost* think that the woman of Proverbs 31 wasn't a real person, or that the proverb really isn't meant to be a to-do list for how a woman might achieve godly perfection.

Couldn't we?

What's Wrong with Proverbs 31? Taking Another Look

What's wrong with Proverbs 31 culture is that it fails to see Proverbs as a particular kind of literature, written when the Israelites had considerable social change and because of it were rethinking their ideas about God. Wisdom literature—of which Proverbs, Psalms, Ecclesiastes, and Job are all part—is characterized by deep, personal experience. In these books, ordinary human events provide the fodder for thinking about God.

Wisdom literature was penned when the Israelites had been brought to their knees. As stronger groups conquered them, they found themselves no longer in control of their own lives but under the thumb of the formidable Babylonians. Known as the period of Exile, many Israelites were forced to leave their homeland and live in Babylon. Psalm 137 expresses their misery: "By the rivers of Babylon— / there we sat down and there we wept / when we remembered Zion... / How could we sing the LORD's song / in a foreign land?" (vv. 1, 4).

Their experience of feeling abandoned by God, exiled in another country and living in a foreign land, caused them to re-evaluate all they thought they knew about God. Prior to this enslavement, the Israelites accepted a theology that said God rewarded those who obeyed and punished those who disobeyed. This belief worked when everything went well, but with their lives in upheaval, they began to question this idea. From a place of exile and bondage, the inference was all too clear: they must have disobeyed, for Babylonian captivity could be no reward for good behavior. Instead of unthinkingly accepting their new circumstances as somehow separate from their understandings of God, the Israelites reconsidered what they believed.

Proverbs and the other wisdom books of the Old Testament are the result of these changing perspectives. For readers thousands of years later, these documents help us see not only their shifting views but also their various perspectives. Proverbs alone reveals its variety through its multiple authors. For example, different wisdom teachers— Agur (Prov. 30:1–14) and Lemuel (Prov. 31:1–9)—provide two passages, while at least one non-Israelite source—the Egyptian Amenemope, whose sayings are echoed in Proverbs 22 and 23–provides others.[17] And with these multiple authors came different points of view. In other words, the ancient Hebrews accepted diversity of opinion.

Despite such variations, however, wisdom literature is remarkably similar in inattentiveness to Israel's history, to the covenant with Moses or Abraham, to the Exodus, and even to kings and prophets. Where sacred literature normally reveals its shared historical memory, the wisdom writings strike a different tone, changing the focus from collective identity to individual experience and behavior. So, the P31 movement is partially right: we should take women's realities seriously. Nevertheless, by isolating the final chapter, separating it from the rest of the book, they fail to see that the Proverbs 31 woman is not human; she is God.

Wisdom and Proverbs

Even as the individual takes center stage in wisdom literature, the key to understanding what it means resides in the relationship of each person to the community. The result of gaining wisdom is not something to be hoarded as individual achievement but is the clue to living well with one's neighbors. Wisdom does not thrive in isolation, but propels people to fully engage with others. In contrast to rugged individualism extolled from many American pulpits, Proverbs calls those who want to be wise to live for the good of the community, to contribute to the benefit of society, and to sacrifice selfish goals for the well-being of one's neighbors.[18]

Framed as instructions to a young man by an older sage, Proverbs is an anthology of insights about living well. Because of his life experiences, the older man passes on valuable knowledge, enabling the younger man to follow a similar path. The father-son image of the text should be no surprise to readers, since this wisdom literature emerged within a patriarchal society. But the metaphor does not necessarily need to be limited in this fashion, and can instead be extended to a master teaching a student.[19] Implied is the idea that the young have much to learn from older, experienced teachers.

As one slice of wisdom literature, the book of Proverbs is composed of brief sayings known in Hebrew as *mashal*, which has multiple meanings: to compare, or to rule over, or to consider a riddle or puzzle.[20] Kathleen M. O'Connor suggests seeing Proverbs as pictures or images. What they mean requires the reader to tease out comparisons and contrasts and to explore multiple perspectives, finally arriving only at tentative understandings. Blithely accepting a checklist to follow in order to become the Proverbs 31 woman would make no sense to Proverbs' early readers, who knew that to gain wisdom one must actively question everything.

The Problem with Proverbs

Two contrasting women are used throughout Proverbs to identify the choice available to the young person seeking to find her or his way. One is portrayed as Folly and the other as Wisdom. While there are redeeming aspects of the Wisdom Woman, there is also the patriarchal lens of this metaphor, of choosing one kind of woman over and against another. Both women are presented through the eyes of masculine biases and female stereotypes, for these are not women as they were then or today. As one-dimensional objects without autonomy or interest, these women are not real, but rather figments of the male imagination. Such dualistic portrayals perpetuate the stereotypes of women as either fully good or fully bad. Such assumptions are harmful to women, especially when these metaphors are used uncritically.[21]

Especially problematic are misogynistic passages in Proverbs, in which Folly is presented as a prostitute who seduces the young man. Such portions of Scripture can serve to reinforce patriarchal privilege at the expense of women who may have few other options for survival and who must find ways of living within systems that disadvantage them in order to maintain the status quo of male dominance. Consider statements such as, "Then a woman comes toward him, / decked out like a prostitute, wily of heart. / She is loud and wayward; / her feet do not stay at home..." (Prov. 7:10–11), or, "Like a gold ring in a pig's snout / is a beautiful woman without good sense" (Prov. 11:22). Ignoring such embedded sexism perpetuates it as acceptable. Much like readers have identified racism in the Bible and realized it represents not the mind of God but rather those who had yet to understand the sin of ethnic oppression, dealing honestly with sexism in the Bible enables us to acknowledge human failure while not judging Scripture to be hopelessly bad news for all women.

The Good News of Proverbs

On the other hand, once we note the problems inherent in portraying good and evil as female figures, we can learn from the personification of wisdom as a woman. Proverbs is not referring to women in general as being good or evil, but is employing a metaphor to suggest that a person becomes wise by making informed choices.

Within this context, the young person is provided two different paths. The way of Folly is one fraught with indecision and waywardness. When fidelity—an echo of the marital metaphor referring to Israel's relationship with God—is abandoned, life takes a turn toward destruction and death. Those who reject the faithfulness of life with God find their paths lead to the shadows, to truncated living (Prov. 2:16–19). The way of Folly sounds good and is enticing. It may be that the bad choice appears to be good, even if the good is short-lived, a momentary or fleeting appearance of a full life, though without the longevity that truly represents the better choice (Prov. 5:1–6).

Proverbs 7:6–27 elaborates on the pleasure of the path of Folly. Shown as sexual seduction and encounter, the temptation is self-gratification. A couch spread with Egyptian linen, perfume of myrrh, aloes, and cinnamon suggest the power of money and material comfort, a path many travel.

A false banquet of stolen water and bread eaten in secret is offered to those who pass by in Proverbs 9:13–18. Those who feast in this way choose the path of death, for it is the way of selfishness. There is no one at this table, for it is created not out of loyalty to God and community, but of living for oneself. What appears to be plenty turns out to be an empty table with no guests.

There is another option, however: to follow the "Woman of Wisdom."[22] In Proverbs, this figure calls out—not from the temple but from the street—to those who will listen: "fear of the LORD is the beginning of knowledge; fools despise wisdom and instruction" (Prov. 1:7). The street, the busiest corner, the entrance to the city gates: these were the places of nitty-gritty living in the ancient world. Gathering crowds, legal transactions, and daily commerce all transpired where Wisdom called. As Kathleen O'Connor suggests, Wisdom announced Her presence "in the thick of life at its shabbiest and its most exciting, in the routine of daily marketing and in the struggles of ordinary people to survive."[23]

What is offered to those who are wise is preferable to silver and gold. Wisdom, Proverbs says, leads to life and peace and is the source for happiness, in contrast to money that the foolish believe will provide ultimate satisfaction (Prov. 3:13–18). In Proverbs 8, Wisdom Woman proclaims Her origin before creation: "Ages ago I was set up, / at the first, before the beginning of the earth... / Before the mountains had been shaped, / before the hills, I was brought forth—" (vv. 23, 25). She offers those listening nothing short of life: "For whoever finds me finds life / and obtains favor from the LORD..."(v. 35).

Two aspects of chapter 8 are especially helpful in understanding Wisdom Woman. In ancient societies, older things were revered by virtue of their age. To say Wisdom existed before creation is another way of saying She has authority to speak and people should highly value what She says. But it isn't just that Wisdom should be heard; She also is intimately related to the world, for She participated in its creation.[24] The world and Wisdom are inseparable, and to honor and respect one is to honor and respect the other. To care for and cultivate the earth is to be working with Wisdom.

Living in relationship to the world means being in community with others. Wisdom Woman demonstrates this in Proverbs 9, in which She issues Her banquet invitation. She prepared the food (slaughtered Her animals), poured the wine, and set the table. Sending out Her servant girls to invite those who have yet to obtain Wisdom (the "simple"), Wisdom Woman offers an open invitation to all who hear. Not everyone decides to attend the banquet, presumably because it takes maturity and insight to gather at this table.[25] This invitation to feasting is in contrast to the stolen water and bread eaten in secret offered by the way of Folly.

The insights of sharing a table are easily missed by those for whom food is readily accessible. But to miss the meaning is unfortunate. When Wisdom Woman invites everyone who hears to Her table She demonstrates Her broad and generous spirit. In contexts in which exclusion because of beliefs or rituals or personal practices is prevalent, suggesting a place to come together without separation offers a radical alternative. When people share a table, they must be willing to split portions and not to hoard; they must be in close proximity to others, maybe even learning each other's names; they reciprocate, sharing their stories and lives, if only momentarily. Table fellowship in ancient society powerfully broke down ethnic, social, and gender barriers. Joining others around a table entailed putting the community ahead of one's personal preferences and/or agendas, a political as well as religious act.

The Proverbs 31 Woman

Only a few seek Wisdom. A rhetorical question indicates as much early on in Proverbs 31: "A capable wife who can find?" (v.

10a). The answer is not many. Those who wish this final proverb to be about the qualities of a Christian woman must disregard the preceding proverbs that work together to help the reader understand the benefits of Wisdom. Such readers must also dismiss the reality that to hold an individual woman in such high regard as Wisdom Woman in Proverbs 31 would have made no sense in the culture from which this writing emerged. Instead, the reader should look for the deeper significance of the woman portrayed: She is Wisdom Woman and Proverbs 31 portrays what life is like for the person who chooses wisdom.[26]

Not only is Wisdom "capable" or "strong" or of "military valor," as several translations indicate, She is more precious than jewels. This phrase is an echo from earlier in Proverbs, where the young seeker was shown the path of Wisdom as being a better path than one with jewels (8:11). Once Wisdom is chosen, trust ensues ("the heart of her husband trusts in her") and all of his needs will be met ("he will have no lack of gain") (v. 11). Living with Wisdom means She cares for him, indicated in the way She (God's Wisdom) provides all the household needs: "She seeks wool and flax, / and works with willing hands" (v. 13); "[God's Wisdom] is like the ships of the merchant, / she brings her food from far away" (v. 14); "[God's Wisdom] rises while it is still night / and provides food for her household / and tasks for her servant-girls" (v. 15); "[God's Wisdom] considers a field and buys it; / with the fruit of her hands she plants a vineyard" (v. 16); "[God's Wisdom] girds herself with strength, / and makes her arms strong. / She perceives that her merchandise is profitable. / Her lamp does not go out at night" (vv. 17–18).

Wisdom provides for Her household and She cares for others: "She opens her hand to the poor, and reaches out her hands to the needy" (v. 20). Because of Her preparation, there is no concern in lean seasons. Instead, they live as royalty: "...for all her household are clothed in crimson. / She makes herself coverings; / her clothing is fine linen and purple" (vv. 21b–22).

Living with Wisdom means being respected: "Her husband is known in the city gates, / taking his seat among the elders of the land" (v. 23). When She speaks, Wisdom and loving kindness are heard, an echo from Hosea, in which God is portrayed through the unending presence of loving kindness: "She opens her mouth with wisdom, / and the teaching of kindness is on her tongue" (v. 26). As She cares for Her household, Her children and husband praise Her (31:28). In choosing the path of Wisdom, the reader of Proverbs should hear the clarion call in the Proverbs 31 Woman: live your life in the web of Wisdom.[27]

Wisdom

Choosing the path of wisdom brings us back to where we started, with a focus on experience and community. Given the ability to choose, Proverbs calls attention to the need of each person to cultivate wisdom through discernment and understanding. Elisabeth Schüssler Fiorenza remarks that "wisdom, unlike intelligence, is not something with which a person is born. It comes only from living, from making mistakes and trying again and from listening to others who have made mistakes and tried to learn from them."[28] Desiring wisdom is good; striving to achieve it is difficult. But, the results of attaining wisdom are clear in Proverbs 31. To choose wisdom is to choose a life with God.

Given the centrality of justice proclaimed by Wisdom Woman, it is ironic when faith communities today offer limited tables, lined like Folly with food that will not sustain. One of the most obvious ways this occurs is in the dismissing of the Divine Feminine who is the one true Proverbs 31 woman. In lieu of celebrating Her presence, theologians and interpreters, pastors and parents have diligently worked to replace Her with false claims about who and what women are supposed to be. In the process, they heap untold portions of guilt on women who will inevitably fail in their attempts to be the very Wisdom of God. Not only is this a detriment to women striving to be all they are meant to be, it is a way of reducing the Divine, of limiting rather than expanding how people conceptualize the Holy One who is our Mother and Father, Wisdom and Grace, and a host of other attributes too numerous to mention.

Language for and images of the Divine Feminine are absent from our liturgies and our hymns, absent from our sermons and our songs. Wisdom Woman is nowhere to be found and people who seek Her are routinely dismissed, their need for this feminine understanding of God rejected as unimportant or something they should seek on their own, outside the communal setting.

When this marginalization happens—and it does more frequently than we know—the table of God is diminished. Not only is Wisdom being truncated, but community suffers from an anemic view of God and a systematic exclusion of groups of people. Women learn to distrust their experiences, signing up for the infinite task of being the

Proverbs 31 woman. No wonder the damage is rampant when so many women believe they are somehow supposed to replicate nothing less than God Herself.

Language and images of God are not minor aspects of faith. How we envision God is reflected in how we treat others and all living things, including the earth. Yet in today's churches, we seldom hear what it means to make Wisdom visible in our everyday lives. Using exclusive language and images for God only serves to make Wisdom invisible; relying almost entirely on masculine portrayals of God, Wisdom has been left in the streets, calling to those who will not hear.

Instead of learning to sit at Wisdom's table, we deliberately warp Proverbs, making lists of things women need to do, all while telling them they are honored and cherished because of who they are (and how well they perform on the Proverbs 31 test). It is an incongruous and dangerous message, one coming not from the heart of God but from the desires of men.

Wisdom Woman's efforts are not in vain. Pockets of Wisdom-seeking communities are emerging, pointing the way to fullness and life. Worship resources helping congregations celebrate Wisdom are becoming more plentiful and accessible. Younger Christians are moving beyond the sexism of their parents' worlds to demand in their churches the justice they already see operating in the workplace and society. In short, their experiences will eventually require a theology that already exists in some Christian traditions, and that will need to be discovered by evangelicals. They will find themselves pouring through the Wisdom literature of the Old Testament and will there discover the path that leads to wise living is one that takes their experiences seriously and celebrates diversity for the benefit of all who sit at Her table.

Chapter Four

When Jesus Was a Man's Man

Jesus was not a sissy.

That's the first premise you need to know if you are to understand Christian masculinity movements: Jesus was not one of those feminine boys who preferred working in the kitchen alongside his mother, nor was a he man who enjoyed peaceful evenings gazing at the moon or serving a gourmet meal to his 5,000 closest fans. If he were walking the earth today, Jesus would be participating in all manner of manly activity: eating barbeque, camping in the backwoods with his disciples, maybe even taking in some Christian Mixed Martial Arts—a chance to show his masculinity by watching men beating each other silly. This is important to recognize, because any man who purports to be godly must follow this particular master, not the one who has been too often feminized by women in the church.

Some might argue that the Christian masculinity movement started from a worthwhile premise: the desire to make church more relevant for men. Churches in the United States, both mainline and evangelical, began hemorrhaging men toward the end of the twentieth century, and, according to Pew surveys, of those in the United States who are affiliated with evangelical Christianity (about 26.3 percent of those surveyed), 47 percent are male and 53 percent are women. While these numbers may not seem too unbalanced, another survey, reported in *Christian Century*, suggested the numbers might be even more skewed, with men comprising only 39 percent of those attending church.[1] This shrinking population of men in the pews heralds trouble for Christian churches that obviously need to draw people in to sustain their ministries. Without a congregation, there is no church.

Prevailing thought suggests, too, that women will come without spouse or family, but men are less likely to do the same. Men are important to the life of the church, and are absolutely essential in congregations in which leadership roles are saved for men alone.

In an attempt to understand why men are not coming to church, a number of evangelicals decided the "feminization" of the church was the culprit. John Eldredge, author of the popular *Wild at Heart,* says, "Christianity, as it currently exists, has done some terrible things to men." Eldredge argues the church has emasculated men, making them "good boys" who don't smoke, drink, or swear, and who are nice to those around them, driving the wildness of a man's heart into remote places and away from the church. Why aren't there more men invested in church? "We have not invited a man to know and live from his deep heart," Eldredge writes.[2]

What exactly does a feminized church look like? It looks like people being forced to greet each other, shaking hands and sharing about their week; because women are by design more relational, even the forced contact of a greeting time reflects the church's propensity toward attracting women. That relational aspect extends to Bible studies and adult Sunday school, which most often revolve around sitting still, reflecting deeply, and sharing with each other.

Also, those praise songs that have become so ubiquitous in evangelical churches? Totally a turn off to most men, especially those that make Jesus into a tender lover we must pursue, a beautiful soul who sends "waves of affection" over us all. Hymns of old that figured Jesus as a strong man heading off into battle are rarely part of an evangelical church's play list—no "Onward Christian Soldier" to inspire strength and courage, no "A Mighty Fortress Is Our God" to fill us with godly fortitude. Indeed, the feminization of the church is so pervasive, it's infecting the pulpit, too, with preachers who would prefer emotion over rational thought, and who are more inclined to wear khakis, not manly denim. Never mind those churches that have hired women as clergy, clearly going against the Bible and God; the pastorate has become increasingly soft, scaring away those men who need a strong, masculine leader, just like Jesus himself.

Here's the truth. The prevalent claims about gender in evangelical popular culture damage men, too. Their relationships are eroded by messages telling them to make women and children submit to male authority, creating unhealthy power dynamics that will result in unhealthy relationships as well. Their self-esteem is altered by ideas suggesting their voices matter most in the church, and that their spiritual leadership skills are far superior to any woman's—even when they are not. Men are boxed in by notions of biblical manhood, and what it means to be a man of God: and those men who don't feel warrior-like, who don't feel especially strong or adventurous, and who would prefer a quiet evening to Christian cage fighting often are denigrated for not embracing God's design for manhood. Such messages about what biblical manhood *really* is have the potential to limit men, making it impossible for them to be all God wants them to be.

Efforts to bring men back into the church by making Jesus and his followers more masculine only intensify these messages about biblical manhood. By applying cultural stereotypes about men to Jesus, contemporary evangelicals let men who do not fit those stereotypes know that they are not in line with their Master, and thus must change if they wish to be true Christ followers. This has meant emphasizing some characteristics of Jesus over others, and, in some cases, ignoring aspects of Jesus' ministry altogether, assuming men would rather follow a leader who overturns tables in a temple than a gentle shepherd seeking the one lost sheep.

If we are to let all people, both men and women, become what God means for them to be, we need to see these cultural messages for what they are: an attempt to return men (and then their families) to church pews, yes, but also an effort to cram men and women into boxes clearly labeled "biblical manhood" and "biblical womanhood." More significantly, we need to understand more fully the richness of Jesus' ministry on earth, and what that ministry might tell us about our own work here, and what it really means to live biblically. For, only when we follow what the gospels tell us will we discover that God calls us each to walk uniquely on this earth, to walk in love, and to walk in right relationship, in ways that allow everyone around us to become all God hopes for them to be.

Becoming a Man, Even as a Boy

Todd grew up in a small Midwest town, where church and football competed for attention every weekend. Most boys played football, by middle school at least, and those who didn't lace on some pads and join the team walked on the margins of school culture; they weren't real boys, learning how to become strong men. Todd was one of those more interested in other pursuits. He excelled at speech and debate, performed in school plays, and achieved near-perfect grades in advanced classes. But in his town, none of these achievements mattered—not for a boy, not in this community, not even in church, where the football coach attended and other players were worshiped with an adoration saved especially for small town heroes. So Todd did what he thought was required of him to be a man, and joined the football team. He couldn't play, and didn't try out for any position. He did what he believed was the next best thing, and for two years he served as the team's manager—gophering for the coach, wiping down muddy footballs during games, and scampering out after kickoffs to retrieve the tee before helmeted kids twice his size bore down on him. He was also miserable, desperate to be included but longing to do those things that actually brought him joy: acting, speech, studying. Only his family's move to the West Coast, and to a community that valued the gifts Todd actually had, saved him from his misery.

It's easy to imagine that Todd's story is replicated in communities everywhere. Without question, there are expectations of how boys are supposed to act if they want to become men. These expectations are embedded in the language we use when we talk to boys: "C'mon, be a man," we might say, or "Real men don't cry," or "Don't act like a sissy; act like a man." They are also embedded in the kinds of behavior we accept from boys, and in our quick judgment of those boys who act outside what we believe is "standard boy behavior." When we assert that someone is "all boy," we know exactly what that means: a kid fueled by adrenaline, climbing chairs and tables, whacking things with sticks, fascinated by sports. By deduction, we are conveying to those boys who are more sensitive, quiet, or sedate that they are somehow less than what we define as "all boy."

These assumptions about what it means to be a boy are intensified by Christian culture—and not only intensified, but also coupled with a sense that those who are "all boy" are also working their way toward godly manhood. As often happens, stereotypes about gender are infused with biblical language, so that those character traits commonly assumed to be inherently boy are considered part of God's great design for those born male. Thus boys who are outspoken, courageous, and athletic are not only "all boy," they are also living into the role God has created for boys; and those who are quiet, reserved, and bookish better learn to "man up" if they hope to fulfill God's plan for their lives.

While Christian children's books teach girls they are to be helpful, thoughtful, kind, and creative, boys are taught to be responsible, brave, and truthful—the character traits they will need as they grow into their spiritual leadership. The book *A Boy After God's Own Heart* (Jim George) promises the reader an "adventure with Jesus," and even though "talking about your heart isn't really a 'guy' thing," the book guides boys on an adventure to see who God wants them to be. Of course, God wants them to be adventurous, as that is part of God's plan, and those cautious boys have some work in store if they want to get themselves right with God.

Many Christian toys marketed to boys reinforce the idea that boys are to be brave and adventurous, while those marketed to girls ask them to imagine being nurturing and demure: just like the Bible says. The now-defunct Vision Forum was perhaps the worst perpetrator when it came to marketing gender-specific toys, using the premise that girls and boys needed to play with toys reminding them of God's design (which might raise the question: If God designed such clear gender roles, do we need to give our children toys that teach them God's design?). At one time on the Vision Forum site, parents could buy toys for "girls" or toys for "boys," much like in other online catalogs—except for a catch. The girls' toys on the Vision Forum site explicitly promised girls lots of "'mommy practice' because we live in a world that frowns on femininity," the site intoned, "that minimizes motherhood, and that belittles the beauty of being a true woman of God."

Interestingly, the toys for boys did not provide "daddy practice," nor prepare boys for a lifetime of mission, service, hospitality, and grace. Instead, the toys prepared boys to go out into the world, contending with the many challenges boys face and "equipping boys for manhood." And this, apparently, is what will make boys into men: action figures that teach them to hunt with a bow and rifle, or wear Camo while riding their motor boats (while the girls, equipped for womanhood, are making them meals back at home). Vision Forum also had a "weapons and gear" link, as equipping boys for manhood apparently meant playing with rifles and handguns, as well as military action sets, which came with guns and missiles, so boys could work on manhood by bombing the crap out of their enemies.

The Vision Forum's distinct toy lines, intended to teach and reinforce God's design for gender, may be gone, but other toy companies have picked up the slack, creating dolls and kitchen sets so girls can learn their place in the home, and action/adventure gear for boys to learn their role as godly providers. While many of these gendered toys are replicated in the broader marketplace—think Lego Friends for girls and militia-geared Lego for boys—Christian toy marketers are more explicit about the ideology undergirding their products, and about the need for their toys to raise up godly girls and godly boys, the latter presumably interested only in being strong and brave, providing for the family through hunting, and blowing stuff up.

This same ideology is threaded through Sunday school curricula created specifically for boys, much of which intends to teach boys "leadership skills"—indicated as strength, trustworthiness, and hard work. Examples of this trend abound, perhaps exemplified best in the "ABCs for Godly Boys" curriculum, which includes crafts, flashcards, activities, and Bible verses that teach boys what it means to grow into godly men. The curriculum is based on the belief that children need to learn early and often about their gender roles, both by the example of their parents and by direct instruction. Boys who do not receive this character instruction will either turn out "hard and abusive or passive and soft," and thus a curriculum that helps them to become godly men is absolutely essential.[3]

Even in mixed-gender Sunday school classes, with a presumably gender-neutral curricula, boys and girls learn exactly what God expects of them. Stories focus on the typically heroic figures in the Bible: Abraham and Isaac; then Jacob and Esau, who wrestle with angels and live off the land; David and Goliath, battling for supremacy; the strong-man Samson; and the disciples who were engaged in physically demanding vocations. Images of Joseph-as-carpenter suggested he had masculine, calloused hands, and that he was familiar with hard work. Zacchaeus, in a white-collar role as a tax collector, is figured a "wee little man," weak in stature and in physique. Flannel graphs featuring characters in the Bible doing less adventurous activities no doubt have far less appeal, but they also do little good in instructing boys to develop into multidimensional men.

If all else fails—if your boy decides he prefers theater over football—parents have prayer as their last, best defense. In list after list of potential prayers one might give on behalf of a son, supplicants are instructed to pray that their sons become godly men, taking on the character traits that once again trend toward the stereotypically masculine. Parents should pray that their boys develop strong work ethics, we are told in one guide to prayer, because boys need to learn the value of hard work and money (girls probably also need to learn the value of hard work, it goes without saying, but work only in service to others).[4] Boys need to be prayed over so they can develop "warrior hearts," strong and active and true.[5] Prayers for sons should focus most on helping them become strong and courageous; to walk with integrity, like King David always did (the Bathsheba stuff not withstanding); to be like Timothy, a leader who was an exemplar to others in his speech, his conduct, and his purity.[6] Only then, we are assured, will our boys be able to fight the enemy who is eroding their confidence, their character.

Only then will they be more like Jesus, the manly man from Galilee.

Becoming a Man

The trajectory toward godly manhood only intensifies as boys reared in the evangelical faith grow older, creeping ever closer to becoming men. What "becoming a man" means chronologically differs, depending on which Bible translation is being interpreted, what interpretation of the Bible is acceptable, and whether denominational fiat demands manhood begin at a certain age, or not. Nevertheless, expectations for boys increase as they move closer to manhood, as do messages about what it means to be a biblical man. By the time a teenager reaches his high school graduation, he will no doubt have a very clear idea of what his elders expect of him as a Christian man, having heard again and again in evangelical Christian culture that someone embracing biblical manhood *must* assume certain character traits, even if those go against who the teenage boy believes himself to be.

A number of gender-specific teen ministries have, as their specific purpose, instruction in helping boys become biblical men. With presumably masculine titles such as "Boys to Men" and "Warrior Training," the ministries endeavor to help teen boys take on the characteristics of biblical manhood, authority, and leadership. At one church, the teenage girl companion for Boys to Men is Diamonds and Pearls. The title is not parallel, despite its clever attempts, though it does reflect the sense that boys will become men, and, hey, girls love their jewelry! At another church, the teen boy ministry is called "The Manly Mecca," a group set apart from female peers because "men need some different food in [their] spiritual diet." At the Manly Mecca, biblical lessons are followed by adventure activities–from camping to barbeques to snowboarding. The leaders of the group love to see the teen boys "take on their noble calling as young men and attempt to find ways to bless the ladies of our youth group, bless the church, and our community."[7] Other teen boy ministries, with names like Conquerors, Royal Rangers, and Man Up Ministry, seem to follow the same model: lots of hardcore activity coupled with biblical teaching and instruction in how to develop into godly men, ready to bless the ladies and the church.

There can be some value to having gender-specific teen ministries that allow girls and boys to interact without the added pressures often accompanying mixed-gender activities. Still, the focus of these ministries suggests girls and boys receive far different kinds of instruction within these programs, and this instruction reflects deeply held beliefs about gender as well as assumptions about what girls and boys want in a youth ministry, and about what they need. Ministries often focus on guiding teens toward becoming biblical men or women, with all the evangelical baggage that comes with those labels. One curriculum for gender-specific teen programs highlights this trend. Called "Guy Talk/Girl Talk," the curriculum promises to provide ten lessons on everyday issues for teens, using "solid biblical truths" as its foundation. But the different foci of the guy talk and the girl talk is telling. For teen boys, this means learning how to "be a man," with lessons in leadership, true strength, fostering God-given gifts, and responsibility; girls learning how to become biblical women can study units on appearance, gossip, kindness, friendship, and girl politics. From the description alone, it's clear to see which group will receive more substantive instruction, potentially deepening their faith and their skills to be Christian leaders, and which group will learn most assuredly that women belong in an entirely different realm, one in which kindness and appearance matter more than strength and responsibility.

Ceremonies marking a boy's transition to biblical manhood are another way that some evangelicals reinforce that God's design for men is far different than that for women. Girls reared in the evangelical faith have their own distinct ceremonies: most often, purity balls, where they learn that, as a biblical woman, their virginal status matters most, and that they are to be protected and saved by the men in their lives. For boys, ceremonies focus not so much on sexual purity (if at all), but on honoring those qualities directing boys into positions of spiritual leadership and power.

Robert Lewis, author of *Raising a Modern-Day Knight*, suggests that, for boys, creating manhood ceremonies at several steps in boys' development might be best, empowering boys to be godly men at every major transition point in their lives: puberty, high school and college graduation, and marriage. For Lewis and his family, this has meant creating a family crest with three distinct sections. One has the image of a sword in the shape of a cross, reflecting "conventional" manhood that must be surrendered to "The Man," Jesus. To the right, there is a crown that represents "authentic" manhood–that is, the "imperatives for real manhood: rejecting passivity, accepting responsibility, leading courageously." In the middle are crosses that represent the ongoing masculine truths each dad offers a son to fight with for an honorable life. In addition to the crest, Lewis also suggests having a ceremony at each stage in the boy's development, a way to reinforce the biblical truths about manhood and assuring the boy remembers the definition of manhood that will guide his life: "A man is someone who rejects passivity, accepts responsibility, leads courageously and expects the greater reward–God's reward."[8] While these "truths" form the foundation of each ceremony, they are also different, starting with a simple dinner when the boy reaches puberty, growing to a dinner and the presentation of a ring at college graduation. The "ring of great price" displays the family crest, reflecting the boy's commitment to Christ and symbolizing his manhood. By comparison, most purity rings of great price for girls reflect a commitment to Jesus via daddy, symbolizing as well the girls' sexual purity.

Even if parents decide not to enact a manhood ceremony, there are still plenty of ways they can help their sons achieve biblical manhood. Once again, of course, Christian writers offer instructions for prayer on behalf of teen sons, that they might develop the skill set they need to become biblical men. Such prayers often focus on helping boys become strong and responsible leaders, men of honor and courage who can take charge. Christian publications also exhort parents to go beyond prayer by helping guide their sons into "heroic manhood," which means teaching them traits such as honor, courage, commitment, and leadership. Moms are encouraged to allow their sons to reject the "feminine energy" through their upbringing, so that, as teens, they can embrace a "masculine energy." After all, *Today's Christian Woman* asserts, "Men are built by men,"[9] and need all the masculine energy they can get. This raises an interesting question: If

God's design for men is to be strong and responsible leaders, men built to be men, and if these character traits are woven into the very DNA of those born male, why are so many people earnestly praying that these traits can be developed in teen boys? Shouldn't they already exist?

Nurturing teenagers to be strong and responsible leaders is certainly a *good* thing. What should be rejected, however, is the notion that these traits need to be encouraged in teen boys alone, and that teen boys need these qualities if they are to become biblical men. Boys who are more reserved, who express their strength in ways other than those prescribed above, and who might prefer an energy that is judged more "feminine" will feel set up for failure, as if they cannot become real men, worthy of the manhood ceremony, the family crest, the rituals that will mark them as truly blessed by God.

If teenage boys haven't gotten the message that they need to develop specific characteristics to become biblical men, hope is not lost. There will be other opportunities, other men's ministries, other messages that let men know exactly who and what they should be. And this is truly unfortunate, especially for those men who cannot fit the mold into which they are asked to squeeze themselves.

Acting Like a Man

Here's one way to get more men into the pews: offer them that most manly of instruments, a gun, along with a steak dinner. Meat and guns? What could be more alluring to a real man? In spring 2014, a Baptist church in Kentucky decided to have a Second Amendment Celebration and Dinner, offering men who attended a free meal and a chance to win one of twenty-five handguns given away at the event. Chuck McAlister, a leader with the Kentucky Baptist Convention, spoke at the inaugural celebration; an avid hunter, he viewed the evening not as a bait-and-switch affair, but as "affinity evangelism," inviting men to come do what they love, and maybe accept Jesus in the process. "So we get in there and burp and scratch and talk about the right to bear arms and that stuff," he said.[10]

Affinity evangelism isn't exactly groundbreaking: women's ministries have been drawing participants by hosting scrapbooking parties, and women's teas, and quilting circles, all activities women presumably enjoy. As churches seek more creative ways to draw men into the pews and keep them there, affinity evangelism has become especially ubiquitous in men's ministries. Drawing on stereotypes about what men like, and what it means to act like a man, these events often involve the outdoors, because every man loves hanging out in the woods.

If someone is going to act like a man—and a godly man at that—it's absolutely essential that he embrace these masculine traits, else he is only giving in to the tyranny of feminism, and to his own feminized destruction. As Christian masculinity has gained more traction in evangelical churches, this message is pervasive and potent: God has designed men to be a certain way, and those men who do not act in this way have some work to do to restore their masculinity. Holding a gun might do the trick. Or eating a steak, sleeping in the woods, and reasserting authority in the home. Those who fail in these endeavors are definitely not acting like the men God created them to be.

For many contemporary evangelicals, acting like a man means calling forth the part of manhood that has always existed, given God's design, but that might be deeply buried because of forces wanting men to act in unnatural ways. That seems to be the premise at the center of Eldredge's *Wild at Heart*, which became a bestseller among evangelicals when it was released in 2001; Eldredge and his wife, Stasi, also wrote a companion book for women, called *Captivating: Unveiling the Mystery of a Woman's Soul.* In *Wild at Heart,* Eldredge outlines his belief that "God *meant* something when he meant man," and that men who want to find themselves, they have to find what God meant dwelling deep in the "masculine heart."[11] What will they discover there? A person who loves adventure, a fierce warrior, and a passionate lover who wants to rescue his beautiful princess. For a man to really act like the man God created him to be, Eldredge claims, he must recover his heart, which has been battered, bruised, and shaped into something the likeness of which he might not recognize. This means a man "must *know* he is powerful; he must *know* he has what it takes." Those men who do not believe themselves to have these characteristics are only fooling themselves, their truest, God-designed self having been buried by contemporary sources who want to weaken them, making them less masculine. A man's heart might "feel dead," Eldredge says, "but it's there. Something wild and strong and valiant, just waiting to be released."[12]

The significance of Eldredge's ideas cannot be emphasized enough. Rather than merely a theory espoused by an evangelical author about the true nature of manhood, *Wild at Heart* became a ready explanation for what men needed to do to act like men: They needed to have a warrior spirit. They needed to protect others. They needed to pursue their princesses—women who, John and Stasi Eldredge tell us in *Captivating*, have a deep need to be pursued and protected by their warrior men. In the last decade-plus since *Wild at Heart* was published, evangelical men's ministries have focused on nurturing these character traits. Sermons use Eldredge's thoughts as the foundation for discussions about biblical manhood. And Christian conferences for men focus on helping them become the wild warriors men were apparently designed to be.

There were evangelical men's Christian conferences before Eldridge, including Promise Keepers, which filled football stadiums with men eager to recommit their lives to Christ, community, and family. Started in 1990, Promise Keepers challenged men to "embrace their calling to lead their families, churches, and communities in worship of, and obedience to, Jesus the Messiah," and, through the 1990s especially, it had a potent ministry, its seven promises asking that men remain steadfast in their commitments to family and faith, that they support their local churches, that they influence and evangelize throughout the world, and that they lean into their callings.[13] None of the original promises seems particularly influenced by the Christian masculinity movement, though clearly they are guided by the idea of male authority and headship within family and church.

Now, though, ideas of masculinity have shaped Promise Keeper rhetoric, so that in 2014 its website announced that the organization was "Unleashing the Warrior" in every man. This announcement was accompanied by the image of a buff man, sporting a knight's armor and a wedding ring, and crossing two swords above his head. "All across America, men have awakened to a new reality," a description of 2014's conference series read. "After years of apathy, weakness, and compromise, a fire has begun to burn in their souls, and these men have arisen to become WARRIORS who will fight for their God, marriages, families, churches, communities, and nation. And it couldn't have come at a better time." Warrior language permeated the conference sessions, with titles such as "Waking the Warrior," "The Warrior's Weapons," "Defending the Homefront," "Band of Brothers," and "Winning the Battle Within." If men are to keep their promises to family, faith, and church, they apparently need to take on the attributes of warriors. This, it seems, will help them become the men of God they clearly were intended to be.[14]

Other Christian men's conferences are more direct in their message and in their intent. For example, the "Act Like Men" conference series lets attendees know straight away that the two-day events will help participants to "man up," becoming the people "God created them to be" by being "loud and ruthless about their own sin" and to "be strong" in their leadership of the family and the church. Those who aren't sure what it means to "Act Like Men" might take direction from the image on the conference home page, which shows a muscled man, deep in prayer, his shaved head bowed deep, a real man's man. (He is also clearly wearing an earring, but, like Mr. Clean, this jewelry only highlights his strength and masculine power.)[15] Pastors at the forefront of the Christian masculinity movement promise to inspire men of all generations to take on the manly character traits they deem biblical and godly. According to a conference review, during a 2013 conference (the Act Like Men folks tour 3–4 cities each year), James MacDonald told the crowd of 6000 plus gathered that to act like men meant four things: not acting like women; not acting like animals; not acting like boys; and not acting like a superhero (though, presumably, acting like a warrior was acceptable).[16]

According to another conference review (one much less complimentary), from a blogger who attended eager to "live out the Gospel of Jesus Christ," the event's speakers compelled men toward manliness by relying on tired stereotypes about women and gays, using the apparent weaknesses of women, for example, to describe the certain strength of men, who are not sissy vegetarians, do not order low-fat lattes (only whole milk for men?), and who are strong leaders to the weak vessels in their midst. The conference organizers also held an "insensitive man" contest, the winners being those men who showed the most insensitivity to others. "Abuse power, demean woman," the blogger wrote. "That's what gives you the prize."[17]

Another Christian men's conference, called The Bravehearted Man, relies on similar warrior imagery on its splash page and the same sense that men need to be set apart from women, their masculinity defined in opposition to the far-too-feminine nature of the church.

The foundational rhetoric of this and other similar men's conferences is that men are under attack, and that if they are to do God's will, men need to reclaim their manhood and face their attackers. For too long, the premise goes, real masculinity has been diluted by the feminist movement and other liberal forces, which have eroded traditional family values, compromised the church, and led to a decline of our great nation. Acting like a man means asserting authority–letting women know who is boss, as it were–and re-establishing the gender hierarchy that has served (some) men well for countless centuries. It involves asserting authority, and then making it clear to everyone that the Bible has sanctified this disproportionate power. Acting like a man means following God's will for men to be leaders, warriors, first-rate protectors.

God wrote these characteristics into men's wild hearts, after all. And removing the layers of detritus placed there by feminists allows men to freely act how God truly intended them to: like insensitive men, humbly seeking God's will by elevating themselves above all others. Lest we think that men's conferences such as these are outliers, or that church leaders such as Mark Driscoll and MacDonald are rare, we need to remember that these are events occurring in mainstream evangelicalism, and that men like Driscoll and MacDonald have large followings, in real life and in social networking. Their muscular Christianity sets the tone for other Christians, helping to shape conversations about gender in the church and compelling many to believe that men must act in definite, stereotypic ways if they wish to be deemed godly–and, as a corollary, that women need to act in different, stereotypic ways that are set up against how men act.

In many ways, too, this ideal of a warrior man, protecting, leading, and pursuing his captivating prey/princess is merely a logical extension of complementarian theology, which argues, fundamentally, that men and women occupy different God-designed spheres and different roles, and that these differences are knit into our very DNA. This is essentially the argument of *Wild at Heart:* that every man has, in his heart, the impulse to be a knight, storming the castle. This is essentially the argument Mark Driscoll has made: that every man must follow his masculinity model, and those who do not are sissies, taking on women's roles instead. And this is essentially the argument conferences such as Act Like Men make: that there is one way to act like a man, and those who choose a different path are outside God's plan, thus unnatural and worthy of derision.

How can this ideology be anything but damaging to both men and women, especially those who do not fit within the roles prescribed for them? Short answer: It can't. And yet the rhetoric of "God's design," the sense that people must fit into clearly prescribed roles, and the mockery of those who are different remains–is amplified, even, when talking about those who assume leadership positions, and whose masculinity must be assured if they are to truly be "Men of God."

When Your Pastor Is a Sissy

Before his downfall and the break-up of his Mars Hill Churches, Mark Driscoll was the contemporary face of muscular Christianity. Driscoll's Mars Hill empire included 14,000 congregants, attending fifteen churches in five states. He was also a top-selling evangelical author and speaker, despite his oft-times abrasive personality and controversial statements—statements that might have contributed to his undoing.* Until his 2014 fall, Driscoll was a leading voice advocating for a stereotypically masculine faith, with a stereotypical masculine Jesus at the center.

One example of Driscoll's muscular posturing came in a July 2011 Facebook post, one that set off a minor Twitter firestorm, resulting in the removal of the post and a lukewarm apology from Driscoll, a man who only rarely admits to being wrong. Driscoll asked his quarter-million Facebook followers the simple question: "So, what story do you have about the most effeminate anatomically male worship leader you have ever personally witnessed?" Driscoll's intent for the post is unclear: Was he looking for sermon fodder? Hoping to reassert his manliness? To judge and mock those his followers deemed "effeminate pastors"? Over six hundred people responded, some of them providing their own narratives about the time they encountered a sissy pastor in the pulpit, and managed to escape. When asked to clarify what he meant by "effeminate," Driscoll provided a definition on his Facebook page: "1: having feminine qualities untypical of a man: not manly in appearance or manner. 2: marked by an unbecoming delicacy or overrefinement."[18] In this clarification, Driscoll clearly played his cards, letting his followers know there was a certain look and behavior that made one manly, and also that "having feminine qualities" is something to be derided, especially if such qualities appear in a pastor. Although Driscoll admits Mars Hills elders "sat him down" to talk about the post, he offered no real

---

*According to Sarah Pulliam Bailey, "Driscoll's fall from grace came after a combination of growing scrutiny of church finances, plagiarism allegations concerning his books and comments he made under an online pseudonym." See "Why Mark Driscoll's fall and Mars Hills' break-up issues a warning for mega-star pastors," *Religious News Service,* November 5, 2014. http://www.religionnews.com/2014/11/05/mark-driscolls-fall-mars-hills-breakup-raises-questions-megastar-pastors/ (accessed Dec. 1, 2014).

apology, saying instead that he should have contextualized his comments better, that Facebook wasn't really the right place for such discussions, and that he was considering a new website where he could provide clarity on his complementarian ideology—an ideology apparently reviling any male pastor who does not look, think, or act like Mark Driscoll's definition of manly.[19]

An outcome of evangelical focus on biblical manhood is the sense that church leaders also have to be masculine in the ways our contemporary culture stereotypically defines masculinity. These cultural stereotypes are then cast as biblical, rather than what they are: contemporary culture's definition of manhood. Driscoll was not acting especially rogue when he posted to Facebook about effeminate pastors, even if his query lacked nuance or care; other evangelicals have likewise asserted that only a certain kind of men—that is, those who have what we would culturally consider masculine traits—are fit to lead the church. Southern Baptist pastor Jared Moore, writing for *SBC Voices*, offered "Ten Reasons Why Sissies and Pastoral Ministry Are a Bad Mix,"[20] letting readers know that becoming a church leader is only for the bravehearted, not for sissies. Certainly church leadership is not for the faint of heart, though the ways the Christian masculinity movement defines traits such as "bravery" and "courage" are informed by cultural assumptions of what means being manly: not one who "acts like a woman," or is one. David Murrow sells DVDs explaining why men hate going to church, and the number one reason is that churches often lack a "manly" pastor. By this, Murrow means a man who "projects a healthy masculinity," including the following traits: "tough, earthy, working guys"; "High achievers, alpha males, risk takers"; "rough-and-tumble men" who don't fit in with "the introspective gentlemen who populate the church today."[21]

The implication is that church leaders who project anything but this masculinity are not only chasing other men away from the church, but they are betraying a lack of biblical manhood embraced by the patriarchs of the Old Testament, and by Jesus and his disciples in the New. We're told sissy pastors may not only chase men away from the church, leaving women who resonate with their emotive men in the pew; they may also delude men and boys into believing they can be less masculine than what the Bible apparently demands. On his Desiring God website, John Piper, whose wide reach in evangelicalism means his every utterance will be embraced, reiterated, and often interrogated, went so far in 2012 as to assert that God gave Christianity a "masculine feel." At a conference hosted by Desiring God, Piper provided a keynote address on the theme of "God, Manhood and Ministry–Building Men for the Body of Christ," asserting, "Now, from all of that I conclude that God has given Christianity a masculine feel. And being God, a God of love, He has done that for our maximum flourishing both male and female."[22] Piper based this argument on the idea that God reveals himself in the Bible as "king, not queen; father, not mother." Jesus is also son, not daughter; all the priests in the Old Testament were men; Jesus chose men as disciples; and God told men that, in marriage, they were supposed to be head of the home. Being true to God's wishes thus means that Christianity must sustain this masculinity, creating leaders who have the manly qualities evident in the Bible to provide for and protect their communities.

Piper's claims had some critics among evangelicals, mostly among egalitarian evangelicals who were troubled by his idea that God endorsed the supremacy of masculinity over femininity in the church, and the sense that the biblical masculinity Piper described looked far too much like cultural masculinity. Others, though, saw nothing wrong with his argument, believing that Piper was just fleshing out complementary theology: of course, if men are leading the church, there is going to be a masculine feel within the church, and of course men will be leading the church. This masculinity is really a positive thing, they say, an opportunity for men and women to live into their design by God, in which men can be truly masculine, and women truly feminine. David Mathias, writing on the Desiring God site, sees Piper's vision as a kind of peaceable kingdom for the church: "If it is done right, this masculine feel creates a space. It is big, it's roomy, it's beautiful, it's peaceful. It's just full and radiates with all the good things of life and in it women, flourishing, will give it that feel. So that as you walk in on Sunday morning and strong singing, led primarily by men, and then a voice from God is heard, and women are loving this, they're radiant, they're intelligent, they're understanding, they're processing, they're interacting." Despite this rather bold assertion, Mathias pulls back in the next paragraph to provide a more nuanced understanding of gender and the church. He writes: "In a community where there is a secure, strong, humble, masculine feel, men are free to be appropriately feminine. And women are free to be appropriately masculine. In other words, when you look at any given human being, the most attractive, interesting, winsome human beings are not all masculine or all feminine." [23]

Clearly, not every leader in the Christian masculinity movement would agree with Mathias' perspective that gender exists along a spectrum. A masculine ideal creates certain expectations for preachers, who must develop their masculinity "cred" however possible, wearing more denim and leather and fewer khakis potentially, or working hard to show that their characters reflect the strong provider-and-protector stereotype that seems to be at the heart of masculine Christianity. For pastors such as Driscoll, increasing masculinity cred means placing around himself the accoutrements of contemporary culture's masculine stereotypes. He drives an SUV, for example, because, "If you drive a minivan, you are a mini-man."[24] He publicly interviewed football players, aligned himself with Christian hard rock bands, and asserted, again and again, that men have the authority and that women need to listen, that wives need to be available for their husband in all ways, and that men who stray in their marriages can blame their ugly wives, at least in part.* The masculine pastor also was not so touchy-feely in his sermons, because leadership that appears too nurturing and gentle will be a turn-off to men, according to Nancy Pearcey, author of *Total Truth: Liberating Christianity from its Cultural Captivity.*[25]

By saying that church leaders need to ascribe to a specific type of masculinity—and by judging what masculinity is and what it is not—leaders in the Christian masculinity movement have helped transform expectations for other evangelical leaders, who feel as if they must meet specific qualifications that have little to do with what it means to be strong church leaders, and everything to do with cultural stereotypes about men and women. In turn, such assertions about "masculine" and "sissy" pastors must surely affect men who do attend church, and who quickly learn what behaviors are acceptable if one is to be considered a godly man; those who are not inclined toward stereotypically masculine traits must change, becoming people God may not intend them to be. Women are also influenced by assertions that only "masculine" pastors are acceptable church leaders, for once again they hear that women are not invited into the boy's club, but

---

*Of evangelical pastor Ted Haggard, who was caught having sex with a male prostitute, Driscoll said, "A wife who lets herself go and is not sexually available to her husband in the ways that the Song of Songs is so frank about is not responsible for her husband's sin, but she may not be helping him either." Quoted in Brendan Kiley, "Church or Cult? The Control-Freaky Ways of Mars Hill Church," *The Stranger,* February 1, 2012, http://www.thestranger.com/seattle/church-or-cult/Content?oid=12172001 (accessed July 14, 2014).

then neither too are men who might appear or act "feminine." Indeed, some blame the erosion of men's participation in church on women, on their admission to seminaries, and on creating Bibles and hymnals that are more inclusive. These trends have created "girly-men" pastors who cannot provide strong male leadership.[26]

Heaven help those pastors who are presumably feminine in any way whatsoever, who wear khaki or drive mini-vans or try to reach out to and nurture suffering congregants. Any pastor who has even a hint of what culture has deemed a "feminine" nature will never be effective church leaders. After all, Mark Driscoll tells us the Bible tells us so.

Warrior Jesus

Figuring the Divine as a mighty warrior is not new; a warrior-God is one of many go-to metaphors used to describe the power of Jesus and his ability to triumph over all evil forces. Yet in evangelical Christian masculinity, Jesus-as-warrior becomes more than just metaphor. In some images of a warrior Jesus, he wears medieval armor and swings a sword; in others, he appears as a warrior on the cross, ready to jump down and pound the enemy. Those who are so inclined can also display pictures of a patriotic warrior Jesus, draped in the American flag as he hangs on the cross. What model of masculinity would not also be full-blooded American, willing to die for God (and country)? A few images of Jesus show a muscle-bound man on the cross, suggesting that Jesus spent hours in the gym pumping iron with his disciples. This could well be an advertisement for the latest kind of "affinity evangelism," a way to draw men into the church by promising them a great workout and a chance to fight the enemy.*

Champions of Christian masculinity movements sometimes use more subtle means to convey this image of a muscular Jesus, embodying the character traits of culturally stereotypic masculinity. Such proponents might not endorse MMA or a taut Jesus hanging from the cross, but they still understand Jesus through a masculinity framework, conveying that being a man must look one specific way,

---

*A movie released in fall 2014, *Fight Club Jesus*, explores the popularity of Christian Mixed Marital Arts or cage fighting. This type of affinity evangelism uses the premise that Jesus was the ultimate cage fighter because he never "tapped out" or quit. See Rod Dreher, "MMA and the Fight Club for Jesus," http://www.beliefnet.com/columnists/roddreher/2010/02/mma-manly-christianity.html

especially for those also proclaiming Christianity. The Council for Biblical Manhood and Womanhood, for example, outlines the characteristics of "The Perfect Man–Jesus," and the list reads like a prototype for every other list of biblical manhood: Jesus was responsible. He wasn't lazy. He was decisive. He showed initiative.[27] While Jesus certainly reflected these traits, the CBMW fails to include other possible components of Jesus' character, ones that would make him appear stereotypically less masculine: his advocacy for the meek, perhaps, or his peacemaking, or his desire to seek out and comfort those who lived on society's margins. Driscoll, in describing Jesus for a 2007 *Relevant* article, said that some contemporary Christians "want to recast Jesus as a limp-wrist hippie in a dress with a lot of product in His hair, who drank decaf and made pithy Zen statements about life while shopping for the perfect pair of shoes."[28] According to Driscoll, this is far from the truth: Jesus, portrayed in Revelation, was a "pride [*sic*] fighter with a tattoo down His leg, a sword in His hand and the commitment to make someone bleed... That is a guy I can worship," Driscoll comments. "I cannot worship the hippie, diaper, halo Christ because I cannot worship a guy I can beat up." His conclusion is that the other Jesus–the hippie, limp-wristed one–has been shaped that way by contemporary culture, not the Bible.[29]

Those who ascribe to a muscular Christianity will often imagine Jesus' crucifixion as the violent act it most certainly was, but with a heroic Jesus triumphing via his warrior strength and power. Although the gospels generally portray the crucifixion as a moment when Jesus accepts his fate and relinquishes his power, this different interpretation features a brazen Jesus, almost trash-talking his captors from the cross. Bryan Fischer of the American Family Association writes of the crucifixion: "The cross represented a cosmic showdown between the forces of light and the forces of darkness, and our commanding general claimed the ultimate prize by defeating our unseen enemy and liberating an entire planet from his [*sic*] bondage." The imagery Fischer uses is of a ferocious Jesus, dealing a "violent blow" to his enemy; and because we are to emulate this "King of kings," we also need to begin recognizing those who resort to wartime violence by "honoring those who kill bad guys."[30]

The Christian masculinity movement, in all its excesses, reveals the ways that any assertions about biblical manhood and womanhood are fundamentally flawed. Evangelicals who doubt the image of a warrior Jesus, killing mortal enemies from the cross, will yet embrace conceptions of God's design for men and women, disregarding this reality: these definitions of what it takes to be a "biblical man" or "biblical woman" are likewise forged by our cultural understanding of masculinity and femininity. They are as culturally conscribed as the idea that Jesus would be a cage fighter, bashing in the face of his opponent. The multitude of messages about what it means to be a godly woman or man are entirely shaped by our Western understanding of gender, not some eternally true part of God's design for humanity.

So long as evangelicals maintain that men are to be protectors of the "weaker vessel," natural leaders who crave adventure and are inclined to physical power, they will be limiting those men who are gifted in different ways: men who will feel the need to change their truest selves, or who will believe themselves less-than-wholly (or godly) men because they cannot fit what their Christian culture wants them to be. So long as evangelicals insist Jesus is a warrior, full of power and domination, men who would seek to emulate his mercy and compassion will not find the fullness of who they are. And, they will miss out on the opportunity to see Jesus in all *his* fullness, in the ways his ministry on earth undermined the existing power structures—upturning religious authority and extending love, grace, and peace to all.

Taking Another Look

Although not a twenty-first–century muscle man, Jesus *is* the most powerful image of God. The good news he brought—news that often conflicts with evangelical culture about him—is conveyed by the four gospels in the New Testament. While each story of Jesus contains overlaps and similarities with the others, each gospel writer paints a distinct portrait of Jesus. These unique portraits of Jesus deserve more attention, we think, to understand who Jesus was in his context and what his life says to our time and place. In other words, we believe that, rather than projecting our culture onto Jesus and making him into a muscle-man and warrior, we should take seriously who he was in his own time and only then seek to understand how to apply his message to our situations.

Portraits of Jesus

Mark's gospel (chronologically, the first one) shows Jesus to be a suffering servant, an important image for a community beset by war as Mark's community was around the year 70 C.E. Instead of reacting to his foes with violence, Jesus embraced suffering as the path of following God. More than any other image, this is the way Mark's gospel wants us to remember Jesus.

An episode toward the end of his life crystallizes Jesus' impending fate and his willingness to suffer. Recorded in Mark 14, the Passover was two days away when Jesus dined in the house of Simon the leper. During the meal, a woman burst on the scene and anointed him with perfume. She poured her expensive ointment on his head, an act offending others at the table. Jesus intervened, telling her accusers to back off because she had anointed him before his burial, an act of love and compassion.

Jesus wasn't being chivalrous, just standing up for a nice woman; he was deliberately violating the purity standards of ancient Judaism. Because Simon was a leper, when Jesus dined at his house he discredited the cultural stipulations of purity. His rejection of purity standards was further emphasized when Jesus accepted the woman's oil and praised her for her kindness—considering physical touch and conversation among different sexes was prohibited. Within the contours of a simple meal, Jesus displayed strength—not the kind of a macho hero—but the kind of inner fortitude that knows how to welcome those societies discard and to welcome others even when it requires going against religious and cultural mores.

In Matthew's gospel, Jesus is primarily portrayed as a figure like Moses, although more important because he fulfills the law and prophets before him. As with Moses, Jesus' key moment takes place on the mountaintop, when he delivers what we call the "Sermon on the Mount" (Matthew 5–7). The message Jesus presents is in stark contrast to what many contemporary Christians convey. There is no love of country or nationalism in his instructions. Instead, Jesus guided the listeners about how to live for the good of community and how to love without limitations.

At the heart of the Sermon on the Mount is a series of three instructions, a method of political action that informed Mahatma Gandhi and Martin Luther King Jr. even as it seems to have escaped many today, who seem to have little concern about using violence. In Matthew 5, Jesus said to resist evil doers, and to turn the other cheek if the right one has been struck; to give one's cloak to anyone who has taken one's coat; and to carry a pack a second mile if someone had required the person to carry it one. Each statement shows how one's actions can provoke the other person to face the injustice involved in the situation. While one might think that power resides in the person who is inherently more powerful, Jesus' teaching shows how the oppressed can utilize power by nonviolent resistance.

Turning the other cheek after the right one has been struck is not merely asking for a second blow. According to biblical scholar Walter Wink, it provides a situation whereby the perpetrator must strike a blow using his fist—an action that in first-century Rome indicated equal status. Hitting a person of lesser status was accomplished with a back-hand, a sign of putting the inferior person in his or her place. A fist used between persons suggested they shared relatively equal status. The assaulted person is not asking to be hit again by turning the cheek; she or he is creating a scenario whereby the assailant must acknowledge the person as an equal in order to strike a second time. Unlike images of a macho Jesus knocking out his enemies with a mean left hook, this understanding of Jesus differs in a fundamental way: Jesus calls on his followers not to be aggressors, not to resist evil, but to overcome evil with good.

A similar act of resistance is created by giving one's cloak. Indebtedness was a huge problem in Jesus' time and the poor often found themselves in vulnerable positions including being sued and having nothing to give except perhaps their outer garments. When Jesus instructed his disciples to give to anyone who asked for one's coat not only the coat but also one's cloak (inner garment) it was a way of demonstrating the absurdity of the position of the poor. Naked, one could enter the courtroom publicly displaying the injustice of the Roman imperial system. Since nakedness was taboo in Judaism (for the party who witnessed it), such actions would clearly shift the attention from the lawsuit in question, to the commotion of a naked defendant whose actions offered the creditor an opportunity to see the absurdity—and oppression—his actions caused.

A comparable strategy resides at the heart of Jesus' final directive. Roman law regulated how soldiers carried their packs. Ordinary people, if they were enlisted by a soldier to carry his pack, were required by law to do so, although it was limited to a mile, clearly marked along Roman roads. Jesus' instructions suggest an action taken to force a potential oppressor to make a decision about how to treat someone deemed inferior. By carrying a soldier's pack longer than the required amount, the person is making a soldier decide whether or not to risk being caught for exploitation and suffer the consequences. Going beyond the distance was not about being nice or doing something for personal satisfaction, but about enabling people to see the problem of oppressing others.

Jesus' teaching in Matthew required inner strength and intellectual fortitude, even as it relied upon nonviolent methods of interpersonal interactions. A far cry from Was Jesus a Man's Man? 81 muscle ministries, Jesus' strength was of a deeper sort. At its heart was justice for all people, not just those who happen to find themselves in positions of power or privilege.[31]

Luke's gospel moves beyond presenting Jesus as greater than Moses to suggest Jesus was a savior, not just for Jews, but for the entire world. Even so, Jesus' actions are no less political than they were in Matthew's gospel.[32] In "The Triumphal Entry" in Luke 19, an event celebrated each year on Palm Sunday worldwide, the subversive undertone of Jesus' ride into Jerusalem on a donkey's back often goes unnoticed.

Roman emperors used public occasions to reinforce their power, often parading soldiers in their armor throughout city streets. Military might displayed on horseback and in chariots sent potent messages about who was in control. Officials decked out in their uniforms provided a contrast to those who lined the streets wearing only worn tunics and dusty sandals. Roman officials used parades of Roman power as ancient billboards, yet when Jesus orchestrated his triumphal entry using a donkey, he created an alternative parade, one that pitted his grassroots movement against Rome's political authority. With followers lined along his path to Jerusalem and calling out "Hosanna" (which means "save us"), they sent a clarion call to Rome. Rather than trusting in Rome's power, they aligned themselves with God, opting for justice and peace rather than oppression and violence.

When Jesus points out the futility of Rome's power with such vivid displays, the reader should not be surprised; the author of Luke pointed to Mary in Jesus' birth narrative, intimating this kind of perspective would be the bedrock for Jesus' life. Prior to Jesus' birth, Gabriel, the angel, spoke to Mary. The visit doesn't take place in a dream or a vision, as often is the case in biblical narratives, but when Mary is wide awake and thinking clearly. Mary did not immediately respond; it is easy to imagine her hesitancy. What does anyone say in response to: "The Lord is with you" (1:28)? Mary found her voice when she heard she would have a son who would be called the Son of the Most High and he would occupy the throne of David. How could this happen, she wanted to know, since she was a virgin? Even though

Gabriel avoided answering her question, instead saying the Holy Spirit would be present, Mary responded that she was willing to participate with God's intention.

Such a decision involved autonomy often not recognized in Mary. Engaged to Joseph at the time, she was already considered his property. Before that she was owned by her father. That Mary did not feel compelled to seek permission from Joseph (or from her father) conveys her independence. She considered Gabriel's claims and acceded to them without following appropriate social protocol.

Later, when she traveled to meet Elizabeth, the mother of John the Baptist, Mary broke into song. Without priestly intervention or a male religious authority, Mary understood the spirit of God's good news. Echoing Hannah's song recorded in 1 Samuel 2, Mary must have been shaped not only by the gracious righteousness of God but also by women before her. Surely Mary knew the ancient stories of Abraham and Moses, was familiar with leaders such as David and Solomon. Yet, when Mary spoke of her faith in God, she used the words of Hannah.

Mary's song in Luke 1, often called Mary's Magnificat, conveys the justice of God seen in Jesus' actions throughout the gospels. It is a theology of reversals, in which the weak become strong, the powerful are brought low, and the hungry are filled. We can imagine Mary knew the lows all too well. She had been on the receiving end of social systems that disregarded groups of people: women, the poor, the sick, the hungry.

Her positive response to Gabriel surely was motivated by what she understood about God. From Hannah she knew God's dream for humanity included freedom and liberation for all. She understood faith in God meant trusting that God would be faithful, and would work to make life more abundant for all. Mary was the perfect person to give birth to God's desire for humanity; in her risky decision, she showed the courage necessary to choose the better way. Mary had no idea what was in store for her as Jesus' mother, and yet she was willing to take a chance on life with God.

As the mother of Jesus, Mary taught him what she knew: how to be stalwart in a world of oppression; how to be compassionate when others looked the other way; how to take a risk that the world would consider as folly. Mary's faith—strong and trusting—formed Jesus and the person he became.

The last gospel to be included in the New Testament, John, shows Jesus as the Incarnation of God. Jesus, in this case, no longer uses parables and one-liners, as he does in the Synoptic gospels (Matthew, Mark, and Luke), and instead relies on long theological essays, speaking often of his Divine status. And yet this disparate portrait of Jesus was included by those who decided which books to use in the New Testament. Therefore, John offers an important aspect in filling out what the early church thought subsequent generations should know about Jesus. It also serves the function of letting readers see the developing nature of the church's theology—a window into the ways beliefs change to fit new contexts and social problems.

According not only to John's author but to all the gospel writers, gender was not a barrier to becoming an evangelist. In every interaction between Jesus and women, Jesus was consistent: no distinction is made based upon gender. From the Samaritan woman in John 4, who has the most developed theological conversation with Jesus of any noted, to Mary and Martha, who worked alongside Jesus, women are held accountable for their own religious convictions and are not released from tasks or commitments because of who they are. Women—like men—are called by Jesus to live lives of faithful fidelity to God and to spread the good news of God.

Even in situations in which a patriarchal preference would argue in favor of men having more importance than women, Jesus demands a counter-cultural approach. The exchange between Mary Magdalene and the risen Christ recorded in John 20 says Mary had gone to the tomb but found the stone rolled away and the tomb empty. Hastily, she left in order to tell Peter and another disciple that Jesus' body had vanished. The three returned to the tomb, where Peter and the other disciple see the linen wrappings in the tomb and return to their homes. Mary, on the other hand, remained at the empty tomb, crying. When she looked inside, she saw two angels sitting where Jesus' body had been and they asked her why she was crying. When she responded that her sorrow was due to Jesus' body being missing, she turned around to see a man standing at the tomb's entrance. This person also asked her why she was weeping. The narrator fills in the details, adding that presumably Mary mistook Jesus for a gardener. She recognized him only when he spoke to her, calling her by name. Their relationship of Rabbi and student established, he instructed her to relay the message of his continuing presence to the disciples.

Mary Magdalene points the way to a full ministry without limits. In each gospel, the women in Jesus' life are the last ones at his tomb and, in his encounters with them, Jesus never limits what he asks them to do. In John, the risen Christ sends Mary back to the disciples. She elects to go, even in a patriarchal age when she and her message to them could be easily dismissed.

The Absence of Hierarchy

Individual encounters between Jesus and women challenge assumptions that women were supposed to be limited in their contributions to the Jesus movement. Still we find those who promote muscle ministries and Jesus as a macho leader, and reinforce these false ideas of hierarchy and patriarchy as somehow ordained by God or evidence of God's male-centric design for the world.

Not only do these assertions discount Jesus' numerous interactions with women, they also fail to take seriously the images Jesus used to instruct his followers about the nature of the community of faith. At the center of Jesus' teaching is the interconnectedness of humanity. The well-known and best-loved stories of Jesus relate this: the feeding of the multitudes, in which fish and bread are shared so that no one goes hungry; the potential for forgiveness and wholeness that comes only when people seek not to be understood so much as to repair broken relationships (as in the story of Zacchaeus); the radical equality in which children are just as important as adults and the supposed greatest is last. At every turn Jesus suggests the dream of God is realized in the reversal of hierarchy: the last shall be first and those who work for a short amount of time are given the same compensation as those who started at dawn.

Love and sacrificing of self for the good of others are at the core of Jesus' instructions. The image of the vine in John's gospel poignantly conveys Jesus' vision for community. In John 15 Jesus teaches that he is the vine, and God is the one who enables the vine to grow. The vine also consists of branches: people who follow Jesus and become part of the ongoing community of God. As Gail O'Day suggests, there are two important clues about this metaphor. First, interconnectedness and mutuality are at the heart of this image. Jesus repeats the verb translated as "abide" multiple times in this passage. To abide means to remain or to maintain one's presence. Jesus elaborates that he abides in God and God abides in him, and those who are part of the vine abide in Jesus. The vine is a web of relationships, woven together in such a way that mutuality is required. Whatever happens to any portion of the vine affects all other parts of it. As O'Day intimates, "Individuals in the community will prosper only insofar as they recognize themselves as members of an organic unit."[33] This emphasis on interconnected relationships and mutuality starkly contrasts any notions of individualism or personal promotion.[34]

A second clue about the nature of Christian community is that it is radically nonhierarchical. There is no one branch that supersedes another, nor can individual branches take over for other branches as more important or more critical to the overall life of the vine. The vine is an organic image that grows or dies together. Its health relies on all the branches, gaining sustenance not from each other but from Jesus. Life grows out from the center: God is the One, who sustains all and who promotes healthy growth by feeding and pruning. Each branch is an integral part of the whole vine, but no one branch gets promoted to head branch or lead branch. All depend on God, and She nourishes and cares for all.[35]

Following Jesus Is Risky Business

For all of the hype around masculine ministries, in which Jesus is touted as a "take no prisoners" kind of guy, there is some truth in the marketing and messages. Jesus had extraordinary strength, and those who followed him did so at considerable personal risk. But the strength and courage required to follow Jesus is not the kind usually portrayed by men wanting, more than anything else, to find acceptance for hyper-masculinity in the person of Jesus.

Despite what his culture demanded, Jesus charted a different course. Compassion and love were central to what he did and taught. Nowhere did he demand special treatment or recognition, and, instead, in every case, he put others before himself. This sacrificial living did not mean treating women as delicate or incapable of making their own decisions. His interactions with women were guided by respect and trust. He held them accountable for their actions, just as he trusted them to be ambassadors of the gospels, evangelists on his behalf. There is not a hint of pedantic condescension in Jesus' relationships with women.

In an era of violence and domination, Jesus showed his disciples to use their creativity and wits to respond to violence with resistance. Rather than being weak in the face of oppression, Jesus called for the strongest actions of all, to offer nonviolent resistance as their response to injustice and coercion. He resisted the cultural wisdom of the day, which encouraged people to use violence as a means of domination and power. Jesus encouraged his followers to take the course he did.

Even as such commitments demanded nonviolence, they also relied on unmatched courage and perseverance.

To live in a way that puts others ahead of oneself is the ultimate test of strength. In choosing the path of suffering and death, Jesus illustrated the depths of his compassion and the extensiveness of new life. From him we learn that strength comes not by the sword, but by choosing peace and justice. From him we also see that this compassion is not simply for those who are part of our communities, but also for those who are not.

To follow Jesus is to give up our own demands and our own justifications about who we are, and instead be willing to be apprentices of the one who pointed the way to God's dream, the reality in which all are loved and welcomed and free.

It's a dream worth pursuing with all of our strength.

Chapter Five

The Problem with Purity

Jessica[1] was like many students who enroll at evangelical universities. Her family was not wealthy, but she was smart and ambitious, driven, just the kind of student colleges are looking for. Her university awarded her a full scholarship based on her leadership potential, and during her four years at the school, she excelled: in the classroom, in her major, in the roles she assumed. Despite her many successes, Jessica also believed herself to be spoiled goods, thanks to a very vivid youth group object lesson.

One night at her church, Jessica's youth leader passed out to every teenager a Jolly Rancher candy. He instructed each person to begin sucking on their candy, though he had quietly told a few girls to refrain, to keep their candy neatly wrapped in their packages. Jessica was one of the girls who began to enjoy her candy, until the youth instructor told them to stop, and put the candy back in its original wrapper. This is impossible to do once a Jolly Rancher has become sticky and deformed, and the wrapper was already mangled in students' hands.

You might see where this story is going.

The youth leader held up the candy still perfectly placed in its wrapper, untouched by those girls he had already instructed. And then, he held up the candy that had been used, no longer fit for the wrapper it had come in. Which piece of candy would the teenagers want now, he asked?

"People who have sex before marriage are like these Jolly Ranchers," he said. "They are used up, unlike the other candy that has yet to be unwrapped. No one wants candy that's already been sucked on. No one delights in that candy." Jessica listened to the youth leader's lesson; she didn't want her friends to know how she was processing this lesson, nor that she had already been sexually active, and thus was no better than a used piece of candy.

While he may have intended to inspire young people, the youth leader conveyed another message: Jessica was worthless because she had made the decision to have sex with a boyfriend. No one would ever prefer her over someone else who had retained her "purity." This campus leader, straight-A student, strong and bright and thoughtful and compassionate young woman believed she was no better than a used-up piece of trash, thanks to an object lesson about the value of remaining a virgin until marriage.

Jessica's story about her youth group's object lesson is not an anomaly. Other young women have reported that, in their youth groups, those who had sex before marriage were likened to chewed-up gum, a rose that's been plucked of its petals, a crisp $20 bill that, once crumpled and stepped on, is no longer as desirable. The message of these lessons can be damaging to women *and* men: those who have had sex before marriage hear they are no longer desirable, and that God (and everyone else) loves them a little less; those who have not had sex hear they will remain loveable, and loved, only if they are able to steer clear of having intercourse before they are wed. When one's sexuality is equated with the sweet, alluring taste of candy, all young women will learn they are only the sum of their bodies, and that their best resource—the one thing they need to hold on to and protect and allow others to savor—rests in their bodies, in their ability to give sexual pleasure to those they marry.

So it is with purity culture, a large and imposing structure that has helped shape the evangelical conversation about sex and sexuality, and has also helped to shape the ways many are led to think about their bodies, and also concepts such as shame and God's grace. Men have certainly been damaged by purity culture, by its demands that godly men protect the virginity of those they love and must not think lustful thoughts. Purity culture has objectified men, too, telling men their sexual impulses are unmanageable, that they are victims of their basest instincts.

Still, the burden of purity culture has been felt acutely by women, to whom most messages about remaining pure are directed. From an early age, women hear purity is their provenance, and that their every decision needs to be informed both by their desire to stay pure and their responsibility to keep any man in their orbit pure, too. The culture also removes women's agency by suggesting purity is something to be protected, that women's bodies are fortresses to be guarded by fathers, boyfriends, husbands. Like other aspects of evangelical popular culture, purity also has become marketable, with a vast line of purity-related products for sale, all intended as reminders of one precious gift.

A precious gift that, once give away, can never, ever be the same, like a used up piece of candy. So we've been told.

The One Ring

The purity ring is arguably the most prevalent symbol of the purity culture. When evangelicals talk about purity, that ring–a marker of one's promise to God and family to remain pure–comes to mind. Both girls and boys wear them, though purity jewelry is much more popular among girls, who have been told that their sexual purity is to be prized above all else, a sure marker of their love for God–and God's love for them. The ring symbolizes a purity they need to guard, nurture, and embrace, because they alone are responsible for what happens with their bodies. Boys are not necessarily prone to the same pressures, nor to the same sense of responsibility. Because boys and men are sexual beings, liable to pursue women whose "immodest dress" invites lust, their purity is not their responsibility, nor the rings they wear a clear indication of their ability to sustain a pure lifestyle.

The purity ring exemplifies the evangelical commodification of sexuality, as the market for purity rings is quite large. A number of companies sell purity rings in a range of prices; Christianbooks.com alone currently has 234 purity ring options. Even corporations such as Walmart and Zales Jewelers have gotten into the act, selling purity rings on their websites for up to $450. Nothing says "purity" like a diamond-studded cross reminding the wearer that true love waits.

Perhaps more significantly, the purity ring reflects the ways in which sexual purity is tied together with notions of male ownership over women and the lack of agency for women. Although purity rings are also available for men, the ritual of the purity ring is focused more on girls, who attend purity balls with their fathers, pledge their purity to their fathers, and more prominently wear the rings as reminders of the promises they've made to their dads, to remain pure until their special men enter the picture.

Purity rings became popular in the 1990s, when abstinence pledges and programs were being considered the best, most successful way to curb teen pregnancy rates. The rings are intended to replicate an engagement or wedding band, but are to be worn by girls before marriage on their right ring finger, though some choose the left hand, showing that they are "taken" (by Jesus, by their fathers) until marriage. Often, slogans such as "True Love Waits" or "Purity" are engraved into the bands.

Purity rings are fairly innocuous on their own—they are just pieces of jewelry. The rituals surrounding the rings and their symbolic intent are problematic. The songs and poems, purity balls and dances (at which the rings are given from fathers to daughters), and the public proclamation that one's virginity is "The Thing" to be celebrated in a girl's life—these remind girls they are to be loved and cherished and celebrated because of their sexual selves, because of what they can give and withhold.

In other words, the purity ring rituals focus on a girl's sexuality, all in the name of avoiding sex.

Let's Dance

A purity ball might seem just like any other teenage dance, minus gawky teen-aged boys. All the accoutrements of a dance are there: Girls wearing their finest new dresses, appearing more grown-up than they really are. A decorated dancing hall with fine china set on tables, ready for the pre-event banquet. Corsages pinned tenderly to each girl's dress or wrapped around her wrist. Soft music and a master of ceremonies, directing couples from dinner to dance.

But look closer, because at a purity ball, these are no ordinary couples, and this is no ordinary dance. In this ballroom, dads dance with their teen-aged daughters, enjoy a meal together, and enact a ritual pledging fathers will protect their daughters' purity from assault. In the upside-down world of purity culture, these balls are the centerpiece, seen by some evangelicals as the hallmark of a father's love for his daughter, replicating God's love for his princesses.

Randy and Linda Wilson are the originators of the purity ball, and since their first ball in 1998, they've developed a small purity-themed industry, hosting purity events for young women and their fathers and a complementary experience for young men. The Wilsons are also available to speak on purity, and have funded their son's purity-focused business, which teaches boys to be men of honor. Three Wilson daughters have also started a similar curriculum for girls, called School of Grace, and have written a book encouraging women to "Awaken their Hearts" through pure living.

At the center of this purity empire is the purity ball, a pseudo-dance at which fathers bequeath their daughters with purity rings, and in exchange promise they will serve as protectors of their daughters until they marry. Although there is no one right way to hold a purity ball, apparently most balls follow a distinct program, starting with dinner shared banquet style between dad and daughter, then dancing, and then the purity ring ritual. Fathers stand in a ring around their daughters, praying for them and for their purity. At most balls, the purity pledge is spoken from father to daughter; at the Generations of Light purity balls, the pledge is this:

> I, (Daughter's Name)'s Father, choose before God to cover my daughter as her authority and protection in the area of purity. I will be pure in my own life as a man, husband and father. I will be a man of integrity and accountability as I lead, guide and pray over my daughter and my family as the high priest of my home. This covering will be used by God to influence generations to come.[2]

This pledge is often followed by the presentation of the purity ring from father to daughter in an act that replicates a wedding's ring ceremony. In purity world, this act intentionally echoes the wedding exchange, as the father is to serve as a husband-by-proxy until a girl's "ownership" can be handed to her real husband.

Although there is no explicit mention of sexuality in the purity pledge, and although the purity ball asserts that its intent to promote all kinds of purity, the emphasis remains focused on a girl's virginity and her father's need to guard that part of his daughter's self over all other things. Purity ball dresses are often white, an imitation of the white wedding dress the girl will one day wear. At some purity balls, too, there are other accoutrements reminiscent of a wedding: processionals, with the daughter walking on her daddy's arm; a church aisle adorned with flower petals; archways under which father and daughter walk, in some cases created by crossed swords; and first dances between father and daughter, a celebration of the vows that have just been spoken.

Some may be quick to point out that a mother-son companion purity event exists, and that sons are also asked to make purity covenants. To some extent, this is true; some Christian organizations have organized "A Knight to Remember" evenings for mothers and sons with the intent of replicating the purity balls taking place country-wide.[*]

What is noticeably absent from description about "A Knight to Remember" and other events is any acknowledgment of a boy's sexuality, of his virginity, or of the need for him to pledge purity. These components also form only one part of "The Brave Heart of a Warrior" ceremony, another invention of the Wilsons as a rite of passage for young boys. This particular manhood ceremony occurs when boys are twelve, presumably mirroring Jesus' own transition from boyhood to manhood. In a nod toward treatment equal to that of girls at purity balls, The Brave Heart of a Warrior ceremony also includes a mother's gift of a purity ring, symbolizing the need for "sons to guard their hearts and walk in purity and call them to live in wholeness and strength in mind, body, and spirit. We call them to protect young women's hearts by living lives of integrity, purpose, and purity. And this ring is to remind him to honor God at all costs."[3] The language here is significantly different than it is for a girl's purity ring; note that for both purity pledges, the male has power; for both, it is the vulnerable female who needs protection, lest someone steals her purity away.

Purity as Consumer Good

Given the wild success of purity rings and purity balls, purity pledges and purity gowns, it's no wonder that purity has become, in a sense, a consumer good: a way for Christian marketers to cash in on products reminding a girl that she is to remain pure. And so, in the years since the abstinence pledge became a key component in a Christian young person's journey toward becoming a sexual being, a number of products now crowd the shelves of Christian stores, both of the online and brick-and-mortar type. Though the product descriptions sometimes make a nod toward including boys as potential

---

[*]See http://generationsoflight.com/html/boys.html (accessed July 11, 2014) for a more expansive description of "A Knight to Remember" events. Boys learn about chivalry and how to treat women, study other men of honor in history, and play ultimate Frisbee and other active games.

buyers, girls remain the primary target for these goods. Girls' purity needs to be guarded in ways a boy's does not, and protecting a girl's purity remains a key function of these products.

Purity rings especially have generated a number of other forms of purity jewelry and clothing, including wristbands and T-shirts announcing that the wearer is pure, virtuous, and priceless.[4] Lockets express to others that "true love waits," with a heart-shaped lock pendant reminding others that a girl's heart is locked tight until the right man holds the key. Other companies mass produce T-shirts a virtuous girl can wear proclaiming that she is a "virgin on purpose" and that she is "virtuous." One T-shirt, surely intended to be clever in its double entendre, seems to instead convey the troubling truth about purity culture: "Notice: No Trespassing On This Property[.] My Father Is Watching."[5]

A number of Christian authors have also entered the purity market, writing devotional books, how-to guides, and easy-to-read polemics intended to help readers remain pure. Some authors have created an entire franchise around the topic of purity; most notable among these is Dannah Gresh, whose *Secret Keeper Girl* line of books has birthed a purity empire. For the *Secret Keeper Girl*, keeping one's purity–and remaining modest–seems the sole *raison d'etre* for a girl's existence. Gresh's site sells a number of her purity-based works, targeted to tweens and teens, women and parents, and even to "boyz," though the Gresh books for boys are, by and large, about how girls can talk to and understand the boys in their lives. Foundational to the entire *Secret Keeper Girl* juggernaut is the idea that women and girls are "a masterpiece created by God," which is all well and good, but this masterpiece seemingly comes with a caveat: that this godly creation works hard to keep her body sexually pure and hidden through modest clothing as a means of "keep[ing] the deepest secret of her authentic beauty a secret." To that end, Gresh's books, her speaking tour, and the *Secret Keeper Girl* pajama parties intend to teach girls and their mothers how best to remain modest to keep "the deepest secrets of her beauty for just one man." Until that man comes around, girls are encouraged to share "all of her heart secrets with her mom at any time."[6]

In some ways, this kind of advice seems like an outlier: surely girls are not being challenged to continually prize, above all, their bodies, modestly covered. Yet a number of Christian books and websites provide all kinds of tests for girls and women to apply to their wardrobes, making sure every skirt is no more than the width of four fingers above the knee, and every top exposes no more than the width of four fingers beneath the collarbone. This rule is offered as the logical standard, although there is no explanation of the rationale behind four fingers (rather than three, or five), nor any sense of what one might do if her fingers are exceptionally skinny or fat. This type of modesty legalism would be hilarious, if it didn't shame women, young and old, who are told their bodies must be constantly concealed, else they lead others into sin. Even more, endless messages about modesty and purity remind women that their bodies are the most important element they hold: capable of great power, of causing considerable temptation. In some ways, modesty rules objectify and sexualize women as much as—if not more—than the "popular culture" they seek to subvert, focusing solely on a woman's body as the sum total of her being.

In "Naked and Ashamed: Women and Evangelical Purity Culture," Amanda Barbee shares the story of a middle school youth group retreat in Georgia, at which a youth leader, hoping to teach a room full of girls and boys about modesty, held a box of donuts up to his chest in a manner so that the donuts remained invisible. He then leaned over so that the entire room could see the donuts, and equated this action to what boys see when a girl leans over. By equating donuts to a girl's cleavage, he somehow hoped to teach middle schoolers to wear clothes that did not reveal and to act in ways that kept boys from seeing one's "goods," while also reminding everyone about the sweet, tempting allure of a woman's chest. Barbee writes, "This metaphor could have provided an opportunity to critique the objectification of women's bodies that is rampant in modern American culture, but like most discussions of male sexuality within the purity movement, the objectification was seen as normative; rather than teaching middle-school boys to respect the bodies of their female peers, these girls are being taught that their bodies are dangerous and tempting."[7]

So dangerous and tempting are their bodies, that girls are taught early and often to alternately revere and revile the very bodies God formed, to cover them up and hide them from everyone who might be peeking up their shorts, because remaining pure remains a girl's highest aim. While purity culture and its drive to make girls modest might intend to celebrate women's bodies and their "gift" of sex for "The One," an unintended consequence is this: shame for one's body and a fear of sexuality and a sense that the woman's body is not–in any way, shape, or form–created in God's very image.

Modesty as Fashion Statement

The evangelical modesty movement puts particular demands on women in terms of dress, believing that it is a woman's responsibility to cover herself as a sign of her own purity and to keep men from falling into lustful temptation. At its extremes, women are compelled by their religious communities to wear long dresses covered by an extra layer of cloth over the front, a cape, which serves as an extra veil over the chest area: think Amish and conservative Mennonites. Yet even many evangelicals believe strongly in the principles of modesty, and though they might not insist on dresses, they still demand of women a certain degree of attention to what they are wearing, lest, by showing too much skin, women lead men astray.

Companies such as Modest Apparel USA sell dresses catering to those for whom clothes at mainstream shops prove too revealing. Like most modest-marketed clothing, the company offers skirts and blouses for both women and girls, but provides only one product for the modest male: a long-sleeved T-shirt, similar to any you might buy at Target or Eddie Bauer. Indeed, if you look at the many websites promising modest clothing, most often you will find nothing suggesting that men themselves need to attend to modesty. Women must always be covered, even when they go swimming, which is why sites selling modest swimwear show girls and women wearing skirts to the knees and short-sleeved, loose swim tops, the perfectly modest ensemble for hot days at the beach.

As maddening as this double standard is for the overtly modest set, the messages about modesty are even more problematic for those who don't require their girls and young women to wear full-length skirts, but expect them to remain modest nonetheless, else they cause men around them to lust. Instructions for wearing "pure" clothing suggest girls can wear clothes similar to what their peers wear, though they must also be constantly vigilant, else they unsuspectingly might lead some man into sin. Proscriptions about what is modest and what is not abound, in books and on blogs and in social networking sites, including Pinterest, which has numerous "modest fashion" sites that appear, almost to the page, no different than other teen fashion sites, save for perhaps fewer sleeveless tops and daisy duke shorts.

The "Modest is Hottest" movement was born from the idea that girls can be fashionable while remaining modest in their clothing. T-shirts proudly proclaim that "Modest is Hottest," even as the words themselves are imprinted across the wearer's chest, drawing attention to that which the shirt presumably is meant to hide. Christian leaders such as Rebecca St. James have leaped on the Modest is Hottest bandwagon, proclaiming that girls are to be modest in all things.[8] Similarly, Christian writer Jarrid Wilson assures readers that modest is indeed hottest, because modesty in dress–"for the ladies," at least– shows that someone is yearning for sexual purity; that modest dress will attract quality "guys" to those who have qualities beyond their bodies; and will mark the wearer as different from every other woman. Wilson then pulls out the binary often used by evangelical culture: women can either follow the model of Proverbs 31, or be a Victoria's Secret model. It's as if there is no in between.[9]

A number of marketers have found ways to brand their swimwear for Christian girls and women who want to be attractively demure at the beach. In summer 2013, Jessica Rey of *Power Ranger* fame gained (or regained?) fame with a new swimwear line that immediately caused a lot of buzz because her clothes promised to be modest; inspired by Audrey Hepburn, the suits were "fashionable but classy." Her presentation at the Christian-based Q Conference compelled women to rush her site, and her swimwear sold out in a few days' time. Using the motto "Who says it has to be itsy-bitsy?" Rey's swimwear was based on the idea that there is power in wearing a bikini, but not the power that women intend; she claimed her suits allowed women to receive more respect from men because, in modest fashion, men will see women less as objects to be desired, and more as equals.[10]

Some folks will no doubt argue that Rey's efforts are good for women. In an era when pop star Miley Cyrus can "twerk" while nearly naked on stage at the Video Music Awards, when little girls' clothing lines sell sex kitten t-shirts and short-shorts, and when the shapes of women's bodies continue to be dissected in every popular culture medium possible, it might seem refreshing for some evangelical Christians to cry "Enough!" and to insist that women can be fashionable, "hot," and still modestly dressed. Yet, fundamentally, what happens in evangelical culture is that women's freedom is judged, demeaned, and removed. They are told they need to be humbled to uphold "modesty standards," presumably built of biblical teaching, else they slip into sexual immorality while also causing their "brothers" to stumble. This is its own kind of objectification, as potentially damaging, if not more so, that the cultural message that women's bodies are their power.

What Teenage Boys Can Tell Us about Modesty

In 2007, brothers Alex and Brett Harris—younger siblings to *I Kissed Dating Goodbye*'s Joshua Harris—initiated a "Modesty Survey" as part of their "The Rebelution" project. The survey, which proposed to foster discussion about modesty between Christian girls and boys, was the brainchild of a fifteen-year-old teenager who solicited questions about modesty from several hundred girls, and she also oversaw data collection with the help of Candace Perry of "Purity Girls," and an expert on "modesty surveys." The survey was shared with Christian young men, who responded in overwhelming numbers to questions about what constituted a modest outfit, whether the way a girl walks can be a "stumbling block" for boys, and whether a girl could wear a necklace without bringing too much attention to her neck.

In just over twenty days, nearly 1600 boys and young men chimed in via an on-line survey, letting everyone know what girls should be wearing. They told girls they will be taken more seriously if they dress modestly, and many suggested they would not even consider dating a girl who they considered immodest. And, according to the males, modesty meant not simply wearing clothes that didn't draw attention to girls' figures. Two-thirds of survey respondents believed that a girl adjusting her bra strap was immodest; almost the same amount believed undergarment lines should not be visible (no panty lines, no hint of a bra strap), else—as one 22-year-old respondent suggested— "we'll think about what you look like in your underwear." Some boys also believed a girl should not bend over, as this might reveal her backside; that girls should not have their chests bounce when walking or running; or stretch their arms over their heads, as this might call attention to their bodies.[11]

Judging by *The Rebelution Modesty Survey*, girls are damned if they stretch when tired, pick something up from the floor, or choose to let their bodies move a little too much when exercising. Anything a girl does might be interpreted as immodest, thereby causing the boys around her to stumble into sexual sin. *The Modesty Survey* reflected well the main message girls receive in purity culture: those born female are responsible not only for their own sexual purity, but for the purity of those born male, too.

The Harris brothers provided a short *Modesty Survey* essay written by an anonymous reader in response to the survey, letting boys know they are responsible when they are tempted and that girls will not be blamed if boys stumble. But even that piece, an apology of sorts, ends with this caveat: "We get tested every day. That's our job wherever we are, whether in the world or in church. But quite honestly, we'd rather do our battles with the world than with our sisters in Christ." This ending salvo foists the responsibility back onto girls, essentially saying that if they weren't forcing men to "battle" their sexual urges by being so immodest, boys could do the *real* work of the church.[12]

And boys and men seem fairly willing to provide their insight about what girls should wear, given the large response to the modesty survey, as well as the many blogs and online articles written by men letting girls know exactly what they should be wearing. Consider, for example, a series of posts written by Ryan Visconti, an Assemblies of God minister in Arizona whose blog promises to deliver the lowdown on "real gospel living." His initial post, "All God's Daughters Wear Bikinis?" expresses disbelief that any Christian woman who has reached physical maturity would even consider wearing a bikini, because, "If we're going to teach young Christian boys to pursue sexual purity and that they should wait till marriage to have sex, and if we're going to teach Christian men to avoid lust and stop viewing pornography, maybe we, as the Church, shouldn't be sending our own women out into the world practically buck-naked, eh? It just seems a little bit cruel. Would you serve whiskey at an AA meeting?"[13]

Visconti unintentionally proclaims what is at the root of purity culture: by seeming to resist the sexual objectification of women, purity culture objectifies women's bodies. Visconti argues women's bodies are not *their* bodies after all: their bodies belong to God, then to their husbands, and *then* to themselves; the bodies of unmarried women are owned first by God and then by *future spouses* (and also by the unmarried women's fathers, who must be responsible for their bodies' purity). By making women responsible for the actions of men, purity culture assumes a great deal about the sexuality of men, too, locking them also in chains.

Another Problem with Purity

In February 2014, the *New Republic* published an article exposing a rape scandal cover-up occurring at one of evangelicalism's prized colleges, Patrick Henry College.[14] Women who reported cases of sexual abuse or rape at the college were not receiving the legal or emotional counsel they needed. Quite the opposite, in fact: women who approached college administrators and faculty about instances of date rape and sexual aggression were being interrogated instead, their motives and behaviors dissected by campus officials eager to blame the victims, rather than the victimizers, for any kind of abuse. The *New Republic* details case after case of students at the school who were violated, who reported the crimes, but who were told that—because of their own actions, because of little evidence, because the male students had apologized—nothing could be done.[15]

When one student, and then another and another, reported cases of sexual assault, it was their own behaviors that received the most scrutiny; they were disciplined if they broke other Patrick Henry rules during the assaults; in several cases, women were disciplined because they were tipsy, or drunk, when they were raped by male Patrick Henry students. In one case, a woman reported that a peer was sending her threatening e-mails, suggesting he wanted to "forcibly take my virginity." When she met with the dean, however, she was told, "The choices you make and the people you choose to associate with, the way you try to portray yourself, will affect how people treat you." Later, according to the *New Republic*, the women's dean at Patrick Henry asked the student "to think about her clothing and 'the kinds of ideas it puts in men's minds.'"[16]

Patrick Henry College has denied these claims, and in a written statement to the *New Republic*, said, "We do not seek to elevate one gender above the other, but to esteem all students as being made in the image of the One who created them."[17] Yet a mountain of evidence, including official and unofficial correspondence, and the personal testimony from female and male students, suggests otherwise. To those familiar with purity culture, what has happened at Patrick Henry—as well as at other institutions—is sobering, but not surprising; Patrick Henry's rape scandal profoundly reflects the problem of purity and modesty.

For, at its center, purity culture is really a shame-based culture, teaching young people they should be at once preoccupied with and ashamed of their sexuality, ashamed of their bodies, ashamed of any self-expression deemed "immodest" by those who might judge them. The messages about sexuality conveyed to young people are in many ways perverse and conflicted. Teenagers especially are taught they should remain sexually pure, at a time when their own hormones make them more interested in sexuality and the potential pleasures of their bodies, and also more curious about intimacy and the possibility of having their new and interesting sexual cravings satisfied. Yet, despite engaging their emerging (and natural) interest in sex, purity culture constantly reminds teens that sexual purity is absolutely what Jesus wants of his followers until marriage, when their reward will be that sex magically becomes amazing and wonderful, the best thing God gives devoted couples.

These conflicting messages serve to further confuse, rather than having the intended effect of inspiring teens and young adults toward living in sexual purity (indeed, by some estimates, fully 82 percent of those who have signed abstinence pledges had, in the words of one federal survey, "retracted their promises").[18] For many, the demands to remain pure and modest fill teenagers with shame. Purity culture fosters tough and shame-based questions within the people it hopes to transform: Why am I having these thoughts and desires, when clearly Jesus wants me to be pure? If the Bible says I should cover my body, else I cause my "brother" to stumble, should I also then despise the body God gave me?

Some will be quick to argue that remaining sexually pure and modest in dress is emotionally, physically, and mentally smart, especially given the risks of sexually transmitted diseases, the damage wrought by a contemporary hook-up culture that often puts the onus of providing pleasure disproportionately on women, and the ways in which sexual intimacy without accompanying maturity can be problematic for both men and women. But it's entirely possible to have conversations about sexual intimacy without resorting to the language of purity culture, a language that is primarily destructive to women. Richard Beck, a professor of psychology at Abilene Christian, explained the extent of that destruction in a 2013 *Atlantic* critique of purity culture. The article states that Beck, "argues that using the metaphor of purity imports a 'psychology of contamination into our moral and spiritual lives,' and this contamination is viewed as a permanent state, one beyond restoration." The *Atlantic* piece continues:

> Moreover, while women are subjected to the language of purity and seen as irreparably contaminated after having sex, the same is not true for men. According to Beck, a boy losing his virginity is seen as a "mistake, a stumbling," a mode of behavior that can be changed and rehabilitated. This, he

argues, exposes a double standard at work in the language of sexual purity: women who have sex are seen as "damaged goods," but men who have sex are not.[19]

This theme of "damaged goods" is threaded throughout purity culture.

But what if we could understand purity in a different way? What if we saw in the Bible another narrative allowing us to affirm our sexual selves and the goodness of our bodies, while acknowledging that women are more than the sum of their (physical) parts? How might another narrative change the mythologies women believe about themselves?

Imagine how that might transform culture for good.

A Second Look at Purity and the Problem of Blood

Jesus said plenty about purity systems, but rather than endorse purity regulations, Jesus debunked them, especially when they reinforced the elite or powerful over the oppressed.

Jesus' critique of Judaism's purity system exists in many gospel stories. It can be seen in the parable of the good Samaritan, in which part of what makes the Samaritan good is his willingness to help a stranded stranger who had been passed over by those duty-bound to their purity system. While this story promotes helping others even when it is inconvenient, it more directly shines a light on the oppression of the Jewish purity system.

The priest and the Levite were obligated to pass by the stranger because of their religious roles. To touch someone who was dead would make these two impure, and therefore would render them unable to perform their temple functions. To maintain purity, each had to pass by the injured man because he might not only be hurt, he might not be alive. In contrast to the religious leaders, the Samaritan (who, ironically, would have been seen by his contemporaries as unclean because of his ethnicity) rendered aid. Thus Jesus' use of this parable illustrates the problem inherent in purity rules originally created as a response to God's holiness.*

---

*As Marcus Borg points out, this parable was a "pointed attack on the purity system and an advocacy of another way: compassion." Marcus J. Borg, *Meeting Jesus Again for the First Time: The Historical Jesus & the Heart of Contemporary Faith* (New York: HarperSanFrancisco, 1994), 55.

Another way Jesus critiqued the purity system was through his dining companions. The Pharisees and others criticized Jesus for eating with unclean people. To not include people socially was a way of pushing outcasts further toward the margins of society. Luke 15 records that while tax collectors and sinners were listening to Jesus, the Pharisees and scribes were grumbling, saying, "This fellow welcomes sinners and eats with them" (v. 2b). Sharing meals with those deemed by the system to be unclean was more than just a nice encounter; it was Jesus' way of making a social and political statement. Eating and drinking with those rejected by society created an inclusive community, a stark contrast from what the purity system promoted.*

Once readers begin to understand the Jewish purity system as part of the indispensible social context for Jesus' life and teachings, they can identify how revolutionary Jesus' message was. One narrative recorded in Mark's gospel (chapter 5) illustrates this and is a useful corrective to many evangelicals' understanding of purity. In the midst of a crowd hanging around, a woman who had been bleeding for twelve years reached out to touch Jesus. She reasoned that, if she could just make contact with his garment, she might be healed. Paying attention to this woman brings into sharp focus a reality with which women contend: blood. More than any other experience, the presence of cyclical bleeding unites women everywhere, not just because of the experience itself, but because of the negative messages women absorb about themselves because of it.

Not all cultures regard menstruation negatively—but those associated with Judaism and Christianity do. Fortunately for most cultures, there are no longer religious rules outlawing female presence in public places of worship during menstruation, but there are lingering messages women hear in jokes about PMS ("stay out of her way; it's that time of the month"), and in marketing ads promising cleanliness and convenience, protection and carefree living. Even the label—feminine hygiene products—suggests women's monthly cycles are a dirty subject in need of cleaning up.

Women get it: menstruation is an obstacle to overcome. How easily the detrimental message seeps into one's consciousness when it pervades unchecked social assumptions. Recently, for example, feminist Debora Spar in *Wonder Women: Sex, Power, and the Quest for*

---

*Borg suggests, "The ethos of compassion led to an inclusive table fellowship, just as the ethos of purity led to a closed table fellowship." Ibid., 56

Perfection claimed that postmenopausal women "should be able to yank a whole slew of concerns off their to-do lists. No more tampons and condoms... Biologically, menopause at last puts women roughly on par with men, freeing them from the bleeding and breeding that have long set them apart."[20] Evangelical women learn early and often that menstruation is the curse of Eve; it is the constant reminder of a secondary status and of differing bodies that keep women down, at least until menopause, if Debora Spar and others are correct.

More than today, menses were an integral aspect of the Jewish purity laws, which originated in Leviticus. The purity laws were largely a collection of rules written by male priests who maintained orderly worship among the ancient Israelites. Since people believed their God to be uniquely holy, they also believed this God required holiness of devotees. The result was that maintaining holiness among the worshiping community became the primary task of priests. Guiding their work was the Divine claim recorded in Leviticus 11:45: "For I am the LORD who brought you up from the land of Egypt, to be your God; you shall be holy, for I am holy." And, in Leviticus 19:2: "Speak to all the congregation of the people of Israel and say to them: You shall be holy, for I the LORD your God am holy." Holiness was deemed not only necessary for true worship of God but also synonymous with purity, separating everything that was impure and thus not holy.

With little knowledge of biological systems, it is easy to see ancient Israelite logic: bodily fluids were mysterious and potentially dangerous. The relationship between significant life events of giving birth, of dying, of monthly cycles, of sexual intercourse, and the presence of blood, saliva, or semen reasonably resulted in their beliefs that something powerful resided in the fluids themselves. Helen Bruch Pearson claims early Hebrews thought blood was "the seat of the soul" and any contact with it was either deeply religious and thus an important part of ritual, or it was terribly dangerous and thus avoided at all costs.[21] The purity laws constructed by the priests determined whether or not blood was pure and appropriate for their worship (such as in sacrifices) or impure and therefore banished from all possible contact.

The goal in these binary distinctions was to make the sacred clear. In practice it would be difficult to imagine how such regulations could be experienced as positive, especially by women. Yet this was the worldview when the woman who had been bleeding for twelve years approached Jesus one dry and dusty afternoon as she struggled through the crowd.

The Bleeding Woman

By law she was unclean and had been that way for a very long time. Most certainly the entire village knew who she was and what was wrong with her. She had been a figure relegated to the fringe of society: people recognized her well enough to know she was to be avoided. Her impure status rendered attendance at synagogue impossible—her presence would make all others unclean and unable to worship a holy God. Joining others in religious observances was out of the question, but so too was simply going out in public. Her life had long been spent in complete and utter isolation.

No wonder that, after having spent all she had trying to get better, the bleeding woman decided to take a chance on the healing touch of Jesus. "If I can but touch his garment," she reasoned, she would be healed. The gospel writer says that at that moment—when she reached out—she received exactly what she had wished. In touching Jesus, she achieved the healing results she desired, although the unclean woman took the risk of making all those around her unclean, including Jesus.

The story does not need to continue if this woman's healing is the primary issue. She was sick and then she was well. End of story. Except, it appears, Jesus wasn't satisfied by the anonymous nature of the healing. Turning around, he asked who had touched him. The disciples quickly dismissed Jesus' question. Surely it was merely the crowd pressing in on Jesus. As readers, we should likewise wonder why Jesus wanted to identify a unique set of hands, a particular person, a specific woman who had been ostracized for twelve years. Rather than dismiss this aspect of the narrative as his disciples did, though, we should sit up and take notice.

Take another look. Because he had been touched by someone unclean, he was now just as impure as she. He was no longer fit to worship in the synagogue; no longer an upstanding Jew because he was unclean, he needed to make proper amends to the Jewish authorities. Is the crowd going to turn on him now because he has become unclean? Or is it possible that Jesus the teacher, now tainted, is too compelling to dismiss out of hand? Just what kind of insurrection might all of this jettisoning of Jewish law cause? It's no wonder the Jewish authorities, along with the Roman officials, became nervous as the crowds increased. Catapulting religious law was serious business.

Notice Jesus' attentiveness to the problem of purity. He identified not just the bleeding woman but the injustice her life represented. Jesus put a public spotlight on her presumed impurity, rather than reviling and isolating her. He brought out into the open the connection between gender/poverty and impurity. A woman who had been ostracized because of her illness, whose exhausted resources meant her impurity would banish her from society for the remainder of her life, suddenly, because of Jesus' actions, had hope for a transformed life. In her renewed reality the crowd would have seen that they, too, were no longer hopeless.

The disciples seemed to overlook all of this in their dismissal of the bleeding woman and their disinterest in the injustice resulting from her unclean status. They were content, it seems, to maintain order and decorum to ensure Jesus had ample crowd control measures in place. The irony of their inability to identify what Jesus saw and its parallel to the evangelical endorsement of contemporary purity schemes is striking. At least in Mark's gospel we realize the disciples are portrayed negatively in part to accentuate the goodness and compassion of Jesus. He not only healed the woman, he also attacked the purity system working to keep her oppressed. The disciples simply wanted him to ignore her; they willingly went along with the ways of society. The contemporary purity culture has no such excuse.

Not Purity But Compassion

Evidently, Jesus had a religious and political agenda in mind that challenged conventional thinking. Rather than succumbing to the injustice created by well-intentioned laws, Jesus modeled compassion for those most negatively affected by religious stipulations. When Jesus asked that this woman acknowledge herself and to affirm she had touched him (thereby making him unclean by the same system), he invited the crowd to embrace an alternative way of viewing the world. By bringing their exchange into public view, Jesus showed people are more important than systems, that compassion rather than judgment was the appropriate response to those marginalized by society.

Similar to the priests of Jesus' day, leaders in today's purity movement use the idea of purity—by which they mean sexual abstinence—to create and maintain order within faith communities and families. Filling young girls' minds with fear-based ideas about sex serves not to create faithful followers of Jesus but rather to teach them that they should protect themselves against all sexual encounters because any sexual act outside of marriage will make them impure, just like the bleeding woman.

In signing abstinence pledges and wearing purity rings and promising to remain pure, young women are in essence held responsible for young boys' sexual activities. As Jessica Valenti points out, "[W]hile proponents of date nights and purity balls argue that they're aiming to protect girls from sexualization, by focusing on girls' virginity they're actually positioning girls as sexual objects before they've even hit puberty."[22] How can young women not see themselves as sexual objects controlled by men? A girl is sandwiched between her father, who holds her accountable for maintaining a pure status, and her male peers, who she is taught are always ogling her as sexual fodder. She is told her peers will always seek the opportunity to pounce when she lets down her guard. If by chance she engages in some kind of sexual activity, is there any way she does not feel it as *her* failure, even when she is a victim of sexual abuse? That, because of it, *she* is unlovable, unworthy, unclean?

At least the purity laws of Jesus' day were in place to protect the worship of God, ensuring people were taking appropriate measures to be holy, a reflection of God's holiness. The purity movement today shifts the focus from God's holiness to the desires of a future husband. As a result, the protection of purity is no longer driven by a Divine reflection but to be acceptable marriage material.

The bleeding woman who approached Jesus was socially and religiously oppressed. The feelings of being ostracized must have been a constant reminder of her impurity. And yet, the purity movement today, rather than assume Jesus' position of dismissing such oppressive laws, reinforces them in ways that are potentially even more demeaning: a woman's sexuality is to be rejected, and yet it is the most important part of who she is. Being a virgin until marriage is now the height of what it means to follow God, at least for many girls and women.

The gospel sets the bleeding woman's initiative at the center, while rejecting the legitimacy of religious oppression. This reversal invites readers to contemplate the vast possibilities of such unconventional wisdom. Like the bleeding woman, women today should hear liberating news in the gospels: not bound by religious laws or obligations, women are free to be the creators of their lives, taking initiative to follow their dreams.

By calling into question the purity movement, we are not suggesting young women seek sexual experiences as some kind of freedom from purity constraints. We think there are many good reasons to avoid sexual experimentation and promiscuity, reasons that have to do with healthy choices and self-fulfillment, with positive feelings of worth and value. Jesus' liberating message to the bleeding woman challenges us to think about women's sex and sexuality in a different way. Rather than focus on sexual purity, we should encourage young women to expand their minds, to be rigorous students and athletes, musicians and poets, people with bodies created in God's image.

Jesus told the bleeding woman to be healed of her disease, to continue to be the author of her destiny. Young women today need to be told they can do and be anything; they are not sexual objects for future spouses. Let's set them free from narrow constraints about their sexuality and instead invite them to make choices allowing them to be all God intended for them: to study well, to be compassionate to those in need, to create healthy bodies through good eating and exercise, and to love God by loving their neighbors. In other words, let's invite women to freely embrace all they are meant to be, recognizing that any idealized pattern—be it labeled Proverbs 31, or purity, or Ruth—may serve far more as a constraint than an instrument of freedom.

Chapter Six

Setting Captives Free

In her 2014 memoir, *Girl at the End of the World*, Elizabeth Esther narrates growing up in The Assembly, a conservative fundamentalist group led by her grandfather, George Geftakys. The details of her upbringing are chilling: Esther was physically abused by her father, a seeming narcissist whose every proclamation was accompanied by biblical admonishment; her mother did little to intervene in the abuse, seeing her role as a helpmeet who must not challenge her husband's authority. Esther was isolated and, for much of her schooling, attended Cornerstone Academy—what amounted to a home-school for Assembly children. Even though she was able to attend a public high school, her father dissuaded her from pursuing activities she enjoyed—including the swim team, where she excelled; and the newspaper staff, which Esther saw as her ticket to college and out of her father's home. Esther experienced long-term emotional and psychological damage after her childhood in The Assembly, and her memoir suggests she continues to work toward healing. She writes that each day she must make an intentional choice to "let God love me," rather than believing herself unlovable, a vile creature worthy of the many abuses she received.[1]

In some ways, Esther's experience in The Assembly is unique, representing an outlier in Christian evangelicalism. And yet, some of the characteristics of Esther's religious upbringing reflect a movement with significant momentum in evangelicalism: Christian Patriarchy. Adherents of the Christian Patriarchy movement believe in the ultimate authority of the Bible, but also the absolute authority of men, asserting that the Bible has designed men to be decisive leaders of family and church. Christian Patriarchy has also had its overpowering

108

personalities, including the likes of Doug Phillips, the defrocked leader of the Vision Forum, a prominent voice in the movement; and it has had its proponents for what amounts to child abuse, including Debi and Michael Pearl, whose book, *Train up a Child*, advises parents to use (among other things) a plumbing tube as a switch to teach ultimate obedience.

Despite this seeming extremism, Christian Patriarchy's influence cannot be ignored, especially as its vocal leaders exert tremendous pressure on more moderate evangelicals, casting judgment on those evangelicals who don't embrace the seemingly more extreme ideas promoted by Christian Patriarchs. Additionally, the much-venerated language many evangelicals use regarding complementarism and God's design for men and women differs only in degree from the Christian Patriarchy. At its core, beliefs for complementarians and Christian patriarchs are based on the assertion that God has designed women and men differently; their roles are distinct and immutable. In God's design, men are created to be leaders and women are created to be helpers. For Christian Patriarchs, these roles are even more clearly defined and more intensified than for complementarians: they are more likely to see any biblical notion about having children as a command to have as many children as possible, a reflection of God's blessing on their lives. Both Christian Patriarchs and their more moderate cousins would agree having children is a woman's highest calling, her very body and soul built to raise children. And both groups would also assert that women, as primary keepers of the home, are charged with the spiritual well-being and obedience of their children, even as men are designed to be providers and protectors.

Although many contemporary evangelicals might eschew the Christian Patriarchy movement's more extreme impulses, the latter definitely informs the former. The complementary gender roles both see as the hallmark of biblical manhood and womanhood work well to keep women in a clearly defined, clearly conscribed space. Rather than considering a woman's gifts or vocational calling, this space carved out by theology is based solely on one's gender, and for both Christian Patriarchs and complementarians, this space is marked as "different" and "special," though clearly less special than the space reserved for men.

By determining God's will for women and families in this way, the Patriarchy movement marginalizes childless couples, as well as infertile and adoptive families.

A History Rooted in Patriarchy

Those with even a cursory knowledge of Christian history will no
doubt be quick to point out that patriarchy has had a long and
cherished tradition within the Church, and that for centuries
Christianity has been built around the belief that men–simply by
virtue of being born male–have Godlike hearts and minds that make
them more capable as leaders in public and private life. Entire
Christian civilizations have been built up around the edifice of
patriarchy.

Still, the Christian Patriarchy movement is somewhat different, in
that it has been born out of twentieth-century evangelicalism and
sustained by dynamic, vocal, and often extraordinarily flawed leaders.
Its ideologies have been propagated through contemporary mediums
such as television, blogs, and online marketing. Its figureheads are just
as likely to be reality television stars such as Michelle Duggar and Phil
Robertson as leaders with significant theological and biblical training.
And the followers of Christian Patriarchy coalesce not necessarily
around denominational beliefs, but around ideals that shape their life
choices about marriage and family, child-rearing, and education.

Manhood resides at the core of Christian Patriarchy, defined as
"biblical manhood" by its proponents. Nearly every tenet in the
Christian Patriarchy movement is shaped by an ideal that endows
men with Godlike status, and that gives God manlike characteristics.
To his family, the man is the head, the commander, the protector, and
savior; he is the arbiter of moral right and wrong; he is the guide and
compass. According to Christian Patriarchs, God has made this so in
the very gender roles designed for men and women. Anyone who
questions this Divine order is pointed to the Old Testament, and to the
patriarchs venerated there: to Abraham and Moses and Noah and
Jacob, among others, who made choices that were God-ordained,
God-blessed, and worthy of replication.

So whether God asks today's "patriarchs" to sacrifice their sons or
lead congregations into a forty-year desert walk or build a massive ark
to avoid worldwide destruction, the decisions men make–Should
daughters go to college? Is it okay to spank one's wife?–are vital, and
only for the Christian Patriarchs to determine.

And what of women in a Christian Patriarch's world? According
to the movement's propaganda, women have a special role in family
life, one God has deliberately designed for each and every woman in

God's kingdom. The rhetoric used to describe this "special role" is nearly identical to that used by complementarians: women are created to be helpmeets to their husbands, vessels for children, creators of a "quiverfull" of offspring. That a woman might remain unmarried or childless is not much of a consideration to those in the Patriarchy movement, because God has not designed women to be single, nor barren. Instead, until a woman is "blessed" with a spouse, she is to remain under the headship of her father, a stay-at-home daughter who foregoes higher education and independence because this is not to be a woman's calling.

These tenets form the core of Christian Patriarchy, a movement that has–in the last two decades–gained significant momentum in great part because of dynamic leaders who have made Christian Patriarchy seem especially attractive to evangelicals seeking a "biblical" approach to living. Leaders in Christian Patriarchy have also used new technologies as powerful tools to spread their message, relying on blogs, social networking, and other Internet tools to bring their men-first message to the mainstream. Their online presence has been coupled with homeschool curricula and conferences for Christians increasingly worried about the standards in public schools, plus their own production of movies and television shows to counter the demonic messages Hollywood seems to peddle. For folks interested in returning to the "finer, holier" times of the Old Testament, Christian Patriarchs seem especially keen on using contemporary technologies to get their messages out into a world they believe is sorely in need of redemption.

A Vision for Patriarchy

At the end of October 2013, Doug Phillips tendered a resignation letter to the board of the Vision Forum, an organization he founded in 1998 and for which he served as president.[2] Phillips's resignation and subsequent closing of the Vision Forum no doubt came as a shock to many of the Vision Forum's followers, who saw in the organization a champion for families, fidelity, and faith. Over the life of the Vision Forum, Phillips had fashioned himself into a crusader for "traditional families," by which he meant a husband who served as the head of household, a wife who served the husband, and as many children as God might offer as "blessings." For the Vision Forum, as for other adherents of Christian Patriarchy, the family's supremacy was part of God's biblical design, a design Phillips reinforced with his many blog posts, conferences, public performances, and spin-off organizations, such as the San Antonio Independent Christian Film Festival.

Phillips' influence was arguably largest among conservative Christian homeschoolers who embraced the many Vision Forum curricular products at one time available on his website. In 2010, the organization published a guidebook for helping parents learn how best to use the Vision Forum DVDs, books, and CDs in ways that would enhance their children's education and their "growth in the Lord." *Building a Winning Curriculum: How to Use Vision Forum Products to Build a Winning Homeschool Curriculum* (Dorys Lee Horn) provided parents all the structure they needed, showing how Vision Forum products could be easily placed into learning categories—including "Creationism and Science," "The History of Christianity," and, "Western Civilization." While these topics might be part of many liberal arts homeschool education, the Vision Forum curricula also included education on "Manly Leadership," "The Nobility of Womanhood," and "The Blessings of Children," suggesting that a Vision Forum education was also one that educated children in the ways of Christian Patriarchy. This indoctrination was both direct and subtle, as even Doug Phillips' interpretation of historical events is seen through the lens of the Patriarchy movement, and the fundamental power white, Western men have to change the world.

In the fifteen plus years the Vision Forum was extant, its influence ran deep into the Christian Patriarchy movement. Doug Phillips' vision for the Christian family helped shape a marketing empire— peddling toys, books, DVDs, and CDs to the evangelical masses. The toys once sold on his website, for example, were categorized by their ability to "equip boys for manhood" and to "equip girls for womanhood." Parents of boys could purchase stagecoach action sets and dinosaur figurines, as well as camouflage hunting trucks and deer hunter action figures, complete with bows and rifles. The site also sold toy weapons for boys to play with and military action sets including toy guns and missiles: toys that suggested something significant about the Vision Forum's ideal of manhood. So too did the toys sold to "equip girls for womanhood," including the Beautiful Girlhood Doll Collection, promising little girls lots of "mommy practice." According to the site's commitment statement, all the toys sold by Vision Forum were specifically created to "rebuild a culture of virtuous womanhood." Their toys achieved this vision "in a world that frowns on femininity, that minimizes motherhood, and that belittles the beauty of being a true woman of God." The toys supposedly cultivated girls' "enthusiasm and industry" (because the beautiful girl "is one who sees her life as a mission of service," and nothing says play like a toy that challenges girls to work hard!); "home and hospitality" (because the beautiful girl is not "driven by wanderlust," like other kids, but finds "true contentment at home," and nothing says playtime like a toy bereft of imagining worlds beyond the home); and "femininity and grace" (because truly biblical girls "enjoy dressing like a lady and being about the business of women").

Beyond toys and homeschool curricula, Doug Phillips worked to spread his message of biblical manhood and womanhood through his outreach efforts, including the San Antonio Independent Christian Film Festival. Judging by some of the festival's winners, this noble mission was coupled with Doug Phillips's interest in "biblical manhood" and his hostility toward anything that would undermine that vision. The movie that won the festival award in 2007, for example, was *The Monstrous Regiment of Women*, a documentary exploring the awful ruin wrought by feminists who "tell women not to submit to a husband, to avoid having children, and that they should listen to their 'inner voice' and chase a career to find true fulfillment." The film explored how feminists' "twisted and irrational teaching has led to disaster for American women, leading many into a frustrating, isolated existence."[3]

Phillips' ministry extended into revising history in a way reflective of his patriarchal world view. He seemed especially fascinated with the Titanic and, in 2012, on the hundred-year anniversary of the Titanic's sinking, the Vision Forum—via its Christian Boys' and Men's Titanic Society—hosted a weekend-long celebration, honoring the Titanic for its "biblical virtue of men sacrificing for women and children." According to Phillips, the Titanic recalled a better age, one in which women and children were considered first, a notion that feminism has ruined in its attempt to destroy Western civilization.

This April 2012 event occurred at the pinnacle of Phillips' power, when his reach and that of the Vision Forum so broad that Phillips was travelling extensively, speaking at homeschooling conventions and building the National Center for Family Integrated Churches, a wide network of Christian Patriarchy congregations spread across the country. He was loved and admired by many evangelicals who embraced his worldview as their own, believing the contemporary threats of socialism, feminism, and secularism might be battled and conquered, leading to the return of a clearer social order, with men serving in headship roles. To his followers, especially, Phillips' resignation in October 2013, and the scandalous details that emerged subsequent to this event, were especially grievous, for it seemed Phillips had succumbed to the temptations against which he so often railed, and that he had abandoned the wife and family he publicly proclaimed as fundamental to his life's calling. By December 2013, the Vision Forum websites had been scrubbed of all its products, blog posts, curricula, and articles; only Doug Phillips's resignation letter and an explanation from the board about Vision Forum's closure remained.*

Children in Abundance: Christian Patriarchy and the Quiverfull

No family has represented the Christian Patriarchy movement more prominently than that of Jim Bob and Michelle Duggar, who as of now have nineteen biological children, with no plans to stop procreating until God makes doing so impossible. The Duggar family was unleashed on American society through a television documentary called *14 Kids and Pregnant Again*, which was followed by several other one-hour specials on The Learning Channel (TLC), detailing more Duggar births. In 2008, the Duggars landed their own television series, *17 Kids and Counting*, which became—in subsequent seasons—*18 Kids and Counting*, and then *19 Kids and Counting*. Their recurring interviews on the *Today Show*, their books and public appearances, and the continued popularity of the television series have kept the Duggar family—and, by extension, the major tenets of the "Quiverfull" movement—consistently in the public eye.

For Jim Bob and Michelle, as for all those ascribing to the Quiverfull philosophy, each child born into a family represents God's blessings, and thus a mother must always be open to the gift of another child in her womb—or, for infertile couples, the obedience to accept when her womb is barren. Those in the Quiverfull movement embrace the passage found in Psalms 127: "Like arrows in the hand of a warrior, / So are the children of one's youth. / Happy is the man that has his quiver full of them; / They shall not be ashamed, / But shall speak with their enemies in the gate" (vv. 4–5, NKJV). Believing that

---

*In March 2014, Doug Phillips threatened to sue his former Vision Forum associates for attempting to "destroy" him. One month later, Lourde Torres filed suit against Phillips, accusing him of sexual misconduct and of aggressively pursuing her, despite her family's attempts to have him cease his efforts to contact and see her.

feminism and other societal ills have pushed Western civilization off track, those seeking full quivers assert that the world needs to be righted through a social structure privileging a male headship model and as many babies as possible who will follow their daddies into the wonderful ways of Patriarchal Christendom.

Given this view of family and birthing, Quiverfull families do not generally practice birth control or even any natural forms of family planning, believing such actions violate the command to be "fruitful and multiply." Otherwise, one Quiverfull writer asserts, "It says to God, 'I want to be in control of this because I don't trust You to make a wise decision in this area…so here's a little help!'"[4] Rather than relying on any kind of family planning, then, a Quiverfull family relinquishes full control of reproduction, believing that attempts to avoid pregnancy reflect a lack of faith in God and God's plan.

Another central tenet in the Quiverfull movement, of course, is the importance of presumably "biblical" gender roles. Women are charged with maintaining a peaceful, happy home, guarding the spiritual well-being of the children and making sure their husbands are comfortable, happy, and satisfied. For Michelle Duggar, this has meant being willing to say "yes" to Jim Bob's advances, even when she is worn down by caring for the couple's nineteen children: "Be available," she told the *Today* show in February 2014. "Anyone can fix him lunch, but only one person can meet that physical need of love that he has, and you always need to be available when he calls."[5]

As members of a fundamentalist Baptist church, the Duggars also embody other tenets of Christian Patriarchy. The Duggars believe in modesty, meaning the girls wear long hair and skirts that fall at least below their knees; swimwear for girls is purchased from a company called Wholesome Wear. Just like many other families in the Christian Patriarchy movement, the Duggars homeschool all their children, with the older children providing instruction and care for their younger siblings. Because there are so many children in the Duggar family, Jim Bob and Michelle cannot give intensive one-on-one attention to each child, but in the Quiverfull mentality, this lack of deep, rich parental attention is mitigated by family bonds, and by the justification that many contemporary two-income couples spend even less time with their offspring, instead shipping them off to public schools and plugging them into electronics when they arrive home.

The Duggars also insist their children ascribe to the courtship model of relationships between males and females. The courtship approach differs from traditional dating in its intent: a man and a woman develop a romantic relationship with the final destination always being marriage. For Quiverfull families, the courtship model allows parental guidance and control in the process of finding one's life partner, for, more often than not, the parents help direct the couple to the ultimate goal of marriage. According to the Institute in Basic Life Principles, an organization propagating Christian Patriarchy principles, those who date capriciously are not informed by the "influence or control" of any authority figures, and thus are more readily led to temptation, irresponsibility, and the quest for personal pleasure.[6] This generally means the influence and control falls to the head of household, who continues to guard his daughter's heart and her purity until she can be wed to another man, who then assumes all control and influence over her, including her reproductive choices.

Most evangelicals would probably hold the Duggar family at a distance, claiming that their Quiverfull lifestyle does not reflect mainstream evangelical belief. Yet although evangelical birth rates generally mirror those of the broader United States population, there is a sense in which the Quiverfull movement only takes fundamental complementarian beliefs to their logical conclusions, especially in that a woman's primary role is as mother—indeed, that above all else God designed women to bear children and to be caretakers. Even more, evangelical popular culture lets women know that their children are gifts God bestows on them, and that anyone who bears children should be considered blessed among women.

Enter almost any Christian church on Mother's Day, and you are likely to hear this message loud and clear: mothers are truly blessed, deserving of all honor and praise for the very difficult work they do. Evangelical popular culture conveys this Mother's Day message every day of the year, and those Christian women who do not have children are considered an anomaly. While there are many reasons for choosing this life direction, childfree women learn from evangelical culture that they are abrogating God's design for women because of their selfishness. Joshua Crutchfield, writing for the Council on Biblical Manhood and Womanhood, articulates well the message conveyed to childfree women when he says:

> It is alarming that Christian couples wish to not have children
> for no other reason but for the purpose of living a selfish

lifestyle. Their ignoring the God-ordained purpose of marriage outright rejects the value of children (Psalm 115:14; and 127:3, 4), God's love for them (Matthew 18:3; 19:13–14; and Mark 10:14), and ultimately undermines His authority (Genesis 1:28). Christian couples will always have excuses, much like non-Christian couples, but they have something different than what other couples have–faith in Christ. Their lives and will are altered by their relationship with Him, and as a result, no excuse should be given for disobedience.[7]

Choosing not to have children, especially for women, is to turn one's back on God and God's design. And, in this sense, evangelical culture's message to women about their role is only amplified by Quiverfull proponents, who assert that God's blessing to a woman must be embraced fully, no matter how many babies God puts in her womb.

Any critique of this problematic message is met with resistance, and with the claim that those who would dare critique the "children are a blessing" ideology must be cold-hearted feminists who hate children. And while it is important to assert that raising children can be life-changing, transformative, amazing, frustrating, and can entirely renew one's relationship to God, it is equally important to note that not everyone is called to be a mother, and that those who choose a different path are just as squarely in God's will as those who choose the messy work of parenting. As mentioned, one result is that the Quiverfull message works powerfully to marginalize those who struggle with infertility or those who choose to build families through other methods, such as adoption; if biological children are indeed a "blessing," those who cannot be thus blessed must believe they have done something wrong and shameful to be cast from God's favor.

Teach Your Children Well

Parents who have a "quiverfull" will obviously need some guidance in how those children can be raised from birth to godly woman- and manhood. And parenting gurus Michael and Debi Pearl are ready to help. It might be well and good to follow the mainstream advice of men like Dr. William Sears (of *The Baby Book*) or Dr. Spock, but those peddlers of parenting help lack the biblical foundation necessary to raise godly children: you know, biblical advice, such as "A spanking (whipping, paddling, switching, or belting) is indispensable to the removal of guilt in your child."[8] "Spare the rod, and spoil the child" has nothing on this kind of advice, which can help parents raise children who are obedient, docile followers of Jesus, the prince of peace.

The Pearls' tips about child-rearing are followed by worshipful parents—those who are certain that children, that "blessing from God," should be switched into submission to learn obedience: to parents, to authority, and, ultimately, to God. The Pearls' ministry, "No Greater Joy," intends to provide child training advice—a mission that seems odd in its very wording, as if children are like animals, fit to be trained, rather than nurtured, loved, encouraged to develop. The Pearls have written several books for parents, and they also claim to be pioneers in the homeschooling movement, teaching children from the home for several decades now. Their books, which include *To Train Up a Child* and *Training Children to Be Strong in Spirit*, and their website provide such gems of advice as using plastic tubing for now-and-then beatings and copious spanking, which—according to a *Seattle Times* article—is "clearly the heart of the book *[To Train Up a Child]*." [9]

The Pearls have developed a following among more conservative parents who see their advice as useful in teaching children obedience—an important character trait for Christians who believe God has created us to be obedient servants of God's holy will. The entire construct of *To Train Up a Child* and the Pearls' parenting philosophy is founded on the idea of obedience to authority as the key ingredient to raising happy, well-adjusted children. According to the Pearls, fostering this kind of obedience requires training rather than discipline, and their methods focus on making a child obedient from a very young age, perhaps even before a child has the capacity to understand the difference between right and wrong.

The Pearls often use their own children and parenting as examples. In one case, they write about "training" one of their five-month-old daughters. She was mobile at an early age and wanted to climb their stairs, putting herself in danger. Each time she began climbing, the Pearls responded by giving her "a voice command of 'No,'" and then switching her on her bare legs. Pearl assures readers "the switch was a twelve-inch long, one-eighth-inch diameter sprig from a willow tree," and, that in time, just laying the switch on the bottom of the stairs had convinced their infant not to climb, as "she had assumed the association of the painful switch to the stairs and my command." [10]

Whether a five-month-old child can learn this lesson is debatable; that a father is communicating his "will" and "resolve" to an infant is problematic. Yet Pearl is sure this is God's way to train up a child, teaching children obedience to authority from an early age. The home is to "mimic the government of God," with parents serving in the role of a judgmental God, one who apparently smacks us with switches or rubber tubing in order to teach us obedience, and by that they say they mean grace. Breaking the rebellious child's will to misbehave is necessary to help teach children a fear of God and a respect for the moral law. The Pearls believe that "only through the naked 'sword' of the law are we pressed into an understanding of grace," and that by following the Pearls' principles, children learn to fear and respect the Lawgiver, the parent and–by extension–God. In the Pearls' world, the parents are Godlike, and how children relate to their parents will reflect how they relate to God. God is also a dominating, judgmental figure in the Pearls' world, quick with a switch as a means of tempering rebellious children. Because of this, using the rod "is not optional with a Bible believer. It is God's design for proper training. The eternal souls of your children are at stake."*

While the Pearls remain on the margins of evangelicalism, their methods for "training up" children are revered by many within the evangelical culture, so their childcare manuals have definite traction with the more conservative members. Their "spare the rod, spoil the child" ideologies reflect the sense that the Bible should serve as a guidebook, its every proverb a checklist for biblical living. The theology is a natural extension of complementarianism: the head of household as the center around which everyone else should turn and to whom everyone else must vow obedience. And this obedience is earned by virtue of position rather than character. In the laws of God's apparent design for gender, men deserve obedience because of their God-given roles as leaders, and they demand obedience because of these same roles. This ideology creates women who are little more than children, lacking agency to act on their own outside a household "rule of law." Their spouses might not switch them, unless they are proponents of domestic discipline, but they are controlled nonetheless, no matter how "special" the roles of women are presumed to be.

---

*From Michael and Debi Pearl, *To Train Up a Child: Turning the Hearts of the Fathers to the Children*, No Greater Joy Ministries, E-book, 2009. In recent years, the Pearls' techniques have come under more scrutiny, in great part because several parents have allegedly killed their children using Michael and Debi Pearls' parenting manual. See Kathryn Joyce, "Hana's Story," *Slate*, November 9, 2013, http://www.slate.com/articles/double_x/doublex/2013/11/hana_williams_the_tragic_death_of_an_ethiopian_adoptee_and_how_it_could.html (acessed July 21, 2014).

Stay-at-Home Daughters

For the Duggar family, as for others in the Christian Patriarchy movement, daughters do not move outside the home until they have been courted and have married a man. In this way, the transfer of influence can occur from one man, the father, to the next, the husband, and a daughter does not need to be bothered with independence or any other problems that might flummox the feminine brain. This also means that most daughters within the Christian Patriarchy movement do not seek higher education, relying solely on their homeschooling to help frame their understanding of the world. As a result, they become stay-at-home daughters, helpmeets who are willing to provide sustenance and care for their fathers (and brothers).

The Botkin daughters, Anna Sofia and Elizabeth, serve as the public face for the Stay-at-Home Daughters movement. Their father, Geoffery Botkin, is a prominent voice in Christian Patriarchy, and he has passed on to his daughters a passion for the primacy of men in Christian households. Anna Sofia and Elizabeth have created a widely read blog, *Visionary Daughters*, to share their ministry, and, in 2005, wrote a book, *So Much More: The Remarkable Influence of Visionary Daughters on the Kingdom of God*, securing their prominence as stay-at-home daughters with a "remarkable influence" on other young Christian women. The Botkin girls believe that "unmarried daughters have the potential to change history," something they can do best, not by getting an education or seeking a vocation outside the home, but through "useful womanhood," defined for the Botkins as a "dominion-oriented femininity": one that is practical, purposeful, and focused primarily—even exclusively—on supporting a family.[11]

For most stay-at-home daughters, this means focusing education on the domestic arts: fostering skills in cooking, cleaning, and sewing as preparation for their roles as spouses and mothers. While the Botkin sisters argue that stay-at-home daughters would do well to learn some history, political science, and theology, these lessons should ideally be done within the home, directing daughters to their house-managing abilities. Higher education is unnecessary for the roles God grants them, and going to college also means leaving the safety of one's home and a father's headship. According to one writer, being on a college campus also means isolating young women from the "real world"—presumably in ways that remaining in her father's home will not similarly isolate her.[12]

A stay-at-home daughter has her parents as primary educators, reinforcing the Christian Patriarchal beliefs her parents hold. Proponents of the movement are fairly keen on insisting that stay-at-home daughters develop their minds, following the curriculum developed by their parents, one heavy on theology and Western classics, and light on topics deemed impure or morally problematic. God provides the best education through Scripture, according to the Botkin sisters at least, and so stay-at-home daughters would do well to study theology and the Bible, because God will "give us more understanding than our teachers."[13]

For a stay-at-home daughter, life revolves around her father and his needs, as well as those of any brothers who might also live in the home, and whose ministry requires support and encouragement. For the Botkin sisters, this has meant caring for their father, keeping a blog, hosting webinars with their father on homeschooling and on beauty, and writing books, including a 2012 follow-up to their first book, the later one titled *It's (Not That) Complicated: How to Relate to Guys in a Healthy, Sane, and Biblical Way.* As promised in the title, the book was intended to explain biblical approaches to male/female relationships, and included a "biblical study of daughterhood." Like other Botkin products, the book received endorsements from a number of leaders in the Christian Patriarchy movement, including R.C. Sproul, Voddie Baucham, and Michelle Duggar and her daughters. The Reclaiming Beauty line of products manages to make beauty secrets biblical, as the Botkin sisters provide their listeners with information on how to create beauty from the inside out. The DVD collection comes with a study guide, so that young women can work their way through their own feelings about their bodies, their understanding of God-given physical assets, and the appropriate colors, fabric, and make-up they should wear on various occasions.

While most evangelicals would assert that the stay-at-home daughter movement is archaic and constrictive (and the Botkins an anomaly within the movement), there remains in many evangelical communities an underlying current of similar theology. While broader evangelicalism would maintain the importance of educating their young women, the message about the secondary place of education in a woman's long-term vocational goals is also fairly prominent. Women hear that going to college will provide them the opportunity to meet future spouses, and the phenomena of women seeking a "Mrs." degree is so widespread that Christian college culture has a name marking its ubiquity: Ring by Spring. The pressure in evangelical universities to land an engagement ring before commencement—and to be married right after graduation—is extraordinarily intense, no matter the many jokes students are inclined to make about the "Ring by Spring" mindset; and women who leave Christian universities single sometimes feel acutely the failure of not finding The One to love and cherish them, certain they will need to face the world and its vagaries all alone.

Arguably, the Ring by Spring mindset mirrors that shared by those embracing a stay-at-home daughter ideology: the sense that a young woman needs to be under the guidance of a man, of her father or husband, and can little succeed in the world without someone to whom she can submit. For those who go to college, that headship is transferred momentarily from father to the university, sometimes seen as *loco parentis,* and then to a husband soon after graduation. Thus evangelicals share the same fundamental belief as adherents to the stay-at-home daughters principle, giving women little agency on their own. Instead, a woman's godly design is as helpmeet to a man, whose own vocation, ministry, and whims need to be met by someone who is inherently skilled to serve him, or who can learn domestic skills, if necessary.

Setting the Captives Free

The past few years have not been entirely kind to the Christian Patriarchs. Some of this has been their own leadership's undoing: the news of Doug Phillips' alleged sexual relationship with his much-younger nanny, his manipulation of her, and his attempts to reframe his conduct as a mutual affair have signaled both the end of Phillips' influence in the movement, as well as the wide reach Vision Forum once had. Another "Patriarch," Bill Gothard, founder of the Institute in Basic Life Principles, also faced scrutiny during a spring 2014 scandal that led to his resignation. It was uncovered that he had molested several female employees, one as young as sixteen years old; nearly three dozen other women who had worked for Gothard said he had sexually harassed them.[14] For both Phillips and Gothard, their undoing came, in part, because of the heady power of their own ideologies. When men hold all control over women and their agency, and that control is deemed part of God's grand design, a certain perversion of right relationship inevitably occurs. In essence, these men believed too much in their own male-centered theology.

Christian Patriarchy has also faced significant media scrutiny, weakening some of its influence within evangelicalism. In 2010, journalist Katherine Joyce wrote an expose on the movement; her book, *Quiverfull,* provided an extensive critique of Christian Patriarchy and evangelical culture. Former members of Christian Patriarchy groups are also telling their stories, including Elizabeth Esther, writing about her life in The Assembly. Others, like Vyckie Garrison, have collated the stories of women who have escaped the Quiverfull movement. Her blog, No Longer Quivering, provides resources for those hoping to be released from the clutches of Quiverfull ideology.

Escape and release are not too harsh of terms to use for women trapped in a family system that relies on Christian Patriarchal ideology. Having been told that God's desire for their lives is to submit to husbands who will guide and protect and lead them, women often lose any ability to act of their own accord. In situations in which physical abuse is sanctified as God-blessed, this must be doubly so. When women are told that God has designed for them a role as biological mothers to as many children as a quiver will hold, going against this design—even when a body is weary of birth, and a soul weary of mothering—becomes even more difficult.

But what if the Bible actually spoke against those tenets of Christian Patriarchy? What if our understanding of the Bible meant not limitation and conscription for women but, instead, opportunity and freedom? Couldn't the Bible offer another message, one that releases women from the chains of patriarchy and empowers them to truly be all God means for them to be?

Let's face it: for most of us as Bible readers, our focus has been pretty narrow. Ample parts of the Bible are generally overlooked. And not just overlooked, but ignored altogether. The patriarchal bias in evangelical churches has blinded many, making it difficult to see other narratives in the Bible. Specifically, despite a growing number of book series about women in the Bible, we rarely cultivate serious interest (in Sunday school curricula, in sermons, in magazine articles and blogs) about biblical women, whose creative actions on numerous occasions speak volumes about their participation in the grand story of God, but also reflect something of God's desire for all humans. In opening our eyes we find people who have much to teach us, and if we are to understand the Bible and the liberating narrative it tells, we must learn how to see.

Taking Another Look: Tamar

Genesis 38 is often considered an interruption to the story of Joseph, the one we normally learn in Sunday school: Joseph with his coat of many colors, the dreamer who irritates his brothers enough that they sell him; Joseph who interprets dreams in the royal court of Egypt and escapes the advances of Potiphar's wife; Joseph who rises to a place of prosperity in Egypt. Somehow, in the midst of learning Joseph's story, we skip over Tamar's.

Tamar, a Canaanite, was secured by Judah to be the wife to his firstborn son, Er. Judah, an Israelite and a patriarch, was one of the twelve sons of Jacob. When his firstborn son died, Judah rightly followed the Israelite custom of levirate marriage, requiring the duty of a brother-in-law to marry the widow and raise a male descendent for the deceased brother. In doing this, he could perpetuate his brother's name and inheritance while also providing security for the widow—in this case, Tamar. But when Onan, Judah's second son, also died, Judah violated the levirate law. He ordered Tamar to "remain a widow in your father's house" (v. 11) and did not follow through by providing his son Shelah once he grew up.

Returning to her father's house empty-handed would have been anything but a celebratory occasion. Tamar had drained the family's resources; presumably her father had provided a dowry when she married Er, and now she was back without a husband or child, and with no prospects for a future. She was a prisoner in her family home. The opportunity for her liberation arrived when she heard Judah was on his way to shear his sheep. Tamar removed her widow's clothing, put on a veil, and waited for Judah on the road.

As he passed by, Judah did not recognize Tamar when he summoned her for a sexual encounter. Seeing only what he wanted to see, Judah assumed Tamar to be a prostitute and he secured her services. As a price for her sexual favor, Tamar requested Judah's signet, cord, and staff. These items identified him later as the source of Tamar's pregnancy. Unaware that he was the father, when Judah was told three months later that his daughter-in-law was pregnant, he asked for a harsher penalty for her than was commonly sought: she was to be burned rather than stoned. In response, Tamar sent Judah's signet, cord, and staff, implicating Judah. Not only was she spared from execution, but Judah acknowledged, "She is more in the right than I" (v. 26).

Securing Justice in a Patriarchal World

People usually see this narrative through a lens of sexuality and incest when reading it for the first time. Yet sexual encounter is not the prism through which the author encouraged his readers to look. Rather, sex was merely the means Tamar used to establish justice when the patriarchal world denied what she rightly should have received.

Judah, as an Israelite patriarch, should have upheld the levirate law. His duty entailed the moral imperative of Israel's God. But as this story illustrates, Judah exchanged this morality for self-interest. It was a cruel move, one that demonstrated the patriarchal mindset of his day. Tamar holds the interpretive key to this complex story by shifting our attention from the presumed major character, Judah, and the assumptions that go along with reading from a perspective of privilege. In doing so, we can see Tamar's courage and initiative.

In the patriarchal world of ancient Israel, Tamar was denied justice. Initially welcomed into his family fold, she was subsequently expelled for reasons she did not create and that were only possible because Judah held power, utilizing it to control her. When it became apparent her rights had been dismissed, Tamar took her chance, throwing off her clothes of mourning and putting on her veil, determined to confront her oppressor.

Readers are not told why Tamar changed her clothing, but most interpreters have been content to assume Tamar wanted to be seen as a prostitute. Judah saw Tamar this way, but readers should be cautioned to consider that he saw, perhaps, only what he wanted to see. In any case, her change of clothing signaled Tamar's transition as she moved from being a victim of patriarchy to a survivor. Tamar took her life into her own hands.

To his credit, Judah eventually admitted that Tamar's actions were appropriate. She was more right than he. Judah's confession amounted to a monumental rejection of supposed male moral supremacy.

If we are to believe proponents of Christian Patriarchy, however, we would need to view Tamar as wrong. Instead of changing her situation, she should have remained stowed away in her father's house indefinitely, prepared to suffer a long life of seclusion and shame, unable to contribute to society beyond her family. She might have been a kind of stay-at-home daughter, protected by men and unable to alter her situation—because Paul says this is how God designed families.

Or, does he?

What Does Paul Really Say?

When his missives are read in order to ascertain "Paul's message today," it is imperative to read with caution because we are mostly eavesdropping on an ancient conversation. In other words, Paul's intended audience is not American Christians living in the twenty-first century, though the New Testament contains a collection of his letters. Even with a collection of Paul's letters in hand, there is no certainty that the ideas conveyed in them represents either the totality of Paul's thoughts or what he may have deemed most important. His writings were conversations with faith communities he founded, and what Paul wrote was driven more by the questions his communities asked than by his determinations about what they—or by extension, we—ought to know.[15]

Paul's letters reveal quandaries not easily explained. For example, Paul makes a bold claim in his letter to the Galatians that, "There is no longer Jew or Greek, there is no longer slave or free, there is no longer male and female; for all of you are one in Christ Jesus" (Gal. 3.28). And from his letter to the Romans it appears Paul put this ethic into practice, mentioning several women and the work they were doing. He commended Phoebe.[16] And he mentioned ten women who were instrumental in his ministry, specifically praising five of them (Rom. 16). Paul also acknowledged Junia as "prominent among the apostles" (16:7), a fact that for years troubled translators, uncomfortable with the idea of a woman apostle. Translators working on the *New International Version* of the Bible mollified their struggle with this by identifying the person as Junias, a male name.

But despite these egalitarian impulses and actions, Paul sometimes was less than clear in how these commitments worked. In 1 Corinthians, Paul assumed women prayed and prophesied in public worship (chapter 11) because he addressed whether or not they should wear veils while doing so. However, even though he stipulated their clothing, he did not back away in that chapter from women being active participants in public worship. Nevertheless, by chapter 14, Paul said women should be silent in churches, subordinate to their husbands, who could, apparently, privately answer any questions they might have.

If one sees Paul's instructions as somehow static and unchanging, it is necessary to adopt a sort of literary amnesia: keeping in mind only passages that portray Paul of one mind on this subject. Yet acknowledging the cognitive dissonance of these contradictory passages is an opportunity to see the challenges of the early Christian movement. Such dissonance allows us to understand, as Dr. Reta Finger points out, that Paul was a work in progress.[17] Realizing Paul and the early Christian community did not have everything figured out enables us to be realistic about what the New Testament letters convey. We no longer need to hold them at arms' length, unwilling to take seriously the foibles of the Christian movement; we can honestly examine how Scripture is a combination of inspired truths and human perspectives. Sometimes these are easy to confuse.

What Paul Doesn't Say

There is significant disagreement among Christians as to whether or not Paul wrote *all* of the letters traditionally ascribed to him. Almost without fail, those who endorse gender roles as God's will see no point in questioning Pauline authorship and instead rely on the idea that Paul was "all things to all people."[*] Part of the reason for resisting questions about Paul's authorship is that these could weaken arguments that women are to be submissive to men. If someone other than Paul wrote the letters collected in the New Testament, perhaps the prohibition doesn't carry as much theological gravitas.

Whether Paul or someone else wrote some of the New Testament epistles attributed to Paul, they are included in the canon and should be studied. But the authorship question is important because not only does it aid in understanding how women participated in the early Christian movement, it also enables a clearer assessment of the movement as a whole, providing insight into its strengths and weaknesses.

The New Testament passages most frequently used to promote women's subordination to men are found in letters many scholars today believe were not written by Paul. Called the "Pastoral Epistles," 1 and 2 Timothy and Titus are not really letters written to specific communities, but are instructions to be followed by church leaders. Although text within the letters contains claims they are written by Paul to his colleagues, Timothy and Titus, there are many convincing reasons these documents should be seen as written well after Paul's

---

[*] *The NIV Study Bible* says, for example, "While the scope of these letters is too limited to draw any firm conclusions about authorship based on vocabulary and style, these features of the Pastorals can be satisfactorily accounted for by considering the different circumstances, addresses and subject matter Paul is dealing with." (Grand Rapids: Zondervan, 2002), 1871.

lifetime, including evidence that pseudonymous authorship–using a respected name to give additional authority to a document–was an accepted and frequent practice in the first and second centuries. To admit to this practice as a possibility in the Pastoral Epistles does not negate their contents, but it does enable a better understanding of the developing Christian movement, including the regression from the egalitarian teachings of Jesus to the restrictive roles prescribed by later New Testament documents.

With writing styles and vocabularies that diverge from the other letters of Paul, 1 and 2 Timothy and Titus also differ from Paul on theology. Earlier we noted how Paul was a work in progress: while he claimed the unrestrictive vision of Jesus evident in the Galatians 3:28 mandate, he also occasionally hinted at restrictive gender norms such as clothing for worship (1 Cor.). Paul argued for the equality of all people, a radical unity to be experienced within the community of faith. He welcomed women as leaders and partnered with them. Paul did not establish a set leadership pattern to be applied to every church. Believing there was little time to squander before Christ's return, Paul encouraged people to remain single, if possible, in order to be more effective.

The Pastoral Epistles argue, on the other hand, for hierarchy in home and church. Marriage and childbirth were heralded as the avenue for women's salvation (1 Tim. 2:15). The church was instructed to be the guardian of right doctrine, an emphasis not evident in Paul's undisputed writings. These remarkable differences are substantive and should not be dismissed as Paul "being all things to all people."[18] It is also difficult to imagine Paul, who spoke so highly of women in the letter to the Romans, as the condescending voice of 1 Timothy, in which widows are readily classified into three groups: the real ones (presumably those who are older and who depend upon the church for support); those who are identified as Christian workers; and those who are young. The latter are not to receive the support of the church because, as this author says, "[W]hen their sensual desires alienate them from Christ, they want to marry, and so they incur condemnation for having violated their first pledge. Besides that, they learn to be idle, gadding about from house to house; and they are not merely idle, but also gossips and busybodies, saying what they should not say. So, I would have younger widows marry, bear children, and manage their households, so as to give the adversary no occasion to revile us" (1 Tim. 5:11–14).

Creating Christian Unity

The desire for unity, whether in the Bible's messages or in contemporary churches, is a powerful motivator, one that can be helpful, but also destructive. Biblical evidence overwhelmingly points to a Christian movement whose identity shifts as it grows and expands into new geographical regions and accepts new classes with higher socio-economic realities. As the context changed, so too did the ways in which it understood itself and implemented its mission.

For Paul, the vision of unity in Christ was most obvious in the dismantling of barriers he identified in Galatians 3:28: Jew/Greek; slave/master; male/female (relationship pairs that are often called household codes because they comprised the households in ancient Greco-Roman society). And yet, when we see Paul in action, it was the Jew/Greek relationship that motivated him most completely. There is little doubt the rapid expansion and perhaps the enduring presence of Christianity itself owes much to Paul's vision to transcend this ethnic and religious barrier. Paul truly was an apostle to the Gentiles.

For the writer(s) of the Pastoral Epistles, unity required embracing a different methodology than Paul's. For this New Testament writer(s), the context had shifted to a later time. Expanded from its earlier origins with Paul, the Christian movement's boundaries now were more clearly drawn between those who were Christian and those who were not. It became the primary responsibility of the church to guard against teachings that were not true by putting into place a church hierarchy of bishops and deacons, official church positions that were absent in the churches Paul founded.

These communities of Timothy and Titus also needed to be understood as benign forces in the Roman world. To accomplish this, it was necessary for Christians to be in accord with governing authorities. By adopting rather than dismantling the Roman household codes long established by Aristotle and others (husbands/wives; slaves/masters; children/parents or fathers), Christians demonstrated their allegiance to the ways of their society. Unity was established by de-emphasizing equality and pointing instead toward similarities to those in power. It was a shrewd move for the longevity of the movement, even as it thereby illustrated a departure from the politics of Jesus.

When leaders of Christian Patriarchy movements and complementarians urge Christians today to accept God-given gender roles to live faithfully, they rely on the Post-Pauline context to make their case. Jettisoning Jesus and Paul for the later New Testament writers, they endorse a particular teaching found in the Pastoral Epistles as paramount, dismissing the counter-cultural teachings in the gospels and the undisputed letters of Paul.

A simplistic approach to the Bible rejects its many nuances and varieties of perspectives in return for the neatness and clarity of a single vision. To argue for a "biblical" view of marriage, of womanhood, of masculinity, or whatever, suggests the Bible has only one thing to say. It's as if the Bible is a great encyclopedia of heavenly advice: search the index for your topic and the answer is easily located. Need an excuse to spank your wife or use plumber piping on your child? Need a reason to assert the primacy of men in the household and church? Need to justify a patriarch-centered dominion whose power trumps all? The Bible will provide, if only you squint your eyes in a certain way, allowing you to see a narrow vision.

But this way to read the Bible reduces it to a kind of document it never purported to be, relying on a sort of myopia affirming a hierarchical vision that establishes men as the only God-ordained leaders. It's no wonder that in several places throughout the gospels, Jesus uses the metaphor of new sight, reflective of transformation wrought by truly seeing.

For some people, relationship with God enhances their desire to also be spouses and partners, mothers or fathers. These are wonderful expression of familial love, and should be acknowledged and celebrated. However, to suggest that women must operate within this context as a requirement to fulfill God's greatest desire is to limit the creativity and expansiveness of God at work. It dismisses the importance of Tamar, who demonstrated the courage it takes to secure justice, especially when it is denied by those in places of privilege.

Despite what the Christian Patriarchs might claim, Jesus did not create special roles for women and call them good, nor did he demand that women stay under the rule of their fathers and husbands, produce a "quiverfull" of children, or subdue their children into obedience with a stiff rod. Instead, Jesus taught that all persons could—and should—embrace the dream of God of loving our neighbors. He never stipulated that following God entailed different responses for women than for men. Only when all Christians embrace our full humanity and giftedness as individuals will we truly see what God means for us to be.

Chapter Seven

What Happens in the Silence

At a mega-church just outside of Portland, Oregon, congregants can enjoy sipping coffee in the fashionably decorated atrium: not bitter church coffee, but Starbucks, served at an on-site cafe that offers a menu almost identical to the Starbucks stores planted on almost every corner of Portland. Women can reapply make-up and nurse babies in a mirrored powder room much larger than the restrooms found at most other churches. In the hallway connecting the central gathering area to Sunday school classrooms, beside flyers announcing church ministries, the church displays its ministerial team in a pyramid of photos featuring the head pastor as the pyramid's top spot. Photos of associate ministers form a row beneath the head pastor, followed by pictures of the men who serve as church elders. Serving as the pyramid's last row are pictures of administrative staff and those who work directly with missions. And only there, in the final row, do any images of women appear.

This display conveys a powerful message to church parishioners and to visitors alike: only men's leadership is honored in this church; only their voices will be heard. Women, the image asserts, can serve in subordinate roles. They can be included, but only in ministry projects directed to other women, to children, or to men living in developing countries, where apparently some "biblical" principles do not necessarily apply.

The composition of this mega-church's predominantly male staff is not unusual. Examine leadership teams found at most evangelical churches, at evangelical parachurch organizations, and at evangelical educational institutions, and the value of women's voices in those places is fairly clear. Women have roles to play in Christian churches, schools, and organizations; and, as evangelicals like to say, those roles are very "special," God-designed, invaluable.

Being heard? Not part of the plan.

This is not startling news. Christians have successfully kept women silent for centuries, privileging only men's voices, their perspectives, and their interpretations of Scripture because, somehow, God deemed that this be so. Disregarding countless biblical passages that assert women are also God's earthly envoys, the church has assured that women remain submissive, many of their gifts and abilities ignored. To imagine a woman might lead a congregation or teach men something substantive from the Bible? In most evangelical circles, that would be heresy, definitely against church history as well as the church's historic interpretations of Scripture and of God's design for women.

Many evangelicals have sustained, perhaps even fortified, the church tradition of keeping women silent. Messages about God's design for women are often built on the presumptions of a woman's silence. She is to be submissive to her husband, as he maintains headship over the home. She definitely cannot speak publicly in church, a role forbidden to her. She should not teach men the Bible, limiting the places she can have influence. Women who ignore messages about keeping quiet are often seen as transgressing God's plan, as unnatural and heretical.

What happens when women are told repeatedly that their voices do not have merit? All too often, such messages serve to erode women's sense of self. In our work as college professors, we encounter young women who have internalized this message, and who believe that their voices—and all those voices symbolize—do not matter: not in the church, not in the classroom, and not in their personal lives, where they often defer to others rather than assert their preferences.

So what happens in the silence?

The Bible as Gag Order

In 2005, an evangelical Friends University hired its first female campus chaplain, over a century after the college itself was founded. The person tabbed for the role was a gifted speaker and leader, with a seminary degree and the experience that made her well qualified for the position. She was also a woman, and this proved to be a significant challenge. Although it was the twenty-first century, and having a woman serving as campus chaplain for an institution of higher learning should (ideally, at least) have caused little controversy, hiring this particular chaplain created quite a stir and, to some, reflected the institution's slide into heresy and secularism.

The chaplain was quickly embraced by some students, who recognized her gifts as a speaker and her skill at creating community. Others rejected her outright, having heard over and over again that women were *not* supposed to assume roles of spiritual leadership. Because college-aged men were part of the chapel audience to which the chaplain would preach several times each semester, having a female in the chaplain role was essentially going against God's plan for men and women. Her dissenters ardently believed the men had nothing to learn from the chaplain, and to even listen might be unbiblical. And so, for several years, whenever the chaplain was slated to speak, her critics refused to attend chapel; or, if they did attend, they made a very public exit when she stepped to the podium, letting her—and the audience—know that her voice mattered not at all.

Protesting a woman's right to speak might be one way to silence her, though in this case the strategy mostly failed. Still, the chaplain's experience, and especially students' resistance to her, compels the questions: Why did eighteen-year-old men believe they could not be taught by someone who was several decades older and educated by a well-regarded evangelical seminary? What made these students assert that God would not speak to them through a woman?

The chaplain's experience is not unusual. Probably every woman who works in a evangelical ministerial capacity can recall an instance when she was silenced by others. Even in our work as university professors, we have been told, implicitly and explicitly, that having men in our classes is unbiblical. This is less common in disciplines *outside* of Bible and religion, but in these professors face resistance every semester from men and women who feel assured that their hearts and minds must remain closed to what is being taught, only because the teachers are women.

But where does that certainty come from?

More than most other kinds of evangelical messaging about gender, the most persistent and powerful idea communicated to women is this: they must be seen, but not heard. This is especially true inside the church, where people learn that only men are called to church leadership, and that a woman speaking from a church pulpit is heretical. The missive to Timothy is dragged out again and again to serve as a biblical gag order, keeping women in their place—silent, submissive, and unable to use the spiritual gifts some of them have so obviously been given.

Endeavoring to deconstruct even a small sampling of these messages is overwhelming, if only because such convictions about a woman's lack of fitness for spiritual leadership are everywhere. They are voiced by the biggest names in evangelicalism, and filtered down into the ideas conveyed by books, blogs, sermons, and women's conferences; they are distilled to the masses who internalize assertions about women in church leadership without questioning the provenance of such problematic claims. Those who very publicly assert that women should not preach reflect a who's-who of contemporary evangelical superstardom:

- Owen Strachan, current president for the Council on Biblical Manhood and Womanhood, argues the biblical teaching of Paul—who demands that men are to teach, and not women—is a teaching "for all time." Men are called "to be the protectors of the family and the church," Strachan says, and men are to "steward the church well," guarding its doctrine from outside sources because they are specially equipped with strength to defend against doctrinal challenges. Women need to be quiet, he suggests, and to own the special, special roles they've been given.[1]

- John Piper, author of over fifty books, founder of DesiringGod. com, and a leading Reformed Christianity voice, has made his position on women and ministry clear in a number of venues. Piper is adamant that there is a "connection between the home and the church," and that there are "role distinctions" for each realm. Paul is explicit in 1 Timothy 2:12, Piper claims, and the functions of "teaching and exercising authority" are reserved for men.[2]

- In the last decade, Mark Driscoll had emerged as one of the leading voices in evangelicalism, and his Mars Hill empire included a church in Seattle and several plants in other states, with 14,000 plus members. Driscoll has been vocal and insistent that most pastoral roles—except for the *special* few reserved for women, such as teaching Sunday school—should be assumed by men. Driscoll argues that because he holds to Scripture as an authority, *of course* women should not serve as church leaders.[3]

- Albert Mohler, president of The Southern Baptist Theological Seminary, and a leading voice in evangelical thought and practice, is likewise emphatic that his beliefs are based solely on the authority of Scripture, and not on cultural trends. Because the Bible "reveals a pattern of distinction between the roles of men and women," evangelicals need to hold firm in sustaining the authority of men in home and church, no matter that culture itself is supporting the "rapid feminization of clergy." He supports his statement by turning to nearly two thousand years of church tradition, as if the continued silencing of women is justified by historical precedent.[4]

Repeatedly, the leadership in contemporary evangelicalism has made it clear: Their beliefs are based on biblical authority, and are unassailable. Women are not to assume leadership roles in the church; they have very special roles within the church, and speaking isn't one of them.

In other words, be quiet already.

The dogmatic assertions of these leaders are echoed in pulpits everywhere, so that those growing up in evangelical traditions learn quickly that God does not wish for women to provide church leadership, nor does God wish for them to preach. It's no wonder such folks are shocked when they first encounter a woman who has been called to the pastorate. They are face to face with what they believe is heresy, incarnate in a skirt-wearing preacher.

What Does It Really Mean to Teach? Splitting Hairs

For some, this potential for apostasy is everywhere, leading Christians to begin to question every moment when a woman has authority over a man, both inside and outside of the church. Those trying to divine whether women are allowed to teach men in one instance, but not in another, turn at times to a kind of evangelical hair-splitting, making presumably biblical claims to assert why a woman's instruction is warranted and acceptable in some situations, but not in others.

Evangelical institutions of higher learning are one place where such pedantry happens often. Having heard since an early age that women are not allowed to have authority over men, young people enter Christian colleges wondering whether it is appropriate for a female professor to teach males in first-year composition classes, or American history, or sociology. Sometimes a student will express his concern outright, telling the professor that he will not be able to accept her instruction on argumentative essays. Often times, discomfort with being taught by a woman is expressed more latently, manifest in behaviors students deem acceptable for female professors but which they would never fathom expressing in male-led classrooms. Bible and religion departments are definitely the on-campus lightning rod for discussions about whether women can have authority over men. And, as such, women who teach in those departments are too often burned by the conversation.[5]

In spring 2013, after Cedarville University in Ohio decided women in its religion department would no longer be able to teach classes in which men enrolled, *Christianity Today* rounded up quotes from several evangelical leaders suggesting that Cedarville was being biblical in its approach—perhaps, even, more biblical than other Christian institutions who continued to allow women to have authority by retaining them in their religion departments and letting them teach the Bible to male students. Owen Strachan, for example, asserted that "teaching roles that are elder-like should be shaped according to biblical eldership,"[6] and thus the requirement that teachers be men should remain. In a dizzyingly circular argument, Wayne Grudem, a theology professor at Phoenix Seminary, said this: "Mixed-gender theology classes should be taught by men. It is illogical to say a woman should train men to be Bible teachers and pastors when she shouldn't be one herself. If women shouldn't be pastors or elders in churches, then they should also not have that role in other contexts."[7] The premise of his entire argument—that women shouldn't be pastors or elders in the church—isn't even questioned, because of course they shouldn't. The Bible apparently tells us so.

Other evangelical institutions have resolved the conundrum of whether women can teach Bible classes by establishing courses of study that allow women to learn how to become ministers—to other women, of course. At Liberty University, the Center for Women's Ministries instructs women in "the basic principles of femininity and equipping today's woman to effectively evangelize and disciple other women living in America and throughout the world."[8] The language Liberty uses is intentionally clear: women will not be instructed in the ungodly work of teaching men, but only *other women*. Similarly, at Southwestern Baptist Theological Seminary, students can enroll in women's programs that instruct in the ways of being a biblical woman and the wife of an equipping minister, two of their disciplinary specialties. Like Liberty, this seminary argues women can be great spiritual influences–solely of *other women*, for sure–and that their degree will give these women the tools to "open God's word and teach eternal truths, engage the culture, and help women and their families come to Christ locally and around the world."[9]

While other evangelical universities may permit women to teach mixed-gender Bible courses, religion departments remain overwhelmingly male, and women often face the resistance of male students who have been told, since childhood, that women have no authority over them. Kendra has written often about her experience as the only woman teaching Bible in a certain evangelical institution, and the ways students express resistance to her, including stonewalling her in class or, conversely, trying to come up with questions that would stump her, making her appear less authoritative about her disciplinary specialty. Colleagues who did not have the same in-class culture discounted the overt hostility students expressed toward a woman teaching them the Bible; as men providing biblical instruction, they were not subject to such resistance, and so could not know what Kendra faced nearly every time she stepped into the classroom.[10] Unfortunately, Kendra's experience is shared by many other women teaching Bible courses at evangelical institutions.[11]

Evangelical universities are not the only places outside the church where these doctrinal battles rage on, and where Christians attempt to draw lines between when it is acceptable for women to teach the Bible, and when it is not. Most evangelicals have settled the debate about whether women can teach children in Sunday school settings. Of course they can, because women have authority over children (also, of course they can, because the edifice of Sunday school itself would collapse without the efforts of women to teach children every Sunday morning). But then the hair-splitting begins. When is it no longer acceptable for a woman to teach a boy? When does a boy become a man? When he is eighteen, and no longer under the authority of his mother? Definitely then, which makes young men's resistance at Christian universities even more understandable. Some argue for an even earlier age, though, because plenty of boys under the age of eighteen are also doing great things for God, and thus, women should no longer teach boys when they are "old enough to understand God's word and be obedient to it in baptism."[12]

How about a mixed-gender Bible study? Some say women should sit quietly, hands in laps, most certainly. There might be opportunity for a woman to speak in such classes, but it depends. At least one organization, Verse by Verse Ministry International, advises that, on rare occasions, a woman could even teach a mixed-gender Bible study if it was obvious to everyone that she remained under authority of a male in the class. What that means practically is less clear: Does the man loom behind her, ready to clamp her mouth shut, should she speak heresy? Another work-around might be to have the woman serve as a co-teacher with a man, but the male leader "should be clearly identified as the leader of the class and the authority over interpretation of the text."[13] How about women presenting at a large Christian conference? Beth Moore and Joyce Meyer have rich (in every sense of the word) ministries teaching the Bible to full arenas, but this is acceptable, as their audiences are other women. Wayne Grudem, co-founder of the Council for Biblical Manhood and Womanhood, emphatically says women speaking at mix-gendered conference is not an option for those who hold fidelity to the Bible.[14]

Although female leadership in churches has been a forbidden realm in evangelical circles, and has been for centuries, new technologies introduce unique conundrums about women's roles. How can 1 Timothy be applicable in a computer age, in which any woman can have her own platform, with the potential to teach? In other words, is it problematic for men to read blogs written by women, especially if those blogs teach men something? In "Should Christian Women Be Instructing Men Through Blogging?" Diana Bucknell wonders how women blogging can get around this "sticky wicket"—or whether they even should. According to Bucknell, it's okay for women to speak in weekly Bible studies or Sunday schools taught by men, though females aren't supposed to actually lead the sessions. Is speaking during a Wednesday night Bible study equal to blogging, or does blogging lend more authority to women, kind of like that forbidden practice of having a woman stand at a pulpit? The writer's husband provides his own opinion in the comments section in an extensive exegesis of Scripture passages his wife only manages to gloss. He lets us know that, as daughters of Eve, women are complicit in "the unspeakable horror that befell the world," and must therefore accept their husbands' authority. Blogging, he decides, is okay, but not women "disjockies [sic] on Christian radio who read Scripture, exhort, teach, and dispense Biblical advice to an audience that is decidedly comprised of Christian men and women."[15] The radio is easy to switch off, though, a ready way to make sure a woman's voice isn't heard.

Even newer technologies will probably demand that Christians continue to revisit the question of when a woman might be permitted to speak. In time, complementarian leaders will probably be debating the relevance of Paul's dictates to Twitter, Instagram, and Snapchat: What if a man reads a Tweet written by a woman, and learns something new about the Bible? Can authority be established in 140 characters? Does the brevity of Twitter, or the ephemeral nature of Snapchat, make such teaching okay?

Surely the Bible will tell us. After all, we may not be able to study Paul's missive in its cultural context, but it is certainly acceptable to allow Paul, writing nearly two thousand years ago, to speak to ours.

All's Quiet on the Home Front

Grace Driscoll, spouse of Mars Hills' pastor Mark, has carved out a nice—that is, acceptable—ministry for herself as a pastor's wife who occasionally blogs, and sometimes speaks at women's conferences or alongside her husband. In 2012, Grace and Mark Driscoll co-wrote *Real Marriage*, a primer on what a godly marriage *really* should look like (one helpful piece of advice: breast augmentation can make for hot, married, godly Christian sex, if needed). By speaking at the side of her husband and penning blog posts primarily for women, Grace has created her own kind of ministry, guiding women toward becoming the excellent, godly wives God obviously calls them to be.

In a 2011 blog post on the now defunct Mark Driscoll site, Grace provided a long discourse on the attributes of an "Excellent (Godly) Wife." Using Proverbs 31, Grace Driscoll argues that, although being an excellent wife is difficult, for she is a "rare and valuable jewel," such is achievable for those who follow her prescription—which is, essentially, that women be gentle, quiet, and submissive. A godly wife is a silent one, and those with a "loud personality" had better get busy at rehabilitation. Driscoll suggests those inclined to speak need to prayerfully weigh their words, and that every word uttered should be directed toward helping and encouraging their husbands, grounded in a gentleness of spirit that seeks to fulfill all others before attending to the self. In that silence of spirit and tongue, women will feel how precious they are to their husbands and to God, a jewel in his/His crown.[16]

Grace Driscoll's understanding of a silent-but-godly woman is not unique: she is merely relying on a long-standing trope among evangelicals of the submissive wife, quietly working to do her husband's and God's will. This trope demands a foil to serve as opposition: wives who have any kind of voice in a marriage, or whose lack of a gentle spirit causes significant marital discord. Thus, a loud-mouthed, argumentative woman might be a Jezebel spirit, an apparent bitch who rebukes God and all others.[17] The loud woman is the proverbial "woman of folly," and will resort to hostility, aggressiveness, and cunning to get what she wants, but a godly woman will be gentle and quiet, where her true beauty resides (though being outwardly beautiful is always useful as well).[18]

So what is to be done if a woman is not, by her very nature, a quiet spirit? Evangelist James MacDonald says a wife can even change her husband by learning to be chaste and quiet, because "changed women help God change husbands." Transformation requires that a woman herself learn to be gentle and quiet, ridding herself of any combative spirit that might lead her to be "blunt in her words or actions," and compelling herself toward being "self-spoken and calm." If a woman insists, "God didn't make me to be quiet," then she must change, allowing her *real* God-given personality to be shown through a quiet spirit.[19]

Although some women *are* naturally quiet, this is certainly not the case for all, and transforming a quality at the core of one's personality seems a nearly impossible task. A young woman named Taylor Holder explained this dynamic well on the *Good Woman Project* website, where she wrote, "For the Girl Criticized for Not Having a Quiet Spirit." In her essay, Holder describes the expectations for godly women she's heard described in the church–that a woman should be quiet and meek in spirit. And although Holder didn't believe she fit this character description, she felt herself changing over time into a quiet person she did not necessarily recognize: she had lost part of herself to these expectations. Now she wonders whether godly women can be loud and strong-willed for the "right causes": for justice and equity, for grace and love. Holder has decided to live an authentic life of faith. She feels she needs to be "a woman with a quiet spirit, but not necessarily a quiet mouth…a woman who challenges those around her, hoping they will challenge her back, because at the end of the day, she just really wants to learn."[20] Taylor Holder is clearly on a significant faith journey, walking against a strong tide of messages telling her that to be godly means being silent.

What Godly Girls Are Made Of

Girls in contemporary culture are reminded that they are expected to be quiet, gentle, and full of "everything nice," and this is doubly true in evangelicalism, where quietness is considered a godly virtue to which girls should certainly aspire. Girls are to be modest both inside and outside, and an unquiet girl—one who voices an opinion, or talks too loudly—is someone who expresses an immodesty of spirit. In her immodesty, she is also going against God's biblical design for women. After all, Eve's big mouth got her in trouble, compelling the fall of humankind; had she followed God's design and kept her mouth shut, the world would be a far different place.

Thus purity culture may demand that girls not call attention to their female bodies, but it also insists that girls not draw others' vision away from Christ and his salvation. Speaking in a loud voice is problematic, because doing so turns others from contemplating Jesus. In an essay advocating that girls rethink their femininity, making it more "Christ-centered," the author (an anonymous "warrior poet") tells girls that a "gentle and quiet spirit" is most esteemed, most beautiful, because it points people toward the One most esteemed. Girls especially must be wary of calling attention away from Jesus, else they grow to become as harlots, women of craft and guile. Those girls who are drawn to Jesus, and whom Jesus loves, will be marked with quiet and gentle spirits.[21] Apparently, Jesus loves everyone, but maybe loves quiet girls just a little bit more.

But what of the loud girls, those who can't just shut up, those who have been given the "gift of gab"? Just like a traditional makeover might make girls more beautiful outwardly, some girls might require a "speech makeover," allowing their interior selves to align with God's design for girls: that they be gentle in spirit, never resorting to speech that might make them more like "one of the guys." Instead, loud girls need to evaluate the ways they talk, the timbre of their voices, the kind of language they use, even whether they resort to fillers such as "like" or "really" or "um," and work to perfect the places their speech seems wanting. Only then will they truly become "Christ-built women," whose speech is "gracious and respectful at all times."[22]

These articles about refining one's speech are predominantly directed at girls, as if girls alone need reformation. A boy who is vocal or talkative is seen as someone who is using his God-given gifts of speech and intellect to inspire others. According to Albert Mohler, writing for Focus on the Family's *Boundless* magazine, a mark of manliness is, in fact, "verbal maturity sufficient to communicate and articulate as a man," and a boy wanting to achieve manliness needs to "learn how to speak before large groups, overcoming the natural intimidation and fear that comes from looking at a crowd, opening one's mouth and projecting words." Similar prescriptions do not exist in advice for a girl to become a godly woman, because women will have little opportunity to speak before large groups, having no propensity or need for leadership—and because girls, by their very nature, will have no need to use their voices. *Boundless* tells us that boys might never become public speakers, but a boy needs the "ability to take his ground, frame his words, and make his case when truth is under fire."[23] In doing so, he fulfills his place as a defender of truth, the role God has designed for every boy becoming a man: serving as a leader and protector for the girl standing silently at his side.

Shame in Silence

When women are told throughout their lives that God desires their silence, that it is their role to be silent, that a loud woman is a Jezebel—when this happens, the consequences can be devastating, on a number of levels. Women learn not to trust their voices nor to believe their opinions, having heard their ideas *might* have merit, but only for a select audience of other women and children. Women who speak when they shouldn't, voicing unpopular beliefs, may become labeled or ostracized, and can internalize the messages they receive about what it means to be female, loud, and thus outside God's design. Repeated proclamations that God created women to be silent shame women who act otherwise, even if they feel called by God to speak about significant truths that might alleviate the suffering of others, might set captives free, might be exactly the words God longs for them to speak.

There are other ways that silencing women can be injurious. When power structures use silencing as a form of control, those who are vulnerable can be more easily wounded, lacking the ability to express the damage being done to them. Nowhere has this been more clear than in the sex abuse cases that have scandalized the Roman Catholic Church—and, more recently, some evangelical churches and colleges as well. In each case, men in leadership used their positions and power to abuse children, then found ways to keep the children mum about the abuse, sometimes for decades. Just as egregious, when abuse *was* discovered, people at the top of the hierarchical chain chose to remain silent, protecting the abusers rather than the victims. At times, these cover-ups were systematic and well organized, suggesting clear intention on the part of those willing to silence already-suffering victims.

Attention has for years been placed on the Roman Catholic Church in its widespread sex abuse scandals, with far less attention being paid to similar stories of abuse unraveling in evangelical churches. Boz Tchividjian, grandson of Billy Graham, has claimed that evangelicalism rivals Catholicism in the numbers of sex abuse cases and in attempts to cover up sexual crimes committed by its leadership. In 2003, Tchividjian started an organization, GRACE (Godly Response to Abuse in the Christian Environment), as a way of investigating abuse cases within Christian organizations and helping the organizations themselves report crime cases, rather than resorting to the silence often used to save face or to protect perpetrators. "The reason why offenders get away with what they do is because we have too many cultures of silence," Tchividjian said in a 2014 interview with Kathryn Joyce. "When something does surface, all too often the church leadership quiets it down. Because they're concerned about reputation: 'This could harm the name of Jesus, so let's just take care of it internally.'"[24] In a long expose for *The American Prospect*, Joyce reported that Tchividjian and GRACE were a little too good at their job. Hired by Bob Jones University to help weed out abuse in the school, GRACE was subsequently fired, presumably because—through the course of over one hundred interviews—GRACE had uncovered a number of sex abuse cases, as well as a systematic attempt to silence and shame those who had come forward to report abuse. At times, Joyce writes, victims were also blamed for being complicit in the abuse, those in charge asking questions about substance use, what the victims were wearing, and whether there might be some underlying spiritual weakness that invited abuse. Before GRACE could file its report, Bob Jones terminated the contract with GRACE, another convenient way of silencing information. When media scrutiny started to focus on possible intent behind the firing, Bob Jones University rehired GRACE to finish its work.[25] The final report from Grace was released in late 2014, claiming that Bob Jones "respond[ed] to rape and abuse claims with woeful ignorance of state law, a near-complete lack of training in psychology and trauma counseling best practices, and an overarching campus culture that blames women and girls for any abuse they suffer, and which paints all sexuality–from rape to consensual sex–as equivalent misdeeds." The report made 26 recommendations for BJU, including a public apology, which was made by newly-hired president Steve Pettit in December 2014.[26]

Attempts to hush abuse victims, either outright or by making them culpable in the crime perpetuated upon them, is not something unique to Bob Jones University.* A number of other Christian institutions have taken a similar tack in recent years, deflecting criticism by suggesting the stories of sexual assault victims have no merit, that their voices do not deserve to be heard. Think Doug Phillips of The Vision Forum, or Bill Gothard from the Institute of Basic Principles, or Sovereign Grace Ministries, or any number of others who have been accused of sexual assaults and the institutions that continued to cover for the crimes of their leaders. The culture that keeps women quiet by saying the Bible demands their silence makes it difficult for victims to come forward. But it also punishes those women who find the courage to speak, questioning their stories and asserting that those stories have little merit. The message from many evangelical institutions is this: If you claim to be abused, you may be called a fornicator, your very soul called into question. If you take your stories to the public, you will be guilty of bearing false witness or, in the least, gossiping about your Christian brothers and sisters. If you remain silent, though, you will be rewarded for your faithfulness, to the institution and, yes, also to God.

Instances in which sexual assault victims are silenced may seem like outliers, as events not really pervasive in Christian culture. But imagine the message other students at Bob Jones and other Christian colleges hear when they see victims of assault expelled, and the institutions assuming the posture of victim, harassed by those with an agenda who want to tell their stories. Imagine the message other women who were faithful to Doug Phillip's Vision Forum must have received when Phillips reframed accusations of sexual abuse into a

---

*For example, Pensacola Christian College came under scrutiny in 2014 for silencing and blaming victims who had been sexually assaulted. See Samantha Field, "God Is Done with You: Pensacola Christian College and Sexual Violence," *Slacktivist*, March 11, 2014, http://www.patheos.com/blogs/slacktivist/2014/03/11/guest-post-god-is-done-with-you-pensacola-christian-college-and-sexual-violence/ (accessed July 12, 2014).

narrative of consensual sex, even if with someone far younger and less powerful than he. Imagine what women learn when they discover any stories about sexual abuse will be questioned, challenged, recast, and thrown into doubt by those who are in power, reminding them that they are a little less loved, a little less blessed, by God.

And then, imagine a culture in which women's voices are accepted as authoritative; in which women hear that God has given them the gift to speak, too; in which women receive messages letting them know their beliefs have merit and deserve to be heard; in which women learn that truth-telling requires the ability to *tell*: to give voice to one's experience, allowing others to be transformed by the stories of others. Think about how that might change even those moments when victims of sexual assault attempt to name their abuse, carrying light to certain darkness.

Taking Another Look: The Canaanite Woman

Women in the Bible have been silenced, too, overlooked and undervalued by readers. Even as they worked for justice, took initiative, labored alongside Jesus and Paul, women have been disregarded as unimportant and uninteresting. And, yet, we have found if we shift our attention to these women in the Bible they come alive once again, teaching us what evangelical culture has muted: women's voices are needed; women should trust their own instincts; women are valuable as persons in their own right.

One such woman is found in Matthew and Mark. In Matthew she was a Canaanite while in Mark she was a Syro-Phoenician. Either way, the point is clear: she was an ethnic outsider. Conflict between Jews and Canaanites (or Syro-Phoenicians) extends back to the Exodus, when the land the Israelites invaded as their own was already occupied by the Canaanites. The ensuing battles of two groups struggling over land form the back-drop of Jesus' interactions with this ethnically marginalized woman.

This unnamed woman's daughter was not well. She was possessed by a demon, and her mother must have been willing to seek Jesus' help despite how she might—or might not—have been received by him. When she approached Jesus, she shouted at him: "Lord, Son of David; my daughter is tormented by a demon" (Matt. 15:22). It appears proper decorum was not as important to her as getting the attention of Jesus, who had a crowd around him. So, she made sure she was heard, referring to him as the Jewish Messiah, an unexpected admission from a Gentile.[*]

The disciples were not keen on her disruption, turning to Jesus and urging him to send her away because "she keeps shouting after us" (v. 23). Their reaction reflected their milieu, one that diminished women. Why should Jesus, a man, respond to her? Given the disciples' lowly status within the Roman Empire, they should have seen her situation differently. They still had much to learn.

But Jesus also was about to learn something, too. While the disciples urged him to send the Canaanite woman away, the narrator explains Jesus said nothing to her. She shouted at him, not something derogatory, but rather a term acknowledging the monarchy of Israel: "Lord, Son of David." He responded by saying nothing.

If this woman was a model of the "good Christian woman," she would have understood Jesus' silence to be her rebuke. She would rightly assume her place, silently relenting to her circumstances, for surely this is what God intended for her. Instead, she stood her ground. When Jesus finally answered her, he said, "I was sent only to the lost sheep of the house of Israel" (v. 24). He did not see her as within his scope of mission.

She responded by kneeling before him (a signal used between a teacher and a student) and saying, "Lord, help *me*" (v. 25, italics added).

In a contemporary context in which autonomy and individualism are accepted as cultural norms, the woman's behavior is unremarkable. She wants something from Jesus and does what she needs to get his attention. In the culture of first-century Palestine, however, where Jews and Gentiles, especially Canaanites, were enemies and where women were not allowed to be in public without an appropriate male escort, this woman has *chutzpah*.

Jesus Changed His Mind

Still, Jesus continued, "It is not fair," he said, "to take the children's food and throw it to the dogs" (v. 26). Jesus had no intention of shifting his focus from his own people—the children of Israel—to those others, the "dogs." Interpreters of this story often resort to complex justifications about how Jesus always planned to help this woman and

---

[*]Amy-Jill Levine suggests by meeting Jesus on his "own turf and on his own terms" the Canaanite woman conveys the superiority of the Jews in God's plan. See "Matthew," in *Women's Bible Commentary*, expanded edition with Apocrypha, ed. Carol A. Newsom and Sharon H. Ringe (Louisville: Westminster John Knox Press, 1998), 346.

was just using an extended conversation to teach his disciples. Or, perhaps, Jesus knew what he was doing and wanted to ensure the woman had the appropriate amount of faith.

Using a derogatory term, Jesus did his best to get rid of what he must have thought was a pesky and persistent woman. Jews had no love for dogs, believing them to be unclean and wild, scouring streets for food. They would not have been allowed into one's house, nor under the table, begging to be fed leftovers. Calling the woman a dog was an insult. But the astute woman diffused his attack by turning his logic on its head. "Even the dogs eat the crumbs that fall from their master's table" (v. 27), she replied.[27] Embracing the position of a dog, the woman was prepared to take even the crumbs left over from Jesus' ministry.

Her argument too compelling, or convicting, or both, Jesus relented and the woman's daughter was healed. In contrast to her, he seems small and petty, focused only on people like himself. She appears broadminded, embracing not only her identity but also the possibility of deeper transformation. Jesus, a Jew, could be her teacher, too.

Whatever the exact details of this conversation were, it is clear that Jesus thought he understood his mission prior to this exchange. However, because of a loud and persistent woman, and because of his humility and flexibility, Jesus changed his mind. This woman had every reason to be silent: she was the wrong ethnicity; she represented the wrong religion; and she was definitely the wrong gender. If Jesus needed to make a test case out of how a woman should act, this was his opportunity. But, instead of silencing her, he listened to her and decided she was right.

When Half the Church Is Silenced

Those who argue that women should not speak in church nor hold leadership positions that might (gasp) create the potential for women to have authority over men skip over gospel accounts such as the Canaanite woman. Instead, they focus attention on Paul's statement in 1 Corinthians that women are subordinate and therefore it is shameful for them to speak in church, and on 1 Timothy, in which women are instructed they should learn in silence with full submission because Eve was deceived.

Isolating passages like these make for easy and frequently convincing arguments for those already predisposed to such positions. Utilizing what appears to be an anomaly in Paul's perspective, proponents of Christian Patriarchy and complementarianism routinely emphasize a few verses Paul may or may not have said in order to keep women silent. Yet to accomplish this point of view, they have to dismiss Paul's claim in Galatians that there are no gender distinctions in the body of Christ, ignore his evangelistic work with numerous women as reported in Romans and Acts, and gloss over his writings that assume women regularly speak in church—*their* prophesying and praying apparently not brought into question in 1 Corinthians.

Instead of isolating such restrictive passages, we think the Bible invites—and demands—deeper analysis. We begin this process by identifying the contradictions, such as the ones occurring in 1 Corinthians, in which Paul mentions women praying and prophesying in church, remarking only a few chapters later that women should be silent in church. We ask why such opposing statements exist even within the same book?

Using this approach, we can identify at least three possible explanations. First, in the original Greek, there were no quotation marks indicating where one person's thoughts begin and end. Is it possible that the Corinthians—not Paul—were the ones making the claim about women not speaking in church? In writing to them, Paul may have quoted their concern first (1 Cor. 14:33b–36) and then responded with his answer (1 Cor. 14:37–40).

If this is the case, the Corinthian church wrote to Paul saying, "As in all the churches of the saints, women should be silent in the churches. For they are not permitted to speak, but should be subordinate, as the law also says. If there is anything they desire to know, let them ask their husbands at home. For it is shameful for a woman to speak in church. Or did the word of God originate with you? Or are you the one ones it has reached?" And Paul's answer was: "Anyone who claims to be a prophet, or to have spiritual powers, must acknowledge that what I am writing to you is a command of the Lord. Anyone who does not recognize this is not to be recognized. So, my friends, be eager to prophesy, and do not forbid speaking in tongues; but all things should be done decently and in order."

Another explanation is that copies were made by monks, who worked by hand and by dimly lit candles. These scribes sometimes made notations in manuscript margins. Over time it is plausible that some of these notes migrated from the margins into the texts themselves. Could this copying process explain the anomaly of Paul's claims about women in 1 Corinthians? Perhaps the divergent narrative there is not his, but instead the ideas of someone who later copied this letter.

Bart Ehrman, a New Testament scholar, suggests the likelihood of this theory, noting the similarities between 1 Timothy 2 and 1 Corinthians 14. Comparing the two reveals they each instruct women to be silent in churches and to be subordinate to men.

Let a woman learn in silence with full submission.

I permit no woman to teach or to have authority over a man; she is to keep silent.

For Adam was formed first, then Eve; and Adam was not deceived, but the woman was deceived and became a transgressor.

Yet she will be saved through childbearing, provided they continue in faith and love and holiness, with modesty. 1 Timothy 2:11–15

Women should be silent in the churches.

For they are not permitted to speak, but should be subordinate, as the law also says.

If there is anything they desire to know let them ask their husbands at home. For it is shameful for a woman to speak in church. 1 Corinthians 14:34–35[28]

Because of the dissimilarities of these two passages from all of Paul's other writings and because they are so strikingly alike in their difference, it may be they were written by the same person, perhaps a scribe who thought it best to have Paul's thoughts conform to the later norms of Christianity in the post-Pauline era.

A third explanation, one more likely to be accepted by conservative evangelicals, is that within the Corinthian community in particular a group of women had become unruly and necessitated being silenced in order for proper worship to be maintained. In this case, Paul's objection to women speaking is curtailed to some degree by the context, and applies today mostly as a cautionary note.

Just like scientific theories that are posed over time as hypotheses to be tested and verified before becoming accepted as facts, these suggestions about discrepancies in Paul's letter are theories. The reason these theories are important, however, is that rather than simply accepting isolated and contradictory statements, these theories provide reasonable explanations of Paul's contrary statements. They also point to the interpretive challenge of extending Paul's instructions from one context to another: from Rome in the first century to North America in the twenty-first.

Silence Is More than Absence

Whether one accepts Paul's statement in 1 Corinthians as the result of parenthetical ambiguity, marginal gloss or addition, or instruction directed to a specific group of individuals, knowing how to make meaning of the admonition is the next step. In the first two cases, the evidence that Paul thought women should be silent is too divergent from his earlier claims that gender should have no distinction in the community of Christ. What makes the most sense in these cases is to accept the plausibility that Paul's injunction against women speaking is not truly Paul's intention. As such, the implication that women should be silent today is not accepted as congruous with Paul's teaching as a whole.

The third possibility, that Paul was concerned about particular women within the Corinthian community, is evangelicalism's most popular theory. In this case, Paul's statement applied to specific individuals, and their distracting behaviors were the problem. Theoretically, the same disorderly conduct could result from men not behaving appropriately, although it is difficult to imagine the same rebukes being accepted and promoted by men, either in Paul's day or today. The meaning now is that people should not be unruly or disorderly during public worship. What applied to a limited group in Paul's community applies to everyone today.

This interpretive conclusion is reasonable and acceptable, except for the hidden, difficult problem. Suggesting women in a particular time and place needed to be silenced (for whatever reason) by those in authority sets precedent for silencing women today and is, we think, an underlying and unacknowledged tendency of evangelical groups to resist women holding positions of power. If it happened before, it can easily happen again. When a corresponding situation for men does not exist in Scripture, it is hard to expunge the patriarchal perspective the Bible appears to endorse.

Elisabeth Schüssler Fiorenza, in *Bread Not Stone*, argues that for women to enjoy flourishing as men do, we must relinquish patriarchy and all its trappings, allowing full liberation for women.[29] To accept the assertion that Corinthian women needed to be silenced is to endorse that men's power and authority over them was appropriate and perhaps even the way God intended. Without identifying this statement in 1 Corinthians as the male-centric perspective it illustrates, the church perpetuates the diminishing of women, the results readily evident as the nascent movement developed into an institution that quickly pushed women to the margins.

Unexamined sexism embedded in the Bible, especially in claims that women be silent and subordinate, no doubt correlates to sexism and abuse in faith communities today. Acceptance of patriarchy, even mild affirmations such as rebellious women in Corinth who needed to be put on notice, reinforces a culture in which men are more suited for authority and women are in need of being silenced, their noisy propensities problematic.

In communities in which patriarchy is believed to be God's intent, the atmosphere is conducive for authority to become abusive, especially where women and men work together (how many church offices are not this way, with a male pastor and a female administrative assistant?) and where women believe they are to be seen and not heard. Having no alternative but to submit to those in charge, women find themselves in situations in which their supervisor has no accountability and where the congregation accepts men's power as given by God while women's questioning is sinful.

1 Timothy: When Silence Turns to Liberation

If the injunction for women to be silent was ambiguous in 1 Corinthians, it appears to be crystal clear in the letter to Timothy. Here women are told to dress modestly, to learn in silence with full submission, to refrain from teaching and having positions of authority, and to be saved through childbearing. It's hardly a list of liberation. As such, it is a favorite among those who maintain patriarchy as God's dream for the world.

This list of restrictive admonitions is an anomaly. Taken as a snapshot in time, these comments reflect a particular moment. But understood as one narrative within the scope of the New Testament, they reveal more about the author conditioned by his historical context than they do about Jesus, the early Christian movement, and surely about God.

Most likely written early in the second century,[30] 1 Timothy promotes a list of gender-based duties designed to undergird and organize a burgeoning movement. Multiple Christian factions had emerged, and this reality made it necessary to provide stronger definition. These unifying measures came in the form of demanding that only bishops could teach, stipulating what was considered Scripture, and determining which beliefs would be codified. The cumulative result of these measures was that rather than adhere to the radical nature of Jesus' teaching there was a reversal: regression away from liberation to cultural accommodation. Women who had been integral to the growth of churches were pushed to the margins, no longer seen as leaders.

One reason for this shift is the difference in where Christians gathered for worship. When Paul created churches, they were initially quite small and met in homes. In ancient Rome, these homes were the spaces where women could exercise their skills; the public places were reserved for men. So, in its infancy, churches met where women were most free.

But as the Christian movement grew, it necessarily met in larger spaces, in public. In these settings, women surely felt reluctant to maintain their previously liberated status. At the same time, those observing the Christian movement would have disdained how Christianity had welcomed the participation of women. They were, according to the thinking of their day, imperfect humans, "men" who had been only partially formed in the womb.[31] Pressure from within and without would have made it difficult for Christianity to maintain its earlier inclusion of women.

Finding a New Way

The easy path, the one traveled by many, is to adopt patriarchy as God's plan for humanity, to claim that men are closer to God and as such are better representatives of God, inherently more qualified to be leaders and teachers, pastors and biblical interpreters. Challenging these assumptions is not easy because this is exactly what we have been told not to do.

But some are waking up to the reality that patriarchy is not God's dream for the world; we are called to embrace freedom. Still, the way is not easy. We start with questioning our surroundings, rubbing our eyes hoping to see more clearly. Only with tentative steps and movement do we begin to explore new possibilities. Learning to navigate our faith free from the constraints of patriarchy requires us to see everything with a new perspective, to realize there will be no easy answers, no path without boulders and snares. We will often be afraid but never without the love of God.

We will come to know that the Bible is a complex collection of writings that are good and bad and that we as readers must not only accept this reality, we need to relish it. For in the messiness of its patriarchy and sexism there is also holiness, justice, liberation, and grace. The Bible can be a source of Divine inspiration, but it also can be the source of immense and abiding pain. To discount the long and dusty desert terrain the Bible often offers women is to perpetuate injustice, to admit we are sorry about the journey while offering no genuine oasis. If we can be honest about the Bible's potential to both harm and to heal, then it can become a genuine source of sustenance.

When read at face value, 1 Corinthians 14 and 1 Timothy 2 are bad news for women. They restrict women's flourishing rather than encourage women to be all that God intends for them. But Scripture is not the final word; it was never intended to be. John's gospel reminds us of our incarnational foundation: Jesus the Word made flesh. The Bible is a guide to assist us in our journey to extend our relationships with others and to strengthen our connection to the Creator who gave us life. This map enables us to chart our course, but it requires our participation and navigational insight.

The path of regression represented by the later New Testament letters, in which the radical equality of Jesus no longer held sway, does not have to be our path. There is the opportunity to learn from the past mistakes of the early church as it accommodated its culture. Sexism does not have to be perpetuated, as in the isolated narratives of 1 Corinthians and 1 Timothy. Instead, these verses can serve as reminders of the limiting vision of self-preservation, of what can happen when one is more concerned with survival than with spreading the good news.

The church often lags behind society in promoting justice: in welcoming the poor and LGBT persons, in addressing our ecological crisis, in admitting to the myriad ways it has endorsed rather than challenged the idols of consumerism. Its history of silencing the marginalized, including women, has resulted in an institution that all too frequently endorses the path of exclusion.

But the Canaanite woman demonstrates how to walk down a different road, one that leads to liberation and wholeness. She shows us how to create a different reality, unrelenting against the forces of tradition and narrow-mindedness. Knowing her daughter's health needed Jesus' attention, she pursued healing until it was within her grasp. But she didn't just take what was hers; she changed Jesus in the process, too.

Moving out of the shadows and into the center, women will continue to find their voices. And, as they do, not only will they see how much it changes them, they will eventually succeed in changing the evangelical church. If the Canaanite woman's passion for the well-being of her daughter can teach us anything, it surely is that we have the power to be all we are meant to be.

Chapter Eight

Princesses, Kingdoms, and God, Oh My!

When Disney introduced its new princess for the 2012 animated movie *Brave*, many parents cheered. Finally, Disney had produced a princess who defied stereotypes. Merida was bold, adventurous, and outspoken, a girl who enjoyed riding horses and shooting arrows, and who was not (very) afraid of the wilderness or its challenges. Unlike the Disney princess whose hair was perfectly styled with ribbons and bows, Merida's red hair sometimes appeared unkempt, reflective of the girl's concerns for more than appearance, beauty, and nifty hair.

Brave's Merida departed from what had become the princess industrial complex, a term created by Peggy Orenstein in *Cinderella Ate My Daughter*. Orenstein argues most young girls who develop a princess obsession between the ages of three and five do so because companies such as Disney have created pink tiaras, gowns, and wands and foisted them onto children. In other words, there is nothing inherently developmental about a princess obsession; it is a social construct, thanks to an industry which has told young girls they are princesses and that princesses are demure creatures, more interested in beauty products than in reigning as rulers. Parents, intent on making their girls happy, only abetted the princess industrial complex, even as they anxiously reviled the princess messages.[1]

This is why Disney's Merida seemed like such a departure, and which is why what happened in May 2013 caused a minor uproar. Before being introduced as part of the princess juggernaut, Disney gave Merida a "glam" makeover: new drawings showed her with tamed hair, a more regal gown (pulled down to provide a glimpse of cleavage), and a slimmer body. Some people—including Merida's original creator–reacted with outrage that an animated girl needed to be made softer and sexier to be included in the princess pantheon. Over 250,000 people signed a Change.org petition, requesting that Disney not make the changes. Brenda Chapman, the film's co-director, said "When little girls say they like it because it's more sparkly, that's all fine and good but, subconsciously, they are soaking in the sexy 'come hither' look and the skinny aspect of the new version. It's horrible! Merida was created to break that mold–to give young girls a better, stronger role model, a more attainable role model, something of substance."[2]

Although Disney responded to the pressure, and the original version of Merida now resides on the Disney Princess website, the "Merida Scandal" reflects well the tensions within the princess industrial complex. There is little room in the princess industrial complex for potential role models who might break the mold by suggesting girls could go on adventures, fight wild animals, have agency in their own lives. And while parents might say they want something different for their daughters, they continue to buy princess products, covering their girls in pink and conveying to them, if only subliminally, that a girl's aspiration should focus on beauty and helpless waiting.

Evangelical Christians have not been immune to the princess industrial complex, nor its ironies and tensions. Like mainstream Americans, they have purchased princess products in spades, feeding the multi-million dollar glittery princess machine. Evangelical toy and book companies have created their own princess products, catering not only to children but to grown women, with Bibles and books, t-shirts for teens and adults, and devotional literature. In some ways, the "God as King" metaphor naturally lends itself to a corresponding "daughter as princess" image, and such images are everywhere, urging women to live a deeper, richer life in God's heavenly castle.

Yet the princess imagery has been shaped and informed not by the Bible so much as by popular culture itself; the Christian princess metaphor has been Disneyfied. Products marketed to Christian women are bathed in pink, and princess-related consumer goods imagine figures more compatible to Snow White and Cinderella than the royal women in the Bible, who were leaders of their people, brave and strong like Merida, rather than quiet denizens of a king, waiting for Prince Charming. Men, constructed as kings and princes, reflect the one True King and one True Prince, God and Jesus, and as such they are closer to God, designed to be leaders and decision-makers, the rulers of every kingdom. Women, as queens and princesses, are not created in God's image, despite what Genesis says; instead, they are indebted to the King and must follow what the King and his representatives (on heaven and earth) demand.

Royalty metaphors are problematic when they assume the extra cultural baggage wrought by the princess industrial complex. Yet many evangelicals continue to use princess metaphors, seeing them as cute and clever, powerful and authentic, in figuring a woman's relationship to God. Like so many other aspects of language, these metaphors shape our reality, so that the very language we use to figure our relationship to the Divine says something about who women and men are supposed to be. A simple assertion that a woman is a "princess of the King" becomes powerful for sure, working to reinforce the hierarchy that evangelical Christian culture craves, in which women have their place—and a comfortable, pretty, pink one at that.

God's Word with Sparkles

A Christian college English professor loves sharing the story of when he was booted from a church for standing on a Bible. In a Sunday school for elderly members at a Quaker church near his home, the professor was speaking on biblical inerrancy. The folks in class were uncomfortable with his questions about whether the Bible was literal or figurative. *Of course* the Bible was factually true, despite the professor's assertions that some of its stories must be mythological in nature.

"I don't know about that," one older woman said, trying to stop the professor's heresy. "I just want to trust, and stand on the Word."

"Oh, you do?" he said. With that, he flung his Bible to the ground and hopped upon it, turning to face the class. "You just *literally* stand on the Word?" His point about the literal and figurative nature of language earned him a hasty invitation to leave the church, for good. No one messes with the perfect Word of God.

Unless you're a marketer of Bibles.

Then any tampering with God's unchanging word might be necessary to make Scripture perfectly suited for the individual in her quest to know God. All one really needs is an online Bible finder that allows searchers to choose not only the biblical version they wish to read, but also the cover color—from burgundy to teal—the type of cover, and the specific audience: from children to tweens to military personnel. Nothing says the literally perfect word of God like a Bible especially tailored for a soldier wanting imitation leather on his camouflage-colored holy book. And the perfect Bible for women is bathed in princess pink. In evangelical marketing, the princess industrial complex expresses itself most clearly in the Bibles sold to the daughters of the King, who surely must need their Scripture framed by reminders that they are pretty princesses, with all the attendant behaviors that royal role entails.

Consider the *God's Little Princess Devotional Bible*, edited by Shelia Walsh, a one-time Christian singing artist who became an evangelist, writer, and inspirational speaker. The premise of this particular Bible is that, in using it, it will "help your little girl blossom into the faithful princess she was created to be."[3] The product description suggests the Bible offers "a good dose of God's truth combined with lots of sparkle," and newer editions of the text have even more shimmer on the cover, something every princess will enjoy as a "daughter of the King." The book also includes features on the Bible's many princesses, memory verse challenges, plays that are easy to perform, and songs girls can sing. An entire section on "beauty secrets" teaches girls how to apply make-up and put on adorable clothes for the "royal subjects" in their lives (that is, "your family, siblings, friends and those in the community"). The book's introduction asserts, "Every girl is a princess," and, "Girls long to be beautiful, to be loved, to be adored, to be wanted and needed, and to give their hearts to their hero."[4] Walsh promises that this particular Bible will help girls on this journey toward what is a narrow view of what girls want, putting girls in a small, passive box.

But Walsh's text is not the only princess Bible on the market. The toddler-targeted book *My Princess Bible* does not hide its affinity for the Disney Princesses, as the cover vaguely resembles a princess lineup from the Magic Kingdom. Produced by Tyndale, the Bible tells the stories of women in the Bible, but its art and storytelling are, according to the publisher's information, "reflective of the modern-day princesses." As with Walsh's Bible, the *My Princess Bible* comes with plenty of sparkles, pink glossy pages, and the affirmation that the small readers are "daughters of a king!" After each story, girls can write their names into the narrative, reinforcing the lesson learned from the biblical princesses; in the story about Eve, "royal" denizen of Eden, girls are asked to fill in these blanks: "_____ is a special princess; _____ is sad when she does something bad." Good thing the Bibles remind little girls that Eve was a trouble-maker, the *real* point of Genesis 3.[5]

These are but two of many entries in a Bible market that seems flooded in pink sparkles. Every major evangelical publisher has its own princess entry, from Zondervan's NIV *Precious Princess Bible: The Holy Bible for Every Princess* to Thomas Nelson's lavender King James *Princess Bible.* For those princesses unable to understand the King's own English, Thomas Nelson also provides an International Children's Bible in a tiara version, "embellished with glitter and sparkly jewels," encased in a "clamshell box with a window to highlight the Bible's beautiful features." We all need to see the bling on our Bibles.

Each Bible promises to highlight the powerful stories of women in Scripture, though the framework placed around these scriptural stories reinforces expectations for what girls should enjoy and reminds them to be passive princesses waiting to be saved. These messages about what it means to be a "daughter of the king!" are amplified when compared to the Bibles marketed to boys, and help to convey exactly what girls should be because of their message about what girls *should not* be.

For example, Shelia Walsh's companion Bible for boys is called *God's Mighty Warrior Bible,* a clear counterpoint to the pink and glittery girls' Bible. The *Mighty Warrior Bible* has a blue cover festooned with shields and swords, and the product itself is targeted to children filled with "energy and imagination," but who may need to "learn how to be strong, honorable, courageous, and true." Rather than lessons on beauty and tips for how to serve one's family, boys learn in the *Mighty Warrior Bible* how to share God's word with friends, building in boys the evangelizing muscles they will need as church leaders; they can also read stories about biblical heroes who are God's mighty warriors, and the boys are given "adventure quests," providing activities to nurture the courageous spirit inherent in any boy.[6]

Walsh may be on the cutting edge of creating the icky-gender-stereotype Bibles, but her Princess and Warrior books opened the door for other competitors in the market. These include different variations of the *Action Bible,* the *Adventure Bible,* the *Super Heroes Bible,* the *Sports Bible,* and a *Mighty Warrior Bible* knock-off, the *Brave Knight Bible,* which creates the royal dichotomy boys and girls long for. According to the product description on Christianbooks.com, the *Brave Knight Bible* encourages boys to "vanquish their fiercest foes" using the "sword of God's Word." Through Scripture, translated in the

King's English, boys learn the character traits of "respect, honor, love, truth, bravery, and other knightly qualities," qualities that boys are clearly called to learn if they are to grow into strong Christian men.

These gendered messages assault children early and often within evangelical culture; conveyed through the Bible, they are intensified. Think about it: children are told that the Bible is the unfailing word of God and that Christians are supposed to venerate everything within biblical texts as sacred, unchanging. Then, girls are given Bibles with pink, glittering covers letting them know they are to serve their subjects; meanwhile, boys are given Bibles covered in swords and shields, letting them know they are to be adventurous and strong. In the minds of children, these messages complement each other: the Bible is God's word, the Bible tells me I am to be a princess, and so therefore I must be. As pernicious as the Disney Princess empire, the mythologies of princesses and princes perpetuated by Christian products help shape the reality of who children believe themselves to be. And God help those girls, or boys, who don't fit into the paradigm provided them by their pink or blue Bibles.

Building Princesses in Church

Samuel Williamson's blog post in July 2013 managed to stir controversy—and nearly one thousand comments—by challenging a Christian institution that many have considered sacrosanct: Sunday school. His post, "Is Sunday School Destroying Our Kids?" and subsequent book of the same title argue that Sunday school curricula "*lie* about God,…about the Bible, and…about the Gospel." Rather than teaching children about grace and love, Williamson says, the Sunday school lessons show children what it means to be "good little boys and girls" and that when they do become good, "God will love us and use us."[7]

When we look at the many princess-and-warrior Sunday school curricula now available for churches to use, Williamson's arguments make sense. In lesson after lesson, children are taught to be good little princesses and strong warriors. Some of this material also includes etiquette training, so that young ones know how to act like the perfect beings God apparently wants them to be. One such curricula typifying this trend is *Princess Training for the King's Glory*, a workbook that, in 2012, received accolades on numerous homeschooling web pages because it helped young girls "truly learn how to be the little princesses God has created them to be." The workbook includes a long section on character study, based on the premise that a girl's good characteristics come from her femininity. The author of *Princess Training* study asserts that, to become a daughter for the king, it's important to "toss" the world's understanding of femininity, and focus on what the Bible says about traits such as industriousness and wisdom, but also submissiveness and moral virtue. Most of the appropriate biblical verses for teaching a child femininity—one of the core principles in the Bible, the study suggests—are in Proverbs 31, of course, the go-to Scripture when it comes to evangelicals and any study of what a woman should do or be. After an initial discussion of femininity, the girls and their mothers are supposed to celebrate this biblical value with ribbons and chocolate treats, because "while hair, make-up, and bows do not teach femininity it does give a sense of the soft and gentle nature God put into women." The author concedes that some girls will not be into pink, but becoming God's princess will demand that mother and daughter spend ample time studying the biblical basis for femininity.[8] At the curriculum's conclusion, a tea party is suggested, because "girls of all ages enjoy a tea party," and "a tea party is synonymous with femininity."

Princess Training for the King's Glory is not the only curricular game in town. The market for religious instruction materials is flush with all manner of princess paraphernalia, as well as corresponding programs for boys. Royal Purpose ministries manages to package curricula for boys *and* girls, though the instructional kits remain separate: Princess Prep School for girls, and Warrior Prince Academy for boys, each promising to help guide children to discover an "identity in Christ" that is fundamentally different and absolutely gendered: one is all sparkles and glitter, the other steely breast plates and swords. In a promotional video for the programs, we learn that boys will learn about "leadership and service," and "how to dress for battle in God's armor." Girls will be instructed in "princess manners," and how they can become "true princesses" using the tools God has given them. The presumably separate but equal ministries have gained a broad following, with three- and five-day Royal Purpose-based camps being held all over Texas.[9]

Although the Royal Purpose ministries purports to help children discover their "true identity in Christ," the entire program is set up to guide girls and boys to identities constructed by a culture that says girls will be one way, and boys will be another. And, those socially constructed identities have been given the "biblical" badge, meaning they must be true, and right, and fixed–definitely *not* something created by the "secular" world, where the princess industrial complex continues to reign.

Women Can Be Princesses, Too

In *Wonder Women: Sex, Power, and the Quest for Perfection,* Debora Spar acknowledges the contradictory messages our culture sends young girls caught up in the princess empire. Most parents do a good job of letting girls know they can be anything they want to be, from a surgeon to an athlete to president of a university–as Spar is–or of the entire United States. The princess industrial complex undermines this message, telling girls they need to be pink, sparkly, a little sexy, and passive, and that a girl's biggest goal in life is to find Prince Charming. These contradictory messages are somewhat different in evangelicalism, in that there is no contradiction. Girls learn God has designed them for specific roles, and being a leader is certainly not among the roles God has in mind. As a daughter of the King, a girl's best bet is to put on the mantle of the princess and keep it there until Prince Charming shows up to save her, at which point she can start cooking and cleaning the castle.

Marketing products to Christian girls already immersed in princess culture might be understandable, but it seems a little more perplexing that grown women continue to buy into the princess mythos. Most women give up pretending to be princesses when they reach adulthood, recognizing–at least at some level–the problems in a billion-dollar industry that has covered the world's daughters in pink. Though Disney counts on some women wanting to connect with their princess pasts, as uber-popular events like the Disney Princess Half Marathon makes clear, few of the women who lace up for the race and even wear a tiara as they run will continue to imagine themselves as royalty when they finish their races.

In evangelical culture, though, many women continue to talk about being princesses, waiting for their heavenly king. In Bible study curricula, women can learn about how they are "all the King's daughters," and thus need "royalty training," which includes having royal tea. A number of blogs and Christian women's sites have writers who proclaim themselves "princesses of the King." Women turn to Tumblr and Pinterest sites with titles like "God's princess" to post pictures of themselves in tiaras, proclaiming they may not be cute or beautiful, but they are "God's princess!" The sites also include sayings about being daughters of the King, poems, Scripture verses, and letters from the King to his princesses, reminding them to be strong for the kingdom. Women are exhorted on these sites to wear their crowns, both visible and invisible, and to keep their heads high, lest their crowns fall off.

Sheri Rose Shepherd might be considered one generator of a princess industrial complex for mature Christian women. Her site, called "His Princess," includes a wide selection of "His Princess" books, information on "Fit for My King" online coaching, and "Daily His Princess Love Letters," which users can receive via text messaging. Shepherd's personal story is inspiring: an overweight child turned beauty pageant champion (she won Mrs. United States), Shepherd was a depressed and eating-disordered young woman who became a best-selling Christian author and a speaker at Christian women's conferences. Her message has also inspired countless women, who have found her resources empowering, giving them opportunities to see themselves as loved by God: a radical message for some, to be sure! Still, Shepherd's Princess books suggest women should assume the "biblical roles" that have become normative in evangelical culture; she relies on royalty metaphors that create a hierarchy, with men serving as kings, ruling over the princess/women as godlike figureheads. This kind of language dilutes Shepherd's empowering message, suggesting that women can be at once strong and capable, but also without much agency. [10]

Shepherd is certainly not alone in her inclination to figure God as a King, a Daddy, a Father in heaven. A cursory glance at blogs by Christian women show this pattern of metaphor so deeply entrenched that we rarely question what it means for women to continue imagining themselves as princesses well into adulthood, nor how women tend to infantilize their relationship to God by believing themselves to be "Daddy's Little Girl." Rather than helping develop a mature relationship with God, these princess metaphors are problematic in the ways they reflect women's understanding of themselves, and the ways they imagine women's understanding of their relationship with God. Coupled with an insistence that boys and men are warriors, fighting as God's righthand men, the princess metaphor conveys messages to girls and women about their place in God's "kingdom," and about the roles they should play. And those messages, embedded deep within the language we use, keep women from being all God intended them to be.

Taking Another Look: Why God Talk Matters

In contrast to Disney's Kings and Princesses, the Bible contains multiple images and names for God. This variety reflects human individuality and uniqueness. Examining the biblical terrain takes us beyond marketing gimmicks to the deeper Divine potentiality in all of us.

We begin this journey with Hagar and her son, Ishmael. Hagar was an outsider: an Egyptian and a slave. Her status meant Sarah and Abraham could use her as they saw fit, illustrated when Abraham reminded Sarah, "Your slave-girl is in your power; do to her as you please" (Gen. 16:6). Sarah did just that, treating her so harshly that Hagar ran away into the desert. While in the desert, an angel appeared to Hagar and told her she would have a son who reflected God's awareness of her affliction. Her child would be called Ishmael because God had heard her despair.

Those conditioned to read this story from Sarah's perspective see Hagar's reassurance as a consolation prize. But when we listen closely, we see this displaced Egyptian slave woman not only heard the angel, she named the Divine presence in her midst. Hagar–not Abraham, not Sarah–identified who had met her in her time of abandonment and need. "You are El-roi" (Gen. 16:13), she remarked, the God who sees me.

Hagar's desert experience comes into sharper focus when compared with Moses' epiphany. While tending his father-in-law's sheep, Moses was stopped by a burning bush with a voice calling out to him, "Moses, Moses!" When he stepped closer, God said to him, "I AM WHO I AM" (Ex. 3:4, 14). Moses, one of the great patriarchs in Jewish and Christian traditions, received this revelation from God. In contrast, Hagar does not merely receive a Divine decree; by naming the Divine, she participates in revelation. She named God and by extension identified God's character: one who sees.

Taking Initiative

Hagar's story involves a shift, from receiver to participant, a move especially difficult for women who have been taught to disregard their experiences and to accept the male naming of God: Father, King, Lord, Master, Shepherd, Son. The pervasiveness of God's maleness is so thorough that questioning its ubiquity is considered heretical in evangelical circles. If you think we are over-stating the situation, try suggesting to any evangelical leader changing the words of a well-loved hymn to be more gender-inclusive, or of asking a pastor to use "heavenly parent" rather than "heavenly father," and measure the response.

Despite such outward resistance, there is also the challenge of trusting one's experience, learning to name God for ourselves.[11] For many women the source of masculine bias is within. We have been so immersed in masculine ways of living and being we struggle to identify the problem. Eventually, however, the contradictions rise to the surface: women, no matter how much we are conditioned to do otherwise, know intuitively that God is not male; that men are not more godly; that our spiritually has been stunted because we have accepted men's experiences and therefore their theologies as our own.

Hagar also knew what it meant to be in the desert, to feel the devastation of isolation. But, she trusted her experience of God enough to identify the Divine being in her midst. Following Hagar's model, we too have the ability to trust ourselves. Instead of accepting the sexism embedded in our churches, we have the capacity to embrace a different way.

The place we must begin is fundamental: it is in how we speak of God.

Speaking of God

Most Christians readily acknowledge God encompasses all gender, and yet they subordinate this confession in practice, using only masculine language and images when referring to God. Countless times we've heard people say, in one breath, "God is not confined by our finite understanding of gender," only with their next breath to pray, "Our Father." The dichotomy between thinking and doing seems almost impossible to correct.

When masculine images and names for God are used exclusively–such as Lord, Master, King, Father, Son–this elevates one aspect of divinity above all others. Fundamentally, to speak of God in one dimension is to limit God, who becomes just another golden calf in a different time and place. If God becomes king or lord, and women his princesses, we begin to see God only as an overseer, someone making the decisions for his subjects, who sit in their castles, waiting for Prince Charming to arrive.

Another consequence of a masculine-only understanding of God is what it says about humans. If God is male, feminist theologian Mary Daly aptly theorized, male is God.[12] Masculine images and language for God support and endorse patriarchal society, with preference for boys and men. Men, by virtue of their maleness, become more closely identified to God. And, while to a patriarchal male this may sound enticing, the reality is that men suffer from this anemic portrayal of God by their shorter life expectancies, their imbalanced work/family expectations, their disassociation with their children, and their unrealistic burdens to be responsible for society and family.

And, of course, a masculine-only understanding of God has detrimental effects on women as well. According to Rev. Dr. Jann Aldredge-Clanton, women who think of God in male terms have a tendency to be more self-abasing than others; they defer to others in relationships, seeing themselves as subordinate.[13] Augustine said as much centuries ago when he claimed that, because of her body, a woman is not made in the image of God. Is there any wonder Simone de Beauvoir coined the term "the second sex" for women?[14]

A benign approach to this challenge of how to speak about God is to avoid using pronouns for God. For years this was Kendra's approach in teaching college Bible courses. With practice, she learned to speak and to write in ways that circumvented the issue; students were none the wiser. They seldom caught on to her tactic and in this way she did not feel guilty for contributing to a masculine portrayal of God; she also didn't find herself in the Provost's office on a daily basis, defending her "unorthodox" view of divinity.

But, over the past few years, we've come to see this approach is problematic because it does nothing to re-conceptualize God. With no countervailing alternatives, the masculine images of God remain too dominant and pervasive to be undone. Additionally, refusing to embrace feminine images and language for God endorses the sexism embedded within us: that women are inferior to men, that to speak of the "womb of God" is somehow too earthy or messy, that to think of God as Mother produces unsettling images. Or, more to the point: a God with breasts is just too sexy, an understanding of God that is flat-out wrong.

To release the patriarchal hold on the Divine, we must take seriously the unlimited ways God is portrayed in the Bible, realizing metaphors are never to be confused with the reality and that metaphors are always approximate and referential. Metaphors help us to identify some aspect of God, but to equate God with one particular metaphor is to substitute the metaphor for God.

The Spirit of God

Spirit is one of the common ways we think of God because this is how we experience the Divine in our ordinary lives: the goose-bumps that surprise us when someone shares her triumph over a struggle, the sense of awe we feel when seeing a roaring waterfall, the unexplainable feeling of transcendence we have when singing a favorite hymn with our faith communities.

In Hebrew, the word for Spirit, *Ruah,* is grammatically feminine, a fact that itself does not indicate femaleness. Nevertheless, *Ruah*'s activities are often reminiscent of things women traditionally did in ancient Israelite society, including forming new life in the womb (Ps. 139:13); crying from the pangs of labor (Isa. 42:14); being a midwife (Ps. 22:9–10); and demonstrating a mother's responsibility (Num. 11:11–12).

Appearing before these images, however, is the poignant yet overlooked one found in the opening verses of Genesis, in which the Spirit is "moving" (alternatively, "fluttering") over the face of the waters. Genesis 1:2 says, "Now the earth was formless and empty, darkness was over the surface of the deep, and the Spirit of God was hovering over the waters" (NIV). A similar picture of God is presented in Deuteronomy 32:11, in which a bird flutters over her young.

How often have we glossed over Genesis 1:2, wanting perhaps to get to the creation of sun and moon or animals and humans, and in our haste ignored the feminine *Ruah* right at the beginning, hovering over her creation? Why have we missed the image of God giving birth to the world as the waters unveil the beautiful landscape and light, plants and animals and humans? She watched all of it with the great care of a mother bird who watches her young break out of their protective shells and into the nest she lovingly built.

Similarly, central to most evangelical understandings of what it means to be a Christian is the image of being born again. Nicodemus, according to the gospel of John, wanted to be born again, and so he asked Jesus how it was possible that someone already born could be reborn (Jn. 3). Surely, he reasoned, one cannot enter a mother's womb again. Jesus could have dismissed the birth metaphor, relying instead on another way of talking about what it meant to embrace the way of Jesus, but instead he maintained the image of birth. "What is born of the flesh is flesh, and what is born of the Spirit is spirit" (Jn.

3:6), he said. The way Jesus explained to Nicodemus the transformation he sought was by describing God's mothering act, bringing new life into the world.

The metaphor in this famous Scripture passage and subsequent usage is obvious. Yet we see the almost complete obliteration of God as Mother, despite the numerous reading clues: to be born is the act of birthing. The water breaks as the womb releases its fluid in preparation for birth. When the time is right the fetus moves through the birth canal to enter the world. God endures the struggle to birth us into being. She brings new life into existence after having nurtured it in her womb.

Another name for Spirit is *Shekinah* used by early Jewish scholars, to mean "to dwell." Derived from the Hebrew verb *shakhan,* the *Shekinah* dwelt among the Israelites as they were led out of exile and wandered in the wilderness (Ex. 25:8 and 29:45–46). A bright pillar of fire at night or a faithful cloud by day, *Shekinah* was steadfast in Her constant presence.[15]

Like Moses in his determination to reach the so-called "promised land," readers have been in too much of a hurry to contemplate the vagaries of desert wandering. The people were without a home and in a most inhospitable place. There is nothing enticing about being in the desert. And yet this is where the *Shekinah* was; as Elizabeth Johnson elaborates, "When the people are brought low then the *Shekinah* lies in the dust, anguished by human suffering." In She-Who-Dwells-Within, the compassion of God is evident.[16]

Feminine Images of God

The Spirit of God hovering over Her creation, bringing all life into being with Her diligent care and Her steadfast presence: these important images have been neglected. Also needing recovering, according to Phyllis Trible and others, is the linguistic relationship between *compassion* and *womb.* To read of God's compassion is to note the womb is trembling, grieved by pain.[17] Failure to see this connection is aided by Bible translations that do not note the relationship, including the *New Revised Standard Version.*

An illustration demonstrates the ease with which the feminine has been masked. Jeremiah 31:20 says, "Is Ephraim my dear son? / Is he the child I delight in? / As often as I speak against him, / I still remember him. / Therefore I am deeply moved for him; / I will surely have mercy on him, / says the LORD." Note the shared linguistic roots of compassion (showing mercy) and womb (deeply moved); it is evident this is a maternal image. God's womb is trembling as She has mercy for Her son. Or, as Johnson translates, "I will truly show motherly-compassion upon him."[18]

Other feminine images for God require much less imagination if, as readers, we are introduced to the plurality of possibilities afforded by the original language. A case in point occurs in the Old Testament, where the Hebrew term *El shaddai* is used for God. Usually translated "all sufficient one," an equally valid translation of *El shaddai* is "the God of many breasts" or "the Many-breasted One." Far from being the God who leads people into battle, the Many-Breasted God conveys a very different impression: One who nurtures and cares for, a God of sustenance and abiding presence.

The most developed embodiment of God's presence in the Old Testament is Wisdom (*Hokmah* in Hebrew, *Sophia* in Greek). Depicted as feminine, Wisdom is described with roles associated with women and women's work in ancient Israel: sister, mother, preparer of food, and eminent hostess. In Proverbs 1, 8, and 9–the three major poems about Wisdom–Sophia is a figure who, while transcendent, also delights in Her creation, calling people to life.

As described in a street preacher metaphor, Sophia in Proverbs 8 displays knowledge and insight. She instructs Her listeners, "For whoever finds me finds life / and obtains favor from the LORD; / but those who miss me injure themselves; / all who hate me love death" (vv. 35–36). Proverbs 9 shows Wisdom, who has built a house, prepared a table, and welcomed others in to dine. The similarity to Jesus' later invitation is hard to ignore. "Come, eat of my bread / and drink of the wine I have mixed" (v. 5), She says.

There is more, of course, but that is our point. Masculine images have dominated our understandings not because the feminine images are absent, but because they have been buried. But we do not have to remain limited by what we have been taught, and can cultivate new understandings of God and ourselves.

Jesus and the Gospels

One of the most ubiquitous excuses for the patriarchal stranglehold on divinity comes from Jesus being a man. Even though some evangelicals assume our feminist convictions mean we think Jesus is problematic for post-patriarchal Christianity, we have no reason to dispute the maleness of the person we know as Jesus from Galilee. The misappropriation emerges, though, if someone extrapolates Jesus' sexuality as normative and other expressions of sexuality as qualitatively different and inferior.

Our understanding of Jesus is that he was an embodiment of God and his sexuality was merely one aspect of who he was, but no more important than his age, race, social location, or anything else. His life provides a glimpse of the story of God in real life. But it wasn't his maleness on display but rather the Wisdom (Sophia) of God showing us the goodness and compassion and justice of God. In this way, Jesus as the Incarnation of Sophia is a remarkable image of mutuality.

Another illustration of balance exists in the three parables found in Luke 15: the lost sheep, the lost coin, and the prodigal son. Of the three, the lost coin has been largely absent in our collective memory, but in it Jesus uses a poor woman to represent God. God is like a woman who searches for her lost coin and then celebrates with her friends when she finds it.

Parables are one way Jesus' teachings survived long after he did. Like a Buddhist *koan,* parables of Jesus require living with a puzzle, a paradox that refuses to be easily unraveled. When Jesus told the parable of the woman searching for her lost coin, we imagine his listeners nodding their heads in agreement as he tells them the woman looked for her coin in her house by lighting a lamp and sweeping the floor. Since women were confined to their homes, not allowed to circulate in public without a man, it made sense to Jesus' audience that the woman was in her house. It would have been poorly lit. Lighting her lamp afforded her some measure of light, but not enough to see her coin. To find it she also needed her broom. Bent over as she carefully drew it across her earth floor, she listened for the tinkling sound it would make when it came in contact with the bristles.

These natural life circumstances created a sense of familiarity. Those listening to Jesus would have thought everything made perfect sense—except for one detail. The shepherd was an established image for God, as was a father. But here, Jesus introduced a new image they would have found shocking. It was the twist. The woman who searched for her coin represented God. God, the good shepherd—sure. God, a father welcoming home a wayward son—of course. God, a poor woman searching her house—unheard of. But this is the picture Jesus painted that day on the dusty outskirts of Galilee.

When God Looks Like Me

The fantasy world of princes and princesses relies on a one-dimensional image of God, resulting in a spiritual immaturity prominently on display throughout much of American Christianity. If people figure themselves only as princesses wearing sparkly tiaras, they remain entrenched in the make-believe world of childhood. As daughters of a King, they miss the opportunity to experience the multifaceted nature of being alive and in relationship with an even more complex God.

Knowing God only as King and Lord promotes one dimension of deity: one that is powerful and controlling, and who takes away women's ability to act in the world. Working around the edges of this patriarchal pattern results in women missing out on understanding Sophia—and themselves—in ways that might make their lives and their relationships richer. A student of ours who experimented with praying to Mother God for one month reflected, "Sometimes when I listen, I hear Her so distinctly. And, at others, He talked over Her. When my Mother speaks She never tries to displace Father, but He tells me She is not real." This student's experience conveys the crux of the challenge we face. Until we take seriously the need for our language and images of God to be fully expressed, sexism will exist in our workplaces, educational institutions, and, most prominently, in our churches.

Chapter Nine

Biblical Womanhood Redefined

The older woman wearing a Navajo print t-shirt had been the audience member every speaker hopes to have. She was attentive, laughing loudly and giving us an "Amen!" now and then, offering sympathetic nods to let us know she understood. Nearly everyone else in the audience followed her cues; we felt like rock stars, playing to a rapt crowd. Okay, so we were only speaking to a crowd of one hundred at a Christian feminism conference; our set, merely a presentation of evangelical popular culture's negative effects on college-aged women.

After our speech, the woman sidled up to us and squeezed us in a huge embrace.

"Thank you for sharing this," she said. "Since I'm kind of outside evangelicalism I had no idea. Don't you get depressed by all the bad messages about women you hear?"

We laughed, out of discomfort and because others had voiced similar concerns about our research already. Then we gave her the answer we'd developed to this familiar question: "Yes." And, "No."

Studying evangelical popular culture and its negative messages about gender can be discouraging. The messages are so pervasive, so damaging. We see the ways evangelical popular culture has eroded the confidence of women we teach, making them less likely to seek out leadership roles, more likely to question their own voices. We see how those messages have affected our friends and family members, compelling people we know and love deeply to second-guess life choices, believing themselves less than fully human. And we have recognized the ways those messages have even complicated our self-conceptions, our ability to succeed in our vocations, and our faith journeys.

So yes, studying evangelical popular culture and its messages about gender has been discouraging. And, yet, we have discovered the key to remaining hopeful, to affirming that these messages can be combated and women can find ways to be all God means for them to be. In great part, we believe reading the Bible can provide an antidote to the one-dimensional, patriarchal narrative that has informed evangelicalism's understanding of gender. Saying good-bye to God as the angry, judgmental king to whom daughters/princesses must pledge fidelity allows us to free ourselves from the shackles of patriarchy, inviting us to understand better the amazingly rich, deep, ever-unfolding mystery of God.

What can be discouraging about that?

We have also reflected on our own spiritual journeys, and on the ways others have helped us become all we are meant to be. We certainly believe this: becoming all God wants us to be cannot be done in isolation, nor can it be easily accomplished without communities of support, with people who affirm the need for gender justice, who recognize the problematic messages women are prone to internalize, who feel convicted to overturn dominant and patriarchal narratives about the Bible, and who remind us, again and again, that we are also, all of us, created in God's image. Right communities also extend an extravagant dose of grace and mercy, taking seriously the core of Jesus' ministry, and the love for *all* people that resides at its center.

This, at least, is nothing about which we might feel discouragement.

Becoming Titus 2

In our time studying evangelical popular culture, we have learned that, as women, we are apparently responsible for sin's entry into the world, thanks to Eve. We discovered that our role model for right living is Ruth, waiting for her Prince Charming, Boaz. We've been told to remain submissive and silent, that men in our lives should take charge. We must imitate the Proverbs 31 woman in what we say or do; we must be all things to all people. These messages of "shoulds" and "oughts" weigh down on us, for we realize—by some standards of so-called "biblical womanhood"—we do not measure up at all.

For these two authors, our Boaz-searching days are far behind us. We've failed as Proverbs 31 women, are not silent women, and we've probably been deceived by an apple-wielding serpent now and again.

We are old in the teeth, or at least middle-aged, and have fallen short
again and again, never living up to becoming the biblical women
evangelical popular culture has asked us to be.

There is still hope for us. As middle-aged women, considered by
all accounts to be "older" in the church, evangelical culture tells us
there is one role we can yet play: that of the Titus 2 woman, based on
Titus 2:3–5: "Likewise, tell the older women to be reverent in
behavior, not to be slanderers or slaves to drink; they are to teach
what is good, so that they may encourage the young women to love
their husbands, to love their children, to be self-controlled, chaste,
good managers of the household, kind, being submissive to their
husbands, so that the word of God may not be discredited."

As with much of evangelical culture, the Titus 2 woman has been
created and commodified, letting us know exactly who and what we
should be, our roles as older women considered "special" and
"important" and "designed by God"–and considerably limited to the
private sphere, where we are to mentor younger women in how they
too might become successful homemakers and mothers.

Mentors can provide significant support and guidance, and we
have both benefited from having mentors in our personal and
professional lives. But books such as *Becoming a Titus 2 Woman* (Martha
Peace) remind us that mentorship is limited to teaching younger
women to excel at housework, at dressing modestly, and at being
better mothers.[1] In *The Titus 2 Woman*, Susan Godfrey asserts a Titus
2 woman rejects "feminism and worldly standards" in favor of "godly
standards," which include being sober and avoiding too much wine,
being chaste, loving their children, and being keepers of the home.
The Titus 2 woman is also supposed to pass these characteristics on to
younger women, and if she does not, she is committing blasphemy.
"When we as Christian women do not act as the women described in
Titus 2," Godfrey writes, "we are blasphemous of our most Holy
God... What makes the situation worse is that many churches are
teaching women to act differently from what Scripture tells them to
act. And, if they're not outright teaching women to do the wrong
thing, they aren't teaching anything at all."[2]

Carolyn Mahaney, in *Feminine Appeal*, writes about how the
passages in Titus 2 provide a "truth" Christian women are desperate
to hear. "More than any other, this Scripture has shaped my own
understanding of biblical womanhood," Mahaney writes. "For the
past twenty-nine years, these words have guided me in my role as wife

and mother." Though older women need to take up the "special" challenge of mentoring, Mahaney suggests women of all ages can instruct others in being godly wives and mothers, as well as being "self-controlled, pure, kind, workers at home, and submissive," all part of God's plan for women.[3] In her book *Sweet Journey,* Teri Maxwell passes along the character traits of a Titus 2 woman en masse; sitting down one-on-one for mentorship appointments is not possible. Maxwell promises to be a Titus 2 woman to her readers, who then can become Titus 2 women for their daughters, who in turn can become Titus 2 women for *their* daughters: a godly pyramid scheme of sorts that will create Titus 2 women into perpetuity.[4]

If an older woman feels ill-equipped to teach her younger charges how to be sober, modest, and submissive, she has plenty of instructional material at her disposal to help her learn. There are Bible studies galore she can work through, as well as self-improvement plans. One Bible study on Titus 2 by John Barnett takes readers through twelve characteristics of an older Titus 2 woman; this writer of the "Being a Titus 2 Woman" plan suggests younger women only need to learn seven of these twelve.[5] Fundamentally, writes Barnett in his Bible study, women who aspire to Titus 2 need to love their husbands, serving them with grace and kindness and making an investment in them; and if a husband is unlovable, it is the responsibility of the Titus 2 woman to figure things out, to train herself to love him if necessary, else she commit a grave sin.[6]

Other Bible studies likewise focus on the Titus 2 woman's love for her husband, as well as the necessity of being a skilled homemaker, so much so that single older women, or older women without children, must feel as if they have nothing to teach younger generations. This exclusive focus on married women with children seems normative in evangelical popular culture: *of course* godly women will be married and have children, which is part of God's design for women.[7]

If a simple Bible study isn't enough to inspire a woman to assume her Titus 2 role, there are entire websites dedicated to the task. At the Titus 2: Women of The Word website, women can learn about the ten principles of Titus 2 womanhood. Another Titus 2 website (titus2mentoringwomen.com) teaches about successful mentorships. Free of charge to women willing to sign a "mentor covenant," the Titus 2 mentorship program is extensive, providing a "12-month track for married women," though the site concedes that some of the principles might work for single women, too.[8] And, over at Titus2.

com, women will be encouraged, equipped, and exhorted to build their families in the principles of Jesus Christ. Primarily for homeschooled families, the site includes resources such as a Titus 2 cookbook and charts that allow moms "stress-free chores" as they manage their households.[9]

What seems to lack clarity is the age at which women slip from Proverbs 31 aspirations to being Titus 2 women. Some evangelical writers assert menopause itself marks this shift, as women are no longer able to bear children and thus are burdened with the stain of old age; for some, a woman can claim Titus 2 status any time she mentors someone younger than she is, including her own daughters. Whatever the appropriate age, Christian marketers are at the ready to sell all manner of Titus 2 inspiration. Pinterest offers numerous Titus 2 sites at which users have pinned inspirational sayings to help spur older women into their mentor roles, including links to "The Ultimate Guide to Titus 2: Mothering" and Titus 2 apron patterns. One woman, writing "in the spirit of Titus 2," composed a chart on "Why Wives Need to Give Their Husbands More Sex," with clear and convicting reasons why sex can be good, from burning more calories to providing a more youthful appearance. Less clear was why this was an important Titus 2 moment: Was the writer mentoring younger women in the art of submission, or that of seduction?[10]

There are plenty of ways to critique Titus 2 Woman products, sermons, blogs, and books. Often, they exemplify the commodification of the Bible, an attempt to get people to hand over money in easy exchange for material goods that, when labeled "biblical," somehow become sanctified. Titus 2 products also create another box to place around women, a box built on a textual interpretation informed by contemporary cultural stereotypes about gender. But we would also argue that evangelical popular culture uses Titus 2 as a way to establish division, separating younger women from the older. Titus 2 has become a way to delineate women who still have a significant role to play in their homes and communities, making a silo of sorts around those who are older, and must now take on the specific–and limited– role as mentors to the young.

This divisive rhetoric is not unusual for evangelical popular culture, which seems to operate best by creating markers suggesting there are insiders and outsiders, the loveable and the reviled, those who deserve grace and those who do not. As we (the authors) have immersed ourselves in evangelical popular culture over the last few years, we have seen over and over again the ways divisive rhetoric has made it clear who belongs with the in crowd, and who must remain on the margins. This language is often clear and definitive, setting one group against another, and establishing that "our" group is somehow better—more loved by God, more godly, more faithful—than those other people.

Often those lines are drawn with language such as "biblical manhood" and "biblical womanhood," or "God's design for gender," or "special gender roles." Often these lines are also drawn with references to Scripture, specifically to those letters presumably written by Paul, telling women to be quiet, to remain in their private spheres, to willfully submit to husbands—and, in the case of Titus 2, to teach younger women the art of homemaking. Often, those lines serve to keep women, both young and old, from becoming all they could possibly be.

When we gave our presentation at the Christian Feminism Today conference in 2012, we most certainly might have seen the older women there as our Titus 2 mentors, showing us the way to act as Christian women. We were considered the young ones at the conference, learning and worshiping with others old enough to be our parents. The woman in the Navajo print t-shirt, sending up an amen now and then for our work? She could have well been our Titus 2 guide, revealing to us the appropriate ways Christian women might navigate the contemporary world. She might even have given us some recipes, some insight into what our marriages might look like, some advice for the difficulties we would face as middle-aged women. Instead, she considered us her equals, peers on our own spiritual journeys, in need of encouragement and support, rather than top-down instruction. Evangelical culture would ask us to see this relationship differently, would ask us to see most of our relationships through the skewed lens of hierarchy and division.

Wherever there is separation, wherever there is hierarchy, wherever there is one group set against another, there is no equity, no sense of the radical community to which Jesus calls us all. So long as there continues to be a divide—in Titus 2 and elsewhere—so long as the Bible is used to "put women in their place," so long as evangelical culture continues to suggest some people are definitely *not* created in God's image, there is no truly Christian community, at least not of the sort Jesus' ministry might compel his believers to create.

And that, most certainly, *is* discouraging.

Taking Another Look

First and Second Timothy and Titus have great appeal to certain segments of American Christians, but what do they tell us about our spiritual heritage, especially if we find their misogynistic tendencies problematic?

The Pastoral Epistles, as these three letters are commonly called, because they contain pastoral advice, reveal the distance the early church had travelled in approximately one hundred years since its inception, a distance marked by Christian expansion and regression. In its early stages, the followers of Jesus were not a threat to Roman power. With their leader executed, only a band of misfits was left, a wandering group of women and men who were poor, whose skills were limited mostly to fishing and tax collecting.

But as they spread geographically and increased numerically, they also assimilated politically and economically elite members. As wealthier people with political clout converted to Christianity, what was once a rag-tag group of religious followers who posed little concern to ruling leaders became a threat to the unity and effectiveness of Roman imperial power.

This shift in who composed the Christian movement was one aspect of its growth in the years following Jesus' ministry. Another aspect involved different assessments of the group's relationship to the Roman Empire, as well as what they thought about family relationships in general and women in particular. These changes occur as the New Testament unfolds. For example, the gospels show Jesus' opposition to Roman authorities, even as later writings appear to dismiss such political dissension in favor of being good and faithful citizens of the empire. Regarding women, Jesus dispelled cultural restrictions, inviting women to cross boundaries of exclusion. The gospels portray women traveling with Jesus, opening their homes to him, providing financial support for his ministry, and becoming evangelists in their own right. Paul also worked closely with women. His letters convey how Christian communities struggled to overcome social norms in order to implement the values of equality. In implementing such counter-cultural groups, these churches drew the attention of those around them.

But later New Testament letters such as the Pastoral Epistles no longer maintain these visions of alternative lifestyles. In their place are affirmations of cultural norms. This regression is one of the primary reasons many biblical scholars do not think Paul wrote 1 and 2

Timothy and Titus. Still, if they were not written by Paul, they are included in the New Testament and should be heard as part of the enduring Christian witness.

Titus Chapter Two

The second chapter of Titus specifies behavior for older men, older women, younger men, and slaves. This vision of a hierarchical household stands in stark contrast to Paul's claim of equality. At odds with the early baptismal formula that no difference exists between women and men in the body of Christ (Gal. 3:28), Titus 2 outlines specific behaviors germane for a distinct group within the community of faith, instructions that stipulate men as superior and women as inferior. Because these instructions are a departure from the vision of Jesus and Paul, we think there is reason to take another look at what such admonitions might indicate before rushing to judgment, deciding they either need to be implemented today as a way to refute feminism or dismissed as sexist and irrelevant to contemporary Christian communities.

Delving into the possibilities behind these instructions provides insight about the changing Christian movement. For example, when the author of Titus instructs women to behave in a submissive manner and be concerned primarily for their households, we wonder whether some women were *not* doing this; who were, rather, operating more like Paul, working as established evangelists and teachers. Their freedom, while acceptable early in the Christian movement, was no longer deemed appropriate.

The presence of this admonishment suggests some communities accepted as necessary a hierarchical household such as the one stipulated in Titus 2, while others continued to live in ways that set them apart precisely because of their rejection of all forms of hierarchy, including not only between women and men, but also slaves and masters.

Bart Ehrman, a well-known New Testament historian, suggests closer analysis of these two distinctly different visions of Christian community offers further clues about women and their lives in ancient Rome.[11] Paul believed Jesus would return from heaven in his lifetime. Because of this, Paul, who himself was single, urged others to also remain unmarried. This decision included a caveat about sexuality—one we can imagine was directed specifically toward men. Paul cautioned that if someone could not remain celibate, then marriage would be a preferable alternative. Women, however, probably heard Paul's instructions differently. For them, the call to celibacy and to a life of evangelism might have held out a new and exciting alternative to marriage. In contrast to social expectations, women in Christianity had a viable option to explore, another life path, one with purpose beyond that of being a wife and mother.

Evidence supporting this alternative vision exists in an ancient narrative that was not included in the New Testament, called *The Acts of Paul and Thecla.*[*] Thecla, according to this account, was engaged to a wealthy man. However, upon hearing Paul preach, she broke her engagement in order to learn more from Paul and, ultimately, to work with him. Even though her fiancé and mother conspired to have her imprisoned, hoping to return her to her proper place as a wife, she survived hazards including being placed in the arena to face down wild beasts. God, the narrative says, enabled Thecla to remain liberated from a family structure.

Whether or not Paul knew about this document or would have recognized within it his vision of Christian community, early Christians popularized it, copying the document in several languages.

Changing Circumstances

Over time, Paul's rationale for remaining celibate weakened. He expected Jesus to return in his lifetime, but it turned out he was wrong. Eventually this conviction of Jesus' imminent return, which required putting off all family matters, abated, replaced by a rationale for how to create a Christian household. No longer was celibacy heralded as the most faithful response to the gospel; restraint from creating a family became creating the right kind of family.

With Paul's death in 64 C.E., the Christian movement entered a new stage. Devoid of Jesus and Paul, and nearly two generations removed from its earliest expressions, the Christian community no longer could assert Jesus was returning soon. And, because of the growth it enjoyed, no longer was it a group easily dismissed by Roman authorities.

---

[*]As Ehrman points out, it is not surprising to find in this document that the people most enticed by an unconventional familial option were women, including Thecla, who appears in this account as Paul's eager disciple, her life a window into what may have been the experience of many women. See Ehrman, 290.
The Acts of Paul and Thecla can be found on various Internet cites, including the following: http://www.pbs.org/wgbh/pages/frontline/shows/religion/maps/primary/thecla.html (accessed December 5, 2014).

This is the political and social context of Titus 2, at which time there were, at a minimum, two minds about the social status of women: one that outlined liberation, including the possibility of singleness and celibacy; and another that advocated for the role of wife and mother. *The Acts of Paul and Thecla* aligned with the former, while the Pastoral Epistles (1 and 2 Timothy and Titus), the ones ultimately chosen to be included in the New Testament, aligned with the latter.[12]

In *The Acts of Paul and Thecla,* not only is Thecla on par with Paul as an evangelist, she has the ability to make her own decisions, to trust she is following what God wants her to do, to experience no familial encumbrances that could inhibit her work in any way. Confirmation of Thecla resided in miracles through which her life was spared, even when she was attacked by beasts. In the narrative, in no way was she secondary to Paul—or to any other person, for that matter.

In contrast, the Pastoral Epistles focused on creating orderly communities, ones without any false teachings or problems. To accomplish this, pastors were instructed to appoint male leaders who were married (1 Tim. 3:2–5; 12) and who kept their households in order (1 Tim. 3:4, 12). Women were told to be silent in churches (1 Tim. 2:12); they were seen as prone to sin and deception (1 Tim. 2:14); they were instructed to be serious and temperate (perhaps suggesting women aren't "serious and temperate" enough) (1 Tim. 3:11); and their salvation was made possible through bearing children, something Jesus never intimated (1 Tim. 2:15). Further, wives were taught to be appropriately submissive (Titus 2:5), and older women were instructed to ensure younger women knew how to keep their households in order and be submissive to their husbands (Titus 2:5). Finally, the author of 1 Timothy stipulated that his leaders should speak out against those who advocated for celibacy, a far cry from Paul's early admonitions, for sure (1Tim. 4:3).

The independent Thecla, and her reliance upon God's revelation, in the end could be no match for the survival techniques necessary to sustain a movement experiencing increasing animosity and opposition because of its successful expansion geographically and socio-politically.

The Good News of Titus Two

Even though the endorsement of Greco-Roman values won the day over the more counter-cultural convictions of Jesus and Paul, some countervailing Christian communities stayed the course. Titus confirms their existence by the instructions it provides. And even though *The Acts of Paul and Thecla* sheds light on this view through the tale of one particular woman in her courageous and faithful determination to follow God, there are other narratives within the New Testament that echo such inclusion.

In Romans 16 Paul calls attention to several people who were instrumental in Rome's faith community. Of the twenty-eight individuals who are named, ten are women: Phoebe, Prisca, Mary, Junia, Tryphaena, Tryphosa, Persis, the mother of Rufus, Julia, and the sister of Nereus. Further, of the ones identified for commendation, five are women: Prisca, Mary, Junia, Persis, and the mother of Rufus. In a society in which women and men routinely cooperate, there is little remarkable about these lists. But in the context of Greco-Roman society, in which men were viewed as superior and women were largely restricted to the private realm, the women in this list take on new significance.

Paul's letter to the Romans even appears to have been carried there by Phoebe, whom Paul identifies in chapter 16. He says she is a deacon of the church at Cenchreae and a benefactor or patron of many, including himself. The term used for deacon means "minister," even though many have distorted it by translating the word as "servant." One can imagine that, as a leader from the Christian community where Paul was currently residing, Phoebe, in addition to reading the letter to the Roman church, would also have ably answered their questions. There is no surprise from Phoebe, from Paul, or from the Romans, that Phoebe provided this ministerial task.

The surprise emerges instead from readers today who misunderstand not only Paul's commitment to equality but also the social context of early Christian worship. While modern-day American Christians usually experience church as distinct from home, this was not the case with the earliest followers of Jesus, who met for teaching and worship in homes. Domestic structures were the birthplace of Christianity, and the realm where women operated most freely.

Households featured prominently, for example, in the gospels as locations for meals and Jesus' intimate teaching. In Paul's letters, Prisca and Aquila have a church in their house (1 Cor. 16:19; Rom. 16:3–5), as does Philemon with Apphia, our sister (Philemon 1:2). Nympha maintains a church in her house in Laodicea (Col. 4:15), while it appears Chloe may also have hosted a regular gathering based on information in 1 Corinthians (1:11). As Carolyn Osiek and David Balch explain, the structures of personal houses in the first century most likely determined the contour of Christian worship.[13] When numbers became too large to fit into a local house, another location was secured. In this way, women who opened their homes to the Christian movement assumed leadership in the community. At the very least, there is no evidence to the contrary, suggesting women may have provided their homes for gatherings but faded into the background while an appropriate male provided oversight.

Not only did women lead in some of the communities founded by Paul, but some were of higher social status than males, and Paul had no problem associating with their positions. Phoebe held one of these positions, according to Romans 16, in which Paul says Phoebe is not only a deacon, but the benefactor of many, including Paul. Patronage was an aspect of ancient Roman society and indicated "a mutual relationship between unequals for the exchange of services and goods."[14] The client provided protection and thereby gained access to political power while the patron acquired political support and gained prestige and stature in the eyes of one's peers.

Even though in general women had lower status than men, it was possible for a woman of higher status to be a patron to a male client with lower status. When Paul notes that Phoebe is his patron, he announces to the Roman church that Phoebe is higher in status than he, which would provide all the more reason for individuals in the Roman church to respond favorably to her presence.

Similar places of privilege would likely have existed for all people who opened their homes to the expanding church. In these situations, the host of the group would take on the position of a patron, especially by offering a place to gather, and she or he would have enjoyed all of the social expectations such a role played. In return, the client (those in the church) responded appropriately with honor and gratitude for the patron.[15]

Contrary to the preference for a patriarchal household in 1 and 2 Timothy and Titus, Paul's endorsement of Phoebe and five other women in Romans 16 is good news—then and today. In the ancient Mediterranean world, male dominance was a daily reality felt by women who at every turn were seen as less than fully human. Despite this overall mindset, economics had the potential to disrupt the patriarchal structure because social status trumped gender. When women owned property or ran businesses or exercised political patronage, they undermined the assumed limitations of gender.

Because of his position as the leading evangelist to the Gentiles, Paul could have stipulated that, despite one's status, women should be subject to male authority or male domination. But he deliberately avoided these opportunities and instead called attention to the fact that some women had a higher status than he, as in the case of Phoebe. Or, when, for example, Paul mentioned Prisca's name before Aquila's (Rom. 16:3), he was acknowledging Prisca's higher status. In other words, when in the rare circumstances women had status that contravened public assumptions and beliefs about women's secondary place in society, Paul sided with women.

This evidence in Paul's letters about women who worked with him reveals the prevailing conviction that the dream of God for all people is centered in freedom. But freedom and counter-cultural living were at odds with the patriarchal household model less than fifty years after Paul died, when the Pastoral Epistles were likely written. By then, it was clear the Christian community would ultimately experience more conflict from Rome if it didn't find a more viable way to be a part of the world in which it existed.

What about Family Values?

Despite the claims of those who portray the Bible as promoting what they call family values (to them, a two-parent household in which the husband provides financial and spiritual support to his spouse who raises several children while keeping the home clean and comfortable), the Bible reveals numerous models of what it means to be a family. And, surprisingly, the family as a social unit receives considerable antagonism from Jesus.

When Jesus' ministry of healing and teaching was gaining steam in Galilee, his family tried to "help" him, to no avail (Mk. 3:21). In another instance, Jesus curtly responded to those who told him his family members were looking for him that his family was only those seated around him, a plain rejection of his biological bonds (Mt. 12:49–50). In other places, Jesus taught that anyone who loves a family member more than Jesus is unworthy (Mt. 10:37; Lk. 14:26). Beyond the synoptic gospels, John reported that Jesus' brothers did not believe in him (Jn. 7:5), even though he was with them in Galilee. It wasn't that Jesus just rejected his family, it was that he taught a different context of faithfulness: to God. Discipleship–being an apprentice of Jesus–meant being willing to subvert all other relationships to the one with God.

On the other hand, the Pastoral Epistles and other letters with household codes (Colossians, Ephesians, 1 Peter) emphasize families, advocating for hierarchical structures. Household treatises popularized since Aristotle reinforced ideals by which males enjoyed authority over women and slaves. Later Christian documents, rather than deconstructing the codes, added a religious underpinning.[16]

The household code in Colossians admonishes the husband to love his wife and to avoid abusing her (Col. 3:19), while the code in 1 Peter 2:11–3:12 instructs the husband to be thoughtful of his wife and to treat her with honor as she is the weaker sex. Ephesians reminds the husband to love his wife as his own body (Eph. 5:28). These mitigating aspects of the codes would have been improvements, to be sure, over codes without them. And, to some degree, the inclusion of benevolence for the dominant male because of his identity in Christ would have, one would hope, resulted in better ethical treatment of the subordinate members of the household: children, slaves, and wives.

The tension between the traditional patriarchal family structure embedded in household codes and the rejection of structure in favor of relationship (Jesus and Paul) existed not only through the ensuing years of the developing Christian movement, but also exists today. Our challenge is not to negate the plurality of voices in the New Testament but to hear within them what we need to be faithful disciples.

What would it mean, for example, to choose the path of radical living, to learn from those who accommodated their cultural circumstance that there are other, better choices?

Embracing All We Are Meant to Be

We know truth is often found in the friction of opposites. Jesus said the cost of discipleship is to jettison one's familial loyalty for fidelity to God. Yet, decades later, New Testament writers were urging Christians to endorse hierarchical households as models of good Roman citizenry. Understanding these disparate and at times opposing voices as Scripture means we invite the depths of costly discipleship in light of our own cultural context. Like the student in Proverbs, we must weigh the options: What is folly? What is wisdom?

We (the authors) as feminist Christians are familiar with the struggle of opposing forces because we know what it means to feel caught in the crosshairs. Because of our feminism we are rejected by traditional, evangelical Christians, and because of our faith we are rejected by feminists. Consequently we inhabit a place fraught with traps and snares. This space is not well worn. Few people have been here and remained.

This struggle, though, is not new. This is merely another verse in the long history of earlier feminist Christians who worked together for justice. As we look back over this journey through different places in the Bible, we realize the depth of conversion that has occurred. Through pages of puzzling texts and layers of patriarchal diatribes, women have nevertheless found themselves, not as mere participants, but as pilgrims on our path home.

The Bible is, after all, the ultimate grand story of liberation. Mixed with this journey to freedom are voices that doubt, voices that call women and men away from deeper truths, voices that tempt us to question who we are and why we are here. These messages perpetuate the false notion that women are created to be less than and subjugated to men; that their value lies in a sexuality that is controlled by men; that women are most godly when they are wives and mothers, serving their husbands and families with little consideration of their own autonomy and individual callings. But these are false assumptions that are not consistent with the biblical call of liberation.

In the summer of 2014, at a conference hotel in St. Louis, a group of feminist Christians—the Evangelical and Ecumenical Women's Caucus—gathered to renew old friendships and cultivate new ones, to celebrate the work of God in our lives, to be inspired to continue the journey of occupying this sparse landscape of feminism and Christian faith.

One might expect such a gathering to be dour, a symposium of stories fraught with disappointment and frustration. This is far from what happened, though. The Spirit of God burst on the scene, spreading an infectious feeling of joy and celebration. It was a sight to behold as the jubilant atmosphere could not be contained with mere clapping and cheering. Sophia led us into a full-blown celebration of Her presence through unrestrained singing and dancing. She, and this vision of an expanding circle of feminist Christians, inspire us to see what previously we (and others) have been taught to ignore.

We are now more convinced than ever that Wisdom Woman stands in the center of the liberating community of Hagar, who named God; of Tamar, who secured her justice when no one else provided it; of Naomi and Ruth, who traveled a long distance together to discover possibilities of new life when old ways were gone; of the bleeding woman, who touched Jesus when all else failed; of the courageous Canaanite woman, who showed Jesus his mission needed expansion; of the woman who found her lost coin.

Wisdom Woman stands in our midst, too, inviting us to be all we are meant to be.

Bibliography

Books

Aldredge-Clanton, Jann. *In Whose Image?: God and Gender.* New York: The Crossroad Publishing Company, 1991.

Borg, Marcus J. *Evolution of the Word: The New Testament in the Order the Books Were Written.* New York: HarperOne, 2013.

_____. *Meeting Jesus Again for the First Time: The Historical Jesus & the Heart of Contemporary Faith.* New York: HarperSanFrancisco, 1994.

_____. *Reading the Bible Again for the First Time: Taking the Bible Seriously but not Literally.* New York: HarperSanFrancisco, 2001.

Campbell, Joseph, with Bill Moyers. *The Power of Myth.* New York: Anchor Books, 1991.

Coogan, Michael D. *A Brief Introduction to the Old Testament: The Hebrew Bible in Its Context.* Second edition. New York: Oxford University Press, 2012.

Daly, Campbell. *Beyond God the Father: Toward a Philosophy of Women's Liberation.* Boston: Beacon Press, 1973.

Ehrman, Bart D. *A Brief Introduction to the New Testament.* New York: Oxford University Press, 2013.

Eldredge, John. *Wild at Heart: Discovering the Secret of a Man's Soul.* Nashville: Thomas Nelson, 2001.

Eldredge, John, and Stasi Eldredge. *Captivating: Unveiling the Mystery of a Woman's Soul.* Revised and expanded edition. Nashville: Thomas Nelson, 2010.

Esther, Elizabeth. *Girl at the End of the World: My Escape From Fundamentalism in Search of a Faith with a Future.* New York: Convergent, 2014.

Farrar, Steve. *Real Valor: A Charge to Nurture and Protect Your Family.* Colorado Springs: David C. Cook, 2013.

Fiorenza, Elisabeth Schüssler. *Bread Not Stone: The Challenge of Feminist Biblical Interpretation.* Tenth anniversary edition. Boston: Beacon Press, 1995.

_____. *In Memory of Her: A Feminist Theological Reconstruction of Christian Origins.* Tenth anniversary edition. New York: Crossroads, 2000.

_____. *Wisdom Ways: Introducing Feminist Biblical Interpretation.* Maryknoll, N.Y.: Orbis Books, 2005.

Gresh, Dannah. *Get Lost: Finding Your True Love in God.* Colorado Springs: WaterBrook Press, 2013.

Gresh, Dannah, and Nancy DeMoss. *Lies Young Women Believe, and The Truth that Sets Them Free.* Chicago: Moody Press, 2008.

Harris, Stephen L., and Robert L. Platzner. *The Old Testament: An Introduction to the Hebrew Bible.* Second edition. Sacramento: McGraw-Hill Higher Education, 2008.

Held Evans, Rachel . *A Year of Biblical Womanhood: How a Liberated Woman Found Herself Sitting on Her Roof, Covering Her Head, and Calling Her Husband "Master."* Nashville: Thomas Nelson Publishers, 2012.

Holmes, Andy, and Sergey Eliseev. *My Princess Bible.* Carol Stream, Ill.: Tyndale Publishers, 2010.

Johnson, Elizabeth A. *She Who Is: The Mystery of God in Feminist Theological Discourse.* New York: The Crossroad Publishing Company, 1992.

Kendall, Jackie. *A Man Worth Waiting For: How to Avoid a Bozo.* Nashville: FaithWords, 2013.

Louth, Andrew, ed. *Genesis 1–11. (Ancient Christian Commentary on Scripture: Old Testament, Volume 1).* Downers Grove, Ill.: IVP Academic, 2001.

McGlothlin, Brooke. *Warrior Prayers: Praying the Word for Boys in the Areas They Need It Most.* E-book. May 2011.

McKinney, Michelle. *In Search of the Proverbs 31 Man.* Colorado Springs: Waterbrook Press, 2003.

Mollenkott, Virginia Ramey. *Omnigender: A Trans-Religious Approach.* Cleveland: Pilgrim Press, 2007.

Newsom, Carol A., and Sharon H. Ringe, eds. *Women's Bible Commentary.* Expanded edition with Apocrypha. Louisville: Westminster John Knox Press, 1998.

NIV Study Bible, The. Grand Rapids: Zondervan, 2002.

O'Connell Killen, Patricia. *Finding Our Voices: Women, Wisdom, and Faith.* New York: The Crossroads Publishing Company, 1997.

O'Connor, Kathleen M. *The Wisdom Literature.* Collegeville, Minn.: The Liturgical Press, 1990.

Omartian, Stormie. *The Power of the Praying Wife.* Eugene, Oreg..: Harvest House Publishers, 2014.

Orenstein, Peggy. *Cinderella Ate My Daughter: Dispatches from the Front-Lines of the New Girlie-Girl Culture.* E-book. New York: HarperCollins, 2014.

Pearl, Michael, and Debi Pearl. *To Train Up a Child: Turning the Hearts of the Fathers to the Children.* Memphis: No Greater Joy Ministries, 2009.

Pearson, Helen Bruch. *Do What You Have the Power to Do: Studies of Six New Testament Women.* Nashville: Upper Room Books, 1992.

_____. *Mother Roots: The Female Ancestors of Jesus.* Nashville: Upper Room Books, 2002.

Petersen, Bettina, and Allyson Jule, eds. *Facing Challenges: Feminism in Christian Higher Education and Other Places.* Cambridge, Mass. Scholars Publishing, Upcoming 2015.

Scanzoni, Letha Dawson, and Nancy A. Hardesty. *All We're Meant to Be: Biblical Feminism for Today.* Third revised edition. Grand Rapids: William B. Eerdmans Publishing Company, 1992.

Shepherd, Sheri Rose, *His Princess: Love Letters from Your King,* Portland, Oreg.: Multnomah Books, 2004.

Spar, Debora L. *Wonder Women: Sex, Power, and the Quest for Perfection.* New York: Sarah Crighton Books, 2013.

Valenti, Jessica. *The Purity Myth: How America's Obsession with Virginity Is Hurting Young Women.* Berkeley: Seal Press, 2009.

Walsh, Sheila. *God's Little Princess Devotional Bible.* Nashville: Thomas Nelson, 2012.

_____. *God's Mighty Warrior Devotional Bible.* Nashville: Thomas Nelson, 2012.

Watters, Candace. *Get Married: What Women Can Do to Help Make It Happen.* Chicago: Moody Publishers, 2008.

Wink, Walter. *Jesus and Nonviolence: A Third Way.* Minneapolis: Fortress Press, 2003.

Articles

Allen, Bob. "Baptists Target Gun Enthusiasts for Outreach." *APBnews.* March 4, 2014. Accessed July 10, 2014. http://www.abpnews. com/ministry/organizations/item/28422-baptists-target-gun-enthusiasts-for-outreach.

Barbee, Amanda. "Naked and Ashamed: Women and Evangelical Purity Culture." *The Other Journal.com: An Intersection of Theology and Culture.* March 3, 2014. Accessed July 11, 2014. http://theotherjournal.com/2014/03/03/naked-and-ashamed-women-and-evangelical-purity-culture/.

Dean, Jamie. "Set Adrift." *World Magazine.* April 5, 2014. Accessed July 8, 2014.
http://www.worldmag.com/2014/03/set_adrift/page1.

Dube, Rebecca. "The Duggars' Tips for Keeping Your Marriage Sexy, Even After (a lot) of Kids." *Today.com.* February 13, 2014. Accessed July 3, 2014. http://www.today.com/moms/duggars-7-tips-keeping-your-marriage-sexy-even-after-lot-2D12106530.

Feldman, Kiera. "Sexual Assault at God's Harvard." *New Republic.* February 17, 2014. Accessed July 11, 2014.http://www.newrepublic.com/article/116623/sexual-assault-patrick-henry-college-gods-harvard.

Fischer, Bryan. "Focal Point," American Family Radio, May 31, 2013. Accessed July 1, 2014. http://www.huffingtonpost.com/2013/05/31/bryan-fischer-men-designed-to-be-breadwinners_n_3367765.html?utm_hp_ref=women&ir=Women.

Gosselin, Suzanne Hadley. "Disillusioned Daughter of Eve." *Boundless.* May 20, 2013. Accessed May 20, 2013. https://community.focusonthefamily.com/b/boundless/archive/2013/05/20/disillusioned-daughter-of-feminism.aspx.

Hodson, Jeff. "Did Hana's Parents 'Train' Her to Death?" *The Seattle Times.* November 27, 2011. Accessed July 21, 2014. http://seattletimes.com/html/localnews/2016875109_hana28m.html.

Irons, Kendra Weddle. "The Alien Among Us: Woman as Prophet." *Christian Feminism Today* 30, no. 1. (Spring 2006): 8–11.

Joyce, Kathryn. "By Grace Alone." *The American Prospect.* April 2014. Accessed July 12, 2014. http://prospect.org/article/next-christian-sex-abuse-scandal.

_____. "Hana's Story." *Slate.* November 9, 2013. Accessed July 21, 2014.

Kiley, Brendan. "Church or Cult? The Control-Freaky Ways of Mars Hill Church." *The Stranger.* February 1, 2012. Accessed July 14, 2014. http://www.thestranger.com/seattle/church-or-cult/Content?oid=12172001.

Liberatore, Paul. "'Brave' Creator Blasts Disney for 'Blatant Sexism' in Princess Makeover." *Marin Independent Journal.* May 11, 2013. Accessed July 14, 2014.

Long, Thomas. "Why Do Men Stay Away?" *Christian Century.* October 20, 2011. Accessed July 14, 2014. http://www.christiancentury.org/article/2011-10/why-do-men-stay-away. http://www.marinij.com/ci_23224741/brave-creator-blasts-disney-blatant-sexism-princess-makeover.

Moon, Ruth. "Should Christian Colleges Let Female Faculty Teach Men the Bible?" *Christianity Today.* May 14, 2014. Accessed July 11, 2014. http://www.christianitytoday.com/ct/2014/may/should-christian-colleges-let-female-faculty-teach-men-bibl.html.

Pierson, Russ. "Mark Driscoll: Gas-Guzzlers a Mark of Masculinity." *Sojourners.* May 9, 2013. Accessed July 14, 2014. http://sojo.net/blogs/2013/05/09/mark-driscoll-gas-guzzlers-mark-masculinity.

Rine, Abigail. "Why Some Evangelicals Are Trying to Stop Obsessing over Pre-marital Sex." *The Atlantic.* May 23, 2013. Accessed July 11, 2014. http://www.theatlantic.com/sexes/archive/2013/05/why-some-evangelicals-are-trying-to-stop-obsessing-over-pre-marital-sex/276185/.

Schneiderman, R.M. "Flock Is Now a Fight Team in Some Ministries." *New York Times.* February 1, 2010. Accessed July 14, 2014. http://www.nytimes.com/2010/02/02/us/02fight.html?_r=0.

Stein, Rob. "Premarital Abstinence Studies Ineffective, Study Finds." *Washington Post.* December 29, 2008. Accessed July 10, 2014. http://www.washingtonpost.com/wp-dyn/content/article/2008/12/28/AR2008122801588.html.

Stephens-Davidowitz, Seth. "Google, Tell Me. Is My Son a Genius?" *New York Times.* January 19, 2014. Accessed July 11, 2014. http://www.nytimes.com/2014/01/19/opinion/sunday/google-tell-me-is-my-son-a-genius.html?_r=0.

"Student Movement." *Baylor Proud.* January 19, 2012. Accessed July 9, 2014. http://www2.baylor.edu/baylorproud/2012/01/student-movement-id-rather-have-a-proverbs-31-woman-than-a-victorias-secret-model/.

Wallace, Michelle. "Soul: The Art of Husbandry." *Living Arlington.* June 2013. Accessed July 1, 2014. http://trendmag.trendoffset.com/display_article.php?id=1430303.

Notes

Introduction: Becoming Who We're Meant to Be

[1]Rebecca Kiser, "Frequently Asked Questions," *Christian Feminism Today,* http://www. eewc.com/faq/inerrancy-of-scripture (accessed July 16, 2014).

[2]"Some in $4.6B Christian industry copy designs, logos," *USA Today,* December 18, 2009, http://usatoday30.usatoday.com/news/religion/2009-12-18-christian-copyright_N. htm (accessed December 1, 2014). According to the Christian Booksellers Association website (cbaonline.org), profits in 2013 had gone up 2.9 percent from the previous year, suggesting sales of Christian products remain strong.

[3]Mary Daly, *Beyond God the Father: Toward a Philosophy of Women's Liberation* (Boston: Beacon Press, 1973), 19.

Chapter One: Saving Eve

[1]For example, see Lynn Japinga, *Feminism and Christianity: An Essential Guide* (Nashville: Abingdon Press, 1999); *Women and Religion: A Feminist Sourcebook of Christian Thought,* ed. Elizabeth Clark and Herbert Richardson (New York: Harper & Row Publishers, 1977; Phyllis Trible, "Eve and Adam: Genesis 2-3 Reread" in *Womanspirit Rising: A Feminist Reader in Religion,* ed. Carol P. Christ and Judith Plaskow (San Francisco, CA: Harper & Row Publishers, 1979) and Rosemary Radford Ruether, *Sexism and God-Talk: Toward a Feminist Theology* (Boston: Beacon Press, 1993.

[2]Tertullian, *De Cultu Feminarum,* "Book 1, Chapter 1," *The Tertullian Project,* http://www. tertullian.org/anf/anf04/anf04-06.htm (accessed July 1, 2014).

[3]John Chrysostom, "Homily 9 on First Timothy," trans. Philip Schaff, in *Nicene and Post-Nicene Fathers,* First Series, Vol. 13, ed. Philip Schaff (Buffalo, N.Y.: Christian Literature Publishing Co., 1889), rev. and ed. Kevin Knight for *New Advent,* http://www.newadvent. org/fathers/230609.htm (accessed July 1, 2014).

[4]Augustine, quoted in *Ancient Christian Commentary on Scripture,* "Old Testament 1 Genesis 1–11," ed. Andrew Louth, gen. ed., Thomas C. Oden (Downers Grove, Ill.: InterVarsity Press, 2001), 68.

[5]John Piper, "The Emergence of Sin and Misery," http://www.desiringgod.org/sermons/the-emergence-of-sin-and-misery (accessed October 8, 2014).

[6]Nancy Leigh DeMoss and Mary Kassian, "True Woman Manifesto," http://www.truewoman.com/?id=980 (accessed October 8, 2014).

[7]Kay Arthur, "It's Your Choice," http://www.truewoman101.com/?period=week-7 (accessed July 2, 2014).

[8]Dannah Gresh and Nancy DeMoss, *Lies Young Women Believe: And the Truth That Sets Them Free* (Chicago: Moody Press, 2008), 24.

[9]John & Stasi Eldredge, *Captivating: Unveiling the Mystery of a Woman's Soul* (Nashville: Thomas Nelson, 2010), 46–49.

[10]"The Danvers Statement," http://cbmw.org/core-beliefs/ (accessed July 1, 2014).

[11]Courtney Reissig, "Confessions of a Recovering Feminist," http://cbmw.org/women/womanhood/confessions-of-a-recovering-feminist-3/ (accessed June 17, 2013).

[12]Ladies Against Feminism, http://www.ladiesagainstfeminism.com/ (accessed July 1, 2014).

[13]Mary Kassian, "You've Come a Long Way, Baby!," (lecture), http://www.truewoman101.com/?period=week-5 (accessed July 1, 2014).

[14]Mary Kassian, "The Genesis of Gender," http://www.truewoman101.com/?period=week-2 (accessed July 1, 2014).

[15]Anna Sofia and Elizabeth Botkin, http://visionarydaughters.com/ (accessed July 2, 2014).

[16]Virginia Ramey Mollenkott, *Omnigender: A Trans-Religious Approach* (Cleveland: Pilgrim Press, 2007).

[17]Mark Driscoll, "A Word to the Men," http://pastormark.tv/2012/01/31/a-word-to-the-men (accessed July 1, 2014).

[18]Michelle Wallace, "Soul: The Art of Husbandry," *Living Arlington* (June 2013), http://trendmag.trendoffset.com/display_article.php?id=1430303 (accessed July 1, 2014).

[19]Owen Strachan, "On Erick Erickson and Differences Between Men and Women," http://www.patheos.com/blogs/thoughtlife/2013/05/on-erick-erickson-and-differences-between-men-and-women/ (accessed July 3, 2014).

[20]Robert Lewis, *Raising a Modern-Day Knight: a Father's Role in Guiding His Son to Authentic Manhood* (Carol Stream, Ill.: Tyndale House, 2007).

[21]Robert Lewis, "The Shaping of a Man," http://www.lifeway.com/Article/student-the-shaping-of-a-man (accessed July 1, 2014).

[22]Letha Dawson Scanzoni and Nancy A. Hardesty, *All We're Meant to Be: Biblical Feminism for Today*, 3d rev. ed. (Grand Rapids: William B. Eerdmans, 1992), 26.

[23]Susan Niditch, "Genesis," in *Women's Bible Commentary: Expanded Edition with Apocrypha,* ed. Carol A. Newsom and Sharon H. Ringe (Louisville: Westminster John Knox Press, 1998), 17.

[24]Scanzoni and Hardesty, 41.

[25]Joseph Campbell with Bill Moyers, *The Power of Myth* (New York: Anchor Books, 1991), 53.

[26]Niditch, 17.

Chapter Two: Waiting for Boaz and Other Myths of Love

[1]Diane Montgomery, "Ruth Is Her Name, and Proverbs 31 Is Her Game," December 2, 2011, http://unlockingfemininity.wordpress.com/2011/12/02/ruth-is-her-name-and-proverbs-31-is-her-game/ (accessed July 7, 2014).

[2]Stephen L. Harris and Robert L. Platzner, *The Old Testament: An Introduction to the Hebrew Bible*, 2d ed. (Sacramento: McGraw-Hill Higher Education, 2008), 339.

[3]Montgomery, "Ruth Is Her Name."

[4]Brad Anderson, "Ruth: A Faithful Woman," March 3, 2014, http://www.faithcycleministry.org/content/ruth (accessed July 7, 2014).

[5]Steve Farrar, *Real Valor: A Charge to Nurture and Protect Your Family* (Colorado Springs: David C. Cook, 2013), 12–13.

[6]Candice Watters, *Get Married: What Women Can Do to Help Make it Happen* (Chicago: Moody Publishers, 2008).

[7]From the marriage preparation page of the-christian-single-woman.com.

[8]John Piper, "Ruth: Strategic Righteousness," (July 15, 1984), http://www.desiringgod.org/sermons/ruth-strategic-righteousness (accessed July 7, 2014).

[9]See Hosea 9:1. See also Amy-Jill Levine, "Ruth," in *Women's Bible Commentary, Expanded Edition with Apocrypha,* ed. Carol A. Newsom and Sharon H. Ringe (Louisville: Westminster John Knox Press, 1998), 88.

Chapter Three: What's Wrong with Proverbs 31?

[1]See the video at https://www.youtube.com/watch?v=4WAFFMF4iZY&spfreload=10.

[2]"Student Movement," *Baylor Proud,* (January 19, 2012), http://www2.baylor.edu/baylorproud/2012/01/student-movement-id-rather-have-a-proverbs-31-woman-than-a-victorias-secret-model/ (accessed July 9, 2014).

[3]"About Us: Proverbs 31 Ministries," http://proverbs31.org/about/ (accessed July 10, 2014).

[4]Ibid.

[5]"Blogs We Read: Proverbs 31 Ministries," http://proverbs31.org/blogs/#sthash.0V6Z TyXA.dpbs (accessed July 10, 2014).

[6]Melissa (pen name), "Is the Proverbs 31 Woman a Career Woman?" July 8, 2013, http://thecrossandthekitchensink.com/2013/07/is-the-proverbs-31-woman-a-career-woman/ (accessed July 9, 2014).

[7]Kelly Crawford, "Making Money from Home: Following the Proverbs 31 Model," January 17, 2013, http://www.ladiesagainstfeminism.com/getting-back-home/making-money-from-home-following-the-proverbs-31-model/ (accessed July 9, 2014).

[8]See http://gilliscoaching.com/how-to-quit-your-day-job-and-come-home-proverbs31-woman/ .

[9]Katy Gillis, "A Proverbs 31 Woman: How Being a Beachbody Coach Fits In," Katy Gillis: Home Focused, http://gilliscoaching.com/a-proverbs-31-woman-how-being-a-beachbody-coach-fits-in/ (accessed July 9, 2014).

[10]Donna Partow, *Becoming the Woman God Wants Me to Be: A 90-Day Guide to Living the Proverbs 31 Life* (Grand Rapids, Mich: Revell, 2008).

[11]Amy Bayliss, *Pursuit of Proverbs 31* (Kindle edition, My Southern Media, 2012; paperback, CreateSpace, 2014).

[12]Michelle McKinney, *In Search of the Proverbs 31 Man: The One God Approves and a Woman Wants* (Colorado Springs: Waterbrook Press, 2003).

[13]Tara Hill, "Christian Women: How to Be a Proverbs 31 Wife in a Modern World," originally on *Yahoo Voices*, August 3, 2009, accessed February 18, 2015 at https://www.facebook.com/OlusteveConcept/posts/616653571710458.

[14]Kylie Bisutti, *I'm No Angel: From Victoria's Secret Model to Role Model* (Carol Stream, Ill.: Tyndale House, 2014).

[15]Janette…ikz, "31 to be Exact," February 16, 2012, https://www.youtube.com/watch?v=IyXSFnZijSs (accessed July 9, 2014).

[16]See "The Ruby Doll: The Proverbs 31 Doll," http://www.doorposts.com/details.aspx?id=20 (accessed July 9, 2014).

[17]Stephen L. Harris and Robert L. Platzner, *The Old Testament: An Introduction to the Hebrew Bible*, 2d ed. (Sacramento: McGraw-Hill Higher Education, 2008), 322–23.

[18]Kathleen M. O'Connor, *The Wisdom Literature* (Collegeville, Minn.: The Liturgical Press, 1990), 51.

[19]Michael D. Coogan, *A Brief Introduction to the Old Testament: The Hebrew Bible in Its Context,* 2d ed. (New York: Oxford University Press, 2012), 382.

[20]O'Connor, *Wisdom Literature,* 37–39.

[21]Ibid., 61–62.

[22]According to biblical scholar Marcus J. Borg, this female personification of wisdom marks the first step in the process of Wisdom/Sophia representing a female image for God in Jewish literature. Marcus J. Borg, *Reading the Bible Again for the First Time: Taking the Bible Seriously but Not Literally* (San Francisco: HarperSanFrancisco, 2001), 150.

[23]O'Connor, *Wisdom Literature,* 70.

[24]Ibid., 66.

[25]Ibid., 74.

[26]Ibid., 77.

[27]Ibid., 78–79.

[28]Elisabeth Schüssler Fiorenza, *Wisdom Ways: Introducing Feminist Biblical Interpretation* (Maryknoll, N. Y.: Orbis Books, 2005), 23.

Chapter Four: When Jesus Was a Man's Man

[1]The *Pew Research Religion and Public Life Project: Religious Landscape Survey* took place in 2007, when Pew surveyed 35,000 United States adults about their religious affiliations. Results

can be found here: http://religions.pewforum.org/. Different statistical numbers were reported by Thomas Long, "Why Do Men Stay Away?" *Christian Century* (October 20, 2011), http://www.christiancentury.org/article/2011-10/why-do-men-stay-away (accessed July 14, 2014).

[2]John Eldredge, *Wild at Heart: Discovering the Secret of a Man's Soul* (Nashville: Thomas Nelson, 2001), 7–8.

[3]*The ABCs for Godly Boys* Bible curriculum, http://theroadto31.com/the-abcs-for-godly-boys (accessed July 11, 2014).

[4]Alecia Simersky, "How to Raise a Boy into a Godly Man," November 25, 2013, http://www.themobsociety.com/2013/11/25/raise-boy-godly-man/ (accessed July 14, 2014).

[5]See, for example, Brooke McGlothlin,*: Praying the Word for Boys in the Areas They Need It Most,* Ebook (May 2011).

[6]Brooke McGlothlin, "Five Scriptural Prayers for your Sons," March 18, 2014, http://proverbs31.org/devotions/devo/five-scriptural-prayers-for-your-son/ (accessed July 16, 2014).

[7]Benjamin Kerns, "The Buried Life: A Fresh Model for Guys' Ministry," January 25, 2012, http://www.averageyouthministry.com/2012/01/25/the-buried-life-a-fresh-model-for-guys-ministry/ (accessed July 14, 2014).

[8]Robert Lewis, "Initiating Sons into Manhood," http://www.focusonthefamily.com/parenting/building_relationships/rites-of-passage-for-your-son/initiating-sons-into-manhood.aspx (accessed July 14, 2014).

[9]Tim Wright, "Boys to Men," http://www.todayschristianwoman.com/articles/2014/january/boys-to-men.html?start=2.

[10]Bob Allen, "Baptists Target Gun Enthusiasts for Outreach," APBnews, March 4, 2014, http://www.abpnews.com/ministry/organizations/item/28422-baptists-target-gun-enthusiasts-for-outreach (accessed July 10, 2014).

[11]Eldredge, *Wild at Heart,* 9.

[12]Ibid., 18. See also John and Stasi Eldredge, *Captivating: Unveiling the Mystery of a Woman's Soul,* rev. and exp. ed. (Nashville: Thomas Nelson, 2010).

[13]"7 Promises," http://www.promisekeepers.org/about/7-promises (accessed July 11, 2014).

[14]Promise Keepers Men's Ministries, http://www.promisekeepers.org/ (accessed July 11, 2014).

[15]See www.actlikemen.com.

[16]Clarence Bouwman, "Act Like Men Conference Review," *Reformed Outfitters,* October 26, 2013, http://reformedoutfitters.com/2013/10/26/act-like-men-conference-review/ (accessed July 14, 2014).

[17]"My Response to Act Like Men," October 26, 2013, http://prestonsteinke.wordpress.com/ (accessed July 14, 2014).

[18]Hemant Mehta, "Christians Go After a Popular Pastor Over His Sexism, Too," July 8, 2011, http://www.patheos.com/blogs/friendlyatheist/2011/07/08/christians-go-after-a-popular-pastor-over-his-sexism-too (accessed July 14, 2014).

[19]See http://robertcargill.com/2011/07/14/mark-driscoll-responds-after-his-elders-sit-him-down-offers-no-apology/ (accessed April 7, 2015).

[20]See http://sbcvoices.com/10-reasons-why-sissies-and-pastoral-ministry-are-a-bad-mix/ (accessed February 25, 2015).

[21]David Murrow, "Why Men Hate Church," http://www.cbn.com/spirituallife/churchandministry/menhatingchurch.aspx (accessed July 14, 2014), excerpt from *Why Men Hate Going to Church* (Nashville: Thomas Nelson, 2005).

[22]Alex Murashko, "John Piper: God Gave Christianity a 'Masculine Feel,'" *Christian Post,* Feb. 1, 2012, http://www.christianpost.com/news/john-piper-god-gave-christianity-a-masculine-feel-68385/ .

[23]David Mathis, "More on the Masculine Feel of Christianity," June 14, 2012, http://www.desiringgod.org/blog/posts/more-on-the-masculine-feel-of-christianity (accessed July 14, 2014).

[24]Russ Pierson, "Mark Driscoll: Gas-Guzzlers a Mark of Masculinity," *Sojourners* (May 9, 2013), http://sojo.net/blogs/2013/05/09/mark-driscoll-gas-guzzlers-mark-masculinity (accessed July 14, 2014).

[25]Quoted in Holly Pivec, "The Feminization of the Church," *biola*, Spring 2004, http://magazine.biola.edu/article/06-spring/the-feminization-of-the-church/ (accessed July 2014).

[26]Ibid.

[27]See http://cbmw.org/uncategorized/jesus-christ-the-perfect-man/ (accessed February 25, 2015).

[28]See http://www.relevantmagazine.com/god/church/features/1344-from-the-mag-7-big-questions (accessed February 25, 2015).

[29]"From the Mag: 7 Big Questions," *Relevant,* August 28, 2007, http://www.relevant-magazine.com/god/church/features/1344-from-the-mag-7-big-questions (accessed July 25, 2014).

[30]Bryan Fischer, "The Feminization of the Medal of Honor," November 16, 2010, http://www.themoralliberal.com/2010/11/16/the-feminization-of-the-medal-of-honor/ (accessed January 27, 2015).

[31]This explanation of Jesus' teachings from the Sermon on the Mount is informed by Walter Wink's *Jesus and Nonviolence: A Third Way* (Minneapolis: Fortress Press), 2003.

[32]Marcus Borg and John Dominic Crossan have been informative in our thinking about Jesus and his context within the Roman Empire.

[33]Gail R. O'Day, "John," in the *Women's Bible Commentary: Expanded Edition with Apocrypha*, ed. Carol A. Newsom and Sharon H. Ringe (Louisville: Westminster John Knox Publishers, 1998), 391.

[34]Ibid.

[35]Ibid.

Chapter Five: The Problem with Purity

[1]Jessica's name has been changed to protect her anonymity.

[2]"The Pledge," March 3, 2014, http://generationsoflight.com/html/thepledge.html (accessed July 11, 2014).

[3]Generations of Light "Manhood Ceremony," http://generationsoflight.com/html/boys.html .

[4]Among several websites offering such fare are Sisters Evolve: Christian Women, Becoming Better Together!, http://www.sistersevolve.com/p/se-t-shirts-get-yours.html and http://www.cornerstonejewelrydesigns.com/pewter-purity-bracelet.html (all accessed April 7, 2015).

[5]See http://www.zazzle.com/waitwear. An even odder artifact in evangelical culture is the Boyfriend Bear, a stuffed animal girls can cuddle until "The One" comes along. You can read more about the Boyfriend Bear at its product site, "Boyfriend Bears: For Girls Who Wait," http://boyfriendbears.org/ (accessed July 11, 2014).

[6]"What is a Secret Keeper Girl?" http://secretkeepergirl.com/what-is-a-secret-keeper-girl/ (accessed July 11, 2014). The "Truth or Bare" section of Gresh's site is an especially interesting foray into the legalism that accompanies modesty and purity culture.

[7]Amanda Barbee, "Naked and Ashamed: Women and Evangelical Purity Culture," March 3, 2014, http://theotherjournal.com/2014/03/03/naked-and-ashamed-women-and-evangelical-purity-culture/ (accessed July 11, 2014).

[8]Rebecca St. James, "Modest is Hottest," *Christian Broadcasting Network*, March 10, 2014, http://www.cbn.com/family/youth/RSJ_Modest.aspx (accessed July 16, 2014).

[9]Jarrid Wilson, "Four Reasons Modest is Hottest," March 10, 2014. The link is no longer available on Wilson's site, though a few months later Wilson wrote a similar post on "Four Reasons Everyone Should Choose Modesty," stating similar principles. See http://jarridwilson.com/4-reasons-everyone-should-choose-modesty/ (accessed July 11, 2014).

[10]Rey Swimwear, http://www.reyswimwear.com/ (accessed July 10, 2014).

[11]Reflections about *The Modesty Survey* remain on the Rebelution website; the survey results appear to have been taken down sometime in Spring 2014. The reflections were written by prominent evangelicals such as John Piper and Nancy Leigh DeMoss, echoing the importance of modesty for girls, and that God desires that girls remain modest above all else. You can find other information and links about the survey here: http://therebelution.com/blog/2007/02/the-modesty-survey-results/#.U77bLo1dWG8 .

[12]Reflections are here: "The Responsibility of Modesty (Part One)," http://therebelution.com/blog/2007/02/the-responsibility-of-modesty-part-one/#.U77b8I1dWG8 (accessed July 10, 2014).

[13]This post has also been removed from Ryan Visconti's website, perhaps after criticism of the post appeared in some progressive blogs. You can see a take on the post "All God's Daughters Wear Bikinis?" on Emily Joy Allison's site in an essay titled "On Bodies as Belongings," http://www.emilyjoyallison.com/2013/08/on-bodies-as-belongings.html (accessed July 16, 2014).

[14]Like many conservative Christian institutions, Patrick Henry College believes strongly in a complementarian understanding of gender. The student handbook even articulates this view of "God's design," quoting Ephesians and asserting that "Husbands are the head of their wives just as Christ is the head of the church, and are to love their wives just as Christ loved the church and gave Himself up for her."

[15]Kiera Feldman, "Sexual Assault at God's Harvard," *New Republic*, February 17, 2014, http://www.newrepublic.com/article/116623/sexual-assault-patrick-henry-college-gods-harvard (accessed July 11, 2014).

[16]Ibid.

[17]Statement by Patrick Henry College to concerned alumni and students

about article in *The New Republic*, PDF, February 18, 2014, http://homeschoolersanonymous.files.wordpress.com/2014/02/phc-statement-to-alumni-and-students-feb-18-2014-1.pdf (accessed July 11, 2014).

[18]Rob Stein, "Premarital Abstinence Studies Ineffective, Study Finds," *Washington Post*, December 29, 2008, http://www.washingtonpost.com/wp-dyn/content/article/2008/12/28/AR2008122801588.html (accessed July 10, 2014).

[19]Abigail Rine, "Why Some Evangelicals are Trying to Stop Obsessing over Pre-marital Sex, *The Atlantic*, May 23, 2013, http://www.theatlantic.com/sexes/archive/2013/05/why-some-evangelicals-are-trying-to-stop-obsessing-over-pre-marital-sex/276185/ (accessed July 11, 2014).

[20]Debora L. Spar, *Wonder Women: Sex, Power, and the Quest for Perfection* (New York: Sarah Crighton Books, 2013), 210.

[21]Helen Bruch Pearson, *Do What You Have the Power to Do: Studies of Six New Testament Women* (Nashville: Upper Room Books, 1992), 99.

[22]Jessica Valenti, *The Purity Myth: How America's Obsession with Virginity Is Hurting Young Women* (Berkeley, Calif.: Seal Press, 2009), 69.

Chapter Six: Setting Captives Free

[1]Elizabeth Esther, *Girl at the End of the World: My Escape from Fundamentalism in Search of a Faith with a Future* (New York: Convergent, 2014), 190.

[2]"The Closing of Vision Forum Ministries," http://www.visionforumministries.org/ (accessed March 25, 2014).

[3]Collin Gunn, Gunn Productions, *The Monstrous Regiment of Women,* http://www.colingunn.com/monstrous (accessed March 28, 2014).

[4]Stacy McDonald, "When Your Quiver Overflows," http://www.quiverfull.com/articles.php/id13/ (accessed July 3, 2014).

[5]Rebecca Dube, "The Duggars' Tips for Keeping Your Marriage Sexy, Even After (a Lot) of Kids," http://www.today.com/moms/duggars-7-tips-keeping-your-marriage-sexy-even-after-lot-2D12106530 (accessed July 3, 2014).

[6]"How Is Courtship Different from Dating?," http://iblp.org/questions/how-courtship-different-dating (accessed July 7, 2014).

[7]Joshua Crutchfield, "Should Christian Couples Choose a 'Childfree' Lifestyle?" http://cbmw.org/public-square/marriage-public-square/should-christian-couples-choose-a-child-free-life/ (accessed July 3, 2014).

[8]Michael and Debi Pearl, *To Train Up a Child* (No Greater Joy Ministries: 1994). E-book.

[9]Jeff Hodson, "Did Hana's parents 'train' her to death?" Seattle Times (Nov. 27, 2011), available online at http://www.seattletimes.com/seattle-news/did-hanas-parents-train-her-to-death/.

[10]Michael and Debi Pearl, *To Train Up a Child: Turning the Hearts of the Fathers to the Children*, No Greater Joy Ministries, E-book, 2009.

[11]Anna Sofia and Elizabeth Botkin, "Visionary Daughters," http://visionarydaughters.com/about-visionary-daughters (accessed April 10, 2014).

[12]Breezy Brookshire, "A Day in the Life of a Stay-at-Home Daughter" (accessed April 25, 2011 and April 15, 2014).

[13]Anna Sofia and Elizabeth Botkin, "The Top Ten Things Girls Should Study (But Rarely Do)," August 21, 2013, http://visionarydaughters.com/2013/08 (accessed July 10, 2014).

[14]Sarah Pulliam Bailey, "Conservative leader Bill Gothard resigns following abuse allegations," *The Washington Post*, March 7, 2014, http://www.washingtonpost.com/national/religion/conservative-leader-bill-gothard- resigns-following-abuse-allegations/2014/03/07/0381aa94-a624-11e3-b865-38b254d92063_story.html (accessed December 1, 2014)

[15]Marcus J. Borg, *Reading the Bible Again for the First Time: Taking the Bible Seriously but Not Literally* (New York: HarperSanFrancisco, 2001), 240.

[16]Marcus J. Borg, *Evolution of the Word: The New Testament in the Order the Books Were Written* (New York: HarperOne, 2013), 125.

[17]Reta Halteman Finger, *Reta's Reflections: Biblical Studies from a Christian Feminist Perspective*, 1 Corinthians Series, http://www.eewc.com/1-corinthians-series-index-retas-reflections/ (accessed July 7, 2014).

[18]Joanna Dewey, *1 Timothy*, in *Women's Bible Commentary*, expanded edition with Apocrypha, ed. Carol A. Newsom and Sharon H. Ringe (Louisville: Westminster John Knox Press, 1998), 444.

Chapter Seven: What Happens in the Silence

[1]Owen Strachan, "1 Timothy 2:12," http://www.godtube.com/watch/?v=F0BJFMNU (accessed July 11, 2014).

[2]John Piper has made this claim repeatedly, but his beliefs about women in ministry are perhaps most emphatic, and condensed, in this short audio excerpt, publishing on his Desiring God site in February 2008: http://www.desiringgod.org/interviews/should-women-become-pastors (accessed July 11, 2014).

[3]Mark Driscoll, "FAQ: Women in Ministry," http://pastormark.tv/2011/09/20/faq-women-and-ministry (accessed July 11, 2014).

[4]Albert Mohler, "Biblical Pattern of Male Leadership Limits Pastorate to Men," July 16, 2009, http://www.albertmohler.com/2009/07/16/biblical-pattern-of-male-leadership-limits-pastorate-to-men-2/ (accessed July 11, 2014).

[5]Cedarville University in Ohio is perhaps the latest, most public example of an institution struggling to define what it means for women to have authority over men. See Ruth Moon, "Should Christian Colleges Let Female Faculty Teach Men the Bible?" *Christianity Today*, May 14, 2014, http://www.christianitytoday.com/ct/2014/may/should-christian-colleges-let-female-faculty-teach-men-bibl.html (accessed July 11, 2014).

[6]Owen Strachan, quoted in ibid.

[7]Wayne Grudem, quoted in ibid. .

[8]Liberty University: Center for Women's Ministries, http://www.liberty.edu/index.cfm?PID=8871 (accessed July 10, 2014).

[9]Southern Baptist Theological Seminary: Women's Programs, http://www.swbts.edu/academics/schools-programs/womens-programs/ (accessed July 10, 2014).

[10]See Kendra Weddle Irons, "The Alien Among Us: Woman as Prophet," *Christian Feminism Today* 30, no. 1 (Spring 2006): 8–11, and the forthcoming "'Man, What a Battle': Facing the Problem of Language as a Feminist Theologian at a Conservative Christian University," in *Facing Challenges: Feminism in Christian Higher Education and Other Places,* ed. Bettina Petersen and Allyson Jule (Newcastle upon Tyne, U.K.; Cambridge Scholars Publishing, forthcoming).

[11]See *Living on the Boundaries: Evangelical Women, Feminism and The Theological Academy* by Nicola Hoggard Creegan and Christine D. Pohl (Downer's Grove, Ill.: Intervarsity Press, 2005).

[12]Kevin Cauley, "Can Women Teach Young Men in Bible Class?" August 24, 2004, http://gewatkins.net/can-women-teach-young-men-in-bible-class/ (accessed July 11, 2014).

[13]Verse by Verse Ministry staff, "Can a Woman Ever Teach a Man?" August 14, 2010, http://www.versebyverseministry.org/bible-answers/can_a_woman_ever_teach_a_man (accessed July 11, 2014).

[14]Wayne Grudem, "Q and A on Women Teaching Mixed-Gender Sunday School," http://cbmw.org/uncategorized/jbmw-forum-q-a-on-women-teaching-mixed-gender-sunday-school/ (accessed July 11, 2014).

[15]Diana Bucknell, "Should Christian Women Be Instructing Men Through Blogging?" August 1, 2012, http://www.theologyforgirls.com/2012/08/should-christian-women-be-instructing.html (accessed July 11, 2014).

[16]Grace Driscoll, "An Excellent (Godly) Wife," October 20, 2011, https://pastormark.tv/2011/10/20/an-excellent-godly-wifehttps://pastormark.tv/2011/10/20/an-excellent-godly-wife (accessed July 11, 2014).

[17]Sophia Christiaan, "Jezebel Versus the Godly Woman," 2013, http://instituteoflove.net/jezebel-spirit/jezebel-versus-the-godly-woman (accessed July 11, 2014).

[18]John Barnett, "Traits of a Godly Wife," June 23, 2008, http://www.crosswalk.com/family/marriage/traits-of-a-godly-wife-11577974.html (accessed July 11, 2014).

[19]James MacDonald, "How a Wife Can Change Her Husband," March 17, 2011, http://jamesmacdonald.com/blog/how-a-wife-can-change-her-husband/ (accessed July 12, 2014).

[20]Holder, Taylor, "For the Girl Criticized for Not Having a Quiet Spirit," March 13, 2013, http://goodwomenproject.com/define-a-good-woman/for-the-girls-criticized-for-not-having-a-quiet-spirit (accessed July 27, 2014).

[21]Anonymous Warrior Poet, "Imperishable Beauty," http://setapartgirl.com/magazine/article/09-1-12/imperishable-beauty (accessed July 12, 2014).

[22]Leslie Ludy, "The Secrets of Social Grace: The Art of Elegant Speech," http://setapartgirl.com/magazine/article/01-1-11/secrets-social-grace-part-threehttp://setapartgirl.com/magazine/article/01-1-11/secrets-social-grace-part-three (accessed July 12, 2014).

[23]Albert Mohler, "The Marks of Manhood," *Boundless Magazine,* October 30, 2009, http://www.boundless.org/adulthood/2009/the-marks-of-manhood (accessed July 12, 2014).

[24]Kathryn Joyce, "By Grace Alone," *The American Prospect,* April 2014, http://prospect.org/article/next-christian-sex-abuse-scandal (accessed July 12, 2014).

[25]Ibid.

[26]Kathryn Joyce, "Report: Bob Jones University Responded to Rape Claims with Woeful Ignorance of the Law, Often Blaming Victims," December 12, 2014. http://prospect.org/article/report-bob-jones-university-responded-rape-claims-woeful-ignorance-law-often-blaming-victims (accessed March 26, 2015).

[27]Canaanites, according to Helen Bruch Pearson, had a different view of dogs than Jews. They adored dogs, especially small ones, and frequently had them in their homes where, presumably, they had opportunity to eat food that fell from the table. Only a Canaanite, Pearson intimates, might have had the insight to respond so adeptly to Jesus' metaphor. See *Do What You Have the Power to Do: Studies of Six New Testament Women* (Nashville: Upper Room Books, 1992), 82.

[28]Bart D. Ehrman, *A Brief Introduction to the New Testament* (New York: Oxford University Press, 2013), 291.

[29]Elisabeth Schüssler Fiorenza, *Bread Not Stone: The Challenge of Feminist Biblical Interpretation*, tenth anniversary edition (Boston: Beacon Press, 1995), xv.

[30]See Ehrman, pg. 281; Stephen L. Harris, *The New Testament: A Student's Introduction*, 7th Edition (New York, NY: McGraw-Hill, 2012), pg. 378; *Marcus J. Borg, Evolution of the Word: The New Testament in the Order the Books Were Written* (New York, NY: HarperCollins, 2012), pgs. 563-567).

[31]As Professor Ehrman explains, "[T]hey differed from real men in that their penises had never grown, their lungs had not fully developed, and the rest of their bodies never would develop to their full potential. Thus, by their very nature, women were the weaker sex." Ehrman, 411.

Chapter Eight: Princesses, Kingdoms, and God, Oh My!

[1]Peggy Orenstein, *Cinderella Ate My Daughter: Dispatches From the Front-Lines of the New Girlie-Girl Culture*, E-book, HarperCollins, 2014.

[2]Brenda Chapman, quoted in Paul Liberatore, "'Brave' Creator Blasts Disney for 'Blatant Sexism' in Princess Makeover," *Marin Independent Journal*, May 11, 2013, http://www.marinij.com/ci_23224741/brave-creator-blasts-disney-blatant-sexism-princess-makeover (accessed July 14, 2014).

[3]From the publisher's website, http://www.thomasnelson.com/god-s-little-princess-devotional-bible.

[4]Sheila Walsh, *God's Little Princess Devotional Bible* (Nashville: Thomas Nelson, 2012).

[5]Andy Holmes and Sergey Eliseev, *My Princess Bible* (Carol Stream, Ill.: Tyndale Publishers, 2010).

[6]Sheila Walsh, *God's Mighty Warrior Devotional Bible* (Nashville: Thomas Nelson, 2012).

[7]Samuel Williamson, "Is Sunday School Destroying Our Kids?," http://www.churchleaders.com/children/childrens-ministry-articles/169293-is-sunday-school-destroying-our-kids.html (accessed July 14, 2014).

[8]"*Princess Training for the King's Glory* Review," *Curriculum Choice: Making Homeschool Decisions Easy*, September 24, 2012, http://www.thecurriculumchoice.com/2012/09/princess-training-for-the-kings-glory-review/ (accessed July 11, 2014).

[9]Royal Purpose Ministries, http://royalpurpose.com/ (accessed July 11, 2014).

[10]Sheri Rose Phillips, "About," hisprincess.com (accessed March 25, 2015).

[11]In her recent TED talk about radical women around the world, Kavita Ramdas suggests one of the challenges of feminism is there isn't a clear, identifiable foe. See Kavita Ramdas, "Radical Women Embracing Tradition," November 2009, http://www.ted.com/talks/kavita_ramdas_radical_women_embracing_tradition (accessed July 17, 2014).

[12]Mary Daly, *Beyond God the Father: Toward a Philosophy of Women's Liberation* (Boston: Beacon Press, 1973), 19.

[13]Jann Aldredge-Clanton, *In Whose Image?: God and Gender* (New York: The Crossroad Publishing Company, 1991), 87.

[14]Simone de Beauvoir, *The Second Sex* (New York: Vintage Books, 1989, 1951).

[15]Elizabeth A. Johnson, *She Who Is: The Mystery of God in Feminist Theological Discourse* (New York: The Crossroad Publishing Company, 1992), 85.

[16]Ibid.

[17]Trible writes, "In its singular form the noun *rehem* means 'womb' or 'uterus.' In the plural, *rahamim*, this concrete meaning expands to the abstractions of compassion, mercy, and love..." Phyllis Trible, *God and the Rhetoric of Sexuality*, quoted in Johnson, *She Who Is*, 101.

[18]Ibid.

Chapter Nine: Biblical Womanhood Redefined

[1]Martha Peace, *Becoming a Titus 2 Woman* (Bemidji, Minn.: Focus Publishing, 1997).

[2]Susan Godfrey, *The Titus 2 Woman: Learning to Be a Godly Woman* (Amazon Digital Services, 2011). Ebook.

[3]Carolyn Mahaney, *Feminine Appeal: Seven Virtues of a Godly Wife and Mother*, kindle edition (Wheaton, Ill.: Crossway Books, 2004).

[4]Teri Maxwell, *Sweet Journey: A Bible Study*, kindle edition (Communication Concepts, 2013).

[5]John Barnett, "Being a Titus 2 Woman," http://www.biblestudytools.com/bible-study/topical-studies/being-a-titus-2-woman.html (accessed July 18, 2014).

[6]Ibid.

[7]The idea that women who do not fulfill their Titus 2 role commit blasphemy is threaded through many Titus 2 Bible studies. See, for example, David Guzik, "Study Guide for Titus 2," https://www.blueletterbible.org/Comm/guzik_david/StudyGuide_Tts/Tts_2.cfm (accessed July 18, 2014).

[8]Titus 2, http://titus2mentoringwomen.com/the-program/ (accessed July 18, 2014).

[9]Titus 2: Encouraging, Exhorting, Equipping Christian Families in Jesus Christ, http://www.titus2.com/ (accessed July 18, 2014).

[10]Jennifer Flanders, "7 Reasons to Prioritize Sex in Marriage," September 21, 2012. http://lovinglifeathome.com/2012/09/21/7-reasons-to-prioritize-sex-in-marriage/ (accessed July 18, 2014).

[11]Bart Ehrman, *A Brief Introduction to the New Testament*, third edition (New York: Oxford University Press, 2013), 289–95.

[12]Ibid., 290.

[13]Carolyn Osiek and David L. Balch, *Families in the New Testament World: Households and House Churches* (Louisville: Westminster John Knox Press, 1997), 33.

[14]Ibid., 48.

[15]Ibid., 97.

[16]Carolyn Osiek, "Family Matters," in *Christian Origins: A People's History*, ed. Richard A. Horsley (Minneapolis: Fortress Press, 2005), 216.

Index

(Scripture citations are included in the subject index and sorted alphabetically. To differentiate verse numbers from page locators, page numbers are in *italics*.)